GOOD PRACTICE IN SUPERVISION

Good Practice in Social Work series

Good Practice in Child Protection
a Manual for Professionals
Edited by Hilary Owen and Jacki Pritchard
ISBN 1 85302 205 5
Good Practice 1

Good Practice in Risk Assessment
and Risk Management I
Edited by Jacki Pritchard and Hazel Kemshall
ISBN 1 85302 338 8
Good Practice 3

Good Practice in Counselling People
Who Have Been Abused
Edited by Zeta Bear
ISBN 1 85302 424 4
Good Practice 4

Good Practice in Risk Assessment
and Risk Management II
Edited by Jacki Pritchard and Hazel Kemshall
ISBN 1 85302 441 4
Good Practice 5

of related interest

Working with Elder Abuse
A Training Manual for Home Care,
Residential and Day Care Staff
Jacki Pritchard
ISBN 1 85302 418 X

The Abuse of Older People
A Training Manual for Detection
and Prevention 2nd Edition
Jacki Pritchard
ISBN 1 85302 305 1

Social Work and People
with Mental Health Problems
Edited by Marion Ulas and Anne Connor
ISBN 1 85302 302 7

GOOD PRACTICE IN SUPERVISION

STATUTORY AND VOLUNTARY ORGANISATIONS

Edited by Jacki Pritchard

Jessica Kingsley Publishers
London and Philadelphia

First published in the United Kingdom in 1995 by
Jessica Kingsley Publishers Ltd
116 Pentonville Road
London N1' 9JB, England
and
325 Chestnut Street
Philadelphia, PA 19106, USA

www.jkp.com

Second impression 1997
Third impression 1998
Fourth impression 2000

Library of Congress Cataloging in Publication Data
A CIP catalogue record for this book is available from the Library of Congress

British Library Cataloguing in Publication Data
A CIP catalogue record for this book is available from the British Library

ISBN 1 85302 279 9

Printed and bound in Great Britain by
Athenaeum Press, Gateshead, Tyne and Wear

This book is dedicated to Philman Miller

CONTENTS

INTRODUCTION

I wanted to edit a book on supervision which would be different and useful, because I have always had very strong views about supervision and feel that it is still not made a priority in many organisations. On reflection, my views about supervision developed from when I started off as a trainee social worker and received supervision on a weekly basis. I was working with terminally ill children in a hospital setting at the time and needed a great deal of practical advice and emotional support. If I had not received good quality supervision I would never have survived and probably would not have wanted to be or ever become a qualified social worker.

I have been very fortunate both as a student and as a practitioner always to have had regular supervision of a high standard. I know this is rare; many workers and managers do not regard supervision as important and do not make it a priority. I have seen the consequences of workers not having supervision and of situations in which colleagues have 'done their own thing'. In these times of high stress levels and low morale, supervision is crucial to all workers. Hence, this book!

Over the years I have had contact with many different agencies and learnt more about the supervision of staff (or lack of it). The literature on supervision has grown enormously in the past two decades but I feel there is still a real gap. The more training of staff I undertake the more I identify the need for better supervision, but also the need to train people about how to supervise and how to be supervised. I believe there is a need for a practical book which will help workers to understand why supervision is important, how it can help them practically and emotionally and how good supervision can be achieved.

One of the main objectives in writing the book was to look at supervision in both statutory and voluntary organisations. I wanted to consider supervision in the context of different work settings and staff groups within agencies. It has *not* been possible to consider every work setting/client group but I hope that the reader will be able to find something useful in each chapter and transfer the knowledge and exercises to their own workplace.

Jacki Pritchard

CHAPTER 1

THE SUPERVISION PARTNERSHIP
A WHOLE GREATER THAN THE SUM OF ITS PARTS

CATHERINE AND DAVID SAWDON

The broad aim of this chapter is to tour the literature relevant to supervision, and to explore some of the models and associated practical ideas that we have encountered on our particular journey. We shall stress the central relevance of what we see as a supervisory partnership. This has the capacity to promote effectiveness and accountability for the agency, and to value the individual worker's contribution and personal development. Our journey represents one menu, attractive to us and also tried and tested by other visitors. It does not aim to be comprehensive, but to examine the relevance to the current political and professional context of social work practice.

CENTRAL AND MARGINAL

'...move from the margin to the centre.' (Hooks 1990)

Supervision is both central and marginal to the practice of social work. It is central because 'the most vital social work resources are the personal resources of the workers' (Payne and Scott 1982), and they need to be controlled and fostered in the interests of effective service delivery. It is marginal in that in practice its purposes and functions are often confused, and its potential efficacy undervalued and undermined by low commitment. Marginality thus leads to unhelpful criticisms that the impact of supervision on practice outcomes cannot be measured, therefore it is of questionable value. A net result is that supervision in terms of regularity, content and outcome is patchy and variable in quality.

This ambivalence about the value of supervision is reinforced by the current political context and its increasing influence on the nature of practice. Critical enquiries into child protection practice, legislative change, and recurring emphasis on the need for business skills to provide value for money tend to render supervision synonymous with bureaucratic control. Issues of accountability, quality control, and management of resources have inevitably become dominant. One purpose of supervision is therefore clear, 'to establish the accountability of the worker to the organisation' (D.H.S.S. 1978). Unfortunately, emphasis on one purpose risks disturbing the fine balance with the other, 'to promote the worker's development as a professional person' (D.H.S.S. 1978). As the two purposes are seen as 'practically and conceptually interwoven' (D.H.S.S. 1978), disruption in practical application leads either to simplistic one-dimensional prescriptions, or confusion, and ultimate ambivalence and resistance. This is not to deny that the two main purposes of supervision have not always been in tension. The challenge has been to wrestle creatively with that tension, and to recognise that each of the three core functions of 'managing', 'teaching', and 'supporting' require a place on the stage as part of the whole, rather than to give one purpose assumed or explicit priority over the other.

This tension or ambivalence around supervision has been addressed in various ways in the now extensive literature. In recent years publishers have tended to encourage practical reference-style handbooks for busy workers to dip into for useful techniques and ideas (eg. Morrison 1993). Some of these build on earlier texts which aimed to provide theoretical frameworks based on empirical research and analysis (eg. Kadushin 1976, Pettes 1967). Some aim to be more pragmatic and context specific (eg. Atherton 1986). In addition and alternatively, there are rich sources of learning and understanding in writing that aims to peel back the diverse layers of human experience and perception (eg. Marshall 1984). These 'deeper' texts may often seem inaccessible to the busy professional because time and reflection, allegedly at a premium, are necessary to make and absorb critical connections. Such commentators can open our minds to new possibilities, addressing as they do socially constructed race and gender differences as basic starting points for making sense of the world. Their work helps us to be concerned with emerging and evolving consciousness about opportunity and oppression in many guises, and not simply with aiming to reach a plateau of complacent understanding.

The would be supervisor is thus confronted with a veritable toyshop of possibilities, and a measure of uncertainty about which models to choose. The dangers, as we have indicated, are that supervision can be reduced to a relatively simple functional analysis, which denies the potential creativity of the supervisory partnership. Most writers seem agreed on the three core functions above. Many add a fourth, mediation, or fifth, notably assessment or appraisal, to reflect a particular context or style. Given such agreement it can be a short step to an intellectual grasp of what's required, and a sense of 'I know therefore I do'. In reality the task is more complex. Practice does not mirror the tidiness of theoretical categorisations. As Herman Hesse put it, 'clarity is violence'.

FUNCTIONS AND SOURCES OF AUTHORITY

It is salutary to read the early texts on supervision if only to appreciate that the theories and principles have not actually changed much since first articulated in a social work context by Virginia Robinson in 1930 (Richards et al. 1991). Pettes (1967) draws on Towle (1963) to highlight the three core functions of 'administration', 'teaching', and 'helping'. Kadushin (1976), Westheimer (1977), and Payne and Scott (1982) adjust these labels to incorporate 'managing' (administration) and 'supportive' or 'enabling' (helping). More recently,

Richards *et al.* (1991) and Morrision (1993) have added a fourth, 'mediation', to reflect the pace of change and the need to work in partnership with other agencies, particularly in work concerned with child protection.

Current emphases on the assessment of competence in social work education (Evans 1990) and performance appraisal in subsequence practice (Sawdon and Sawdon 1991) suggest that a fifth function, 'assessment', may now be to the fore where previously it has tended to be subsumed within the core three. It can be seen as a potential driving force, geared to producing measurable outcomes and improved effectiveness through a focus on staff performance. The literature on appraisal (eg. Harrison 1988, Stewart and Stewart 1977) draws intrinsic connections with the practice of supervision whether the motivation is towards improved profits and service delivery or staff care and development. The pace of introduction of staff appraisal schemes within social services seems likely to quicken.

This range of functions harbours tensions, ambiguities, and overlapping complexities. A key area for exploration by several writers has thus been the sources and use of authority to sustain credibility in the role. Pettes (1967) reminds us that the agency in general terms derives its authority within a framework of community. Within the agency 'there is administrative authority, the authority of knowledge, and authority derived from personality'. Payne and Scott (1982) build on this analysis by observing that hierarchical notions of authority have been legitimately challenged by, amongst other things, more participative organisational structures. They suggest, therefore, three definitions of authority:

- positional or legalistic authority
- sapiential authority, or that which is derived from wisdom, experience, and acknowledged skills
- the authority of relevance, or that authority which arises 'from the possession of knowledge relevant to the client's own feeling of well-being' (Webb and Hobdell 1980).

Their definitions imply 'that a more democratic and egalitarian approach to work and organisations is both desirable and attainable' (p.10).

A central element of this debate, extended by Richards *et al.* (1991), is the extent to which the staff supervisor is able to recognise her/his limitations as well as their capabilities – 'they are not omniscient'. Delegation and experimentation with a variety of supervision approaches are seen as essential. Moreover, the context of teams, and the varying distribution of authority within teams not only suggests but demands that a wider set of definitions of authority will be required. Each of the models and the language used reflects the stage in social work developmental history at which it was written. Today, the notion of 'sources of authority' within agencies and teams must be seen in the context of institutional oppression and who holds or is denied power on the basis of their colour, gender, age, abilities, sexual orientation, religion or class. Such differences of experience and perspective should no longer be denied. Such considerations must clearly overlay the 'traditional' model and open up alternative possibilities.

In our current roles as training consultants we have shared these long-standing, yet evolving frameworks with various groups of supervisors from a range of settings and found much to confirm their relevance as analytic tools. Many agencies in search of a clearer job specification have made the post of staff supervisor explicitly managerial. One of the implications, and in some cases a direct consequence of such 'clarity', is that management functions inevitably acquire predominance over the 'educative' or 'supportive'.

As Richards *et al.* (1991) observe 'first line management is often seen to involve *control* over people and resources with *monitoring* and ensuring that agency procedures are adhered to. It is seen as less to do with *empowering, nurturing* and *supporting* staff, managing feelings and stress and assisting staff with their *learning* and professional development generally.' The divorce of management from caring, eloquently described by Grimwood and Popplestone (1993) and others (eg. Coulshed 1990) where supervisors are often 'cut off from the pain in clients lives' (Hanmer and Statham 1988) offers clarity for some, but more noticeably a sense of loss and bewilderment to others. To deny that the developmental and support functions of supervision are integral to good practice, and to imagine that control and accountability can ensure quality, is both short sighted and oppressive.

The majority of those who use scarce training and education opportunities to explore the meaning of supervision competence recognise in theory and practice a willingness to achieve a balance of interrelated functions. They want to be able to tolerate the ambiguities and tensions involved. Such a stance reflects what they experience in terms of their own expectations and the demands of those they supervise. Their often expressed sense of loss and bewilderment, far from being a pathological indicator of weakness, appears to stem more directly from imposed reductionist structures which do not want to recognise either the complex nuances of responsibility or individual strengths and needs. Statements of this order often attract the criticism of 'whingeing' and invitations to leave the heat of the kitchen. Continuous restructuring, permanent instability and resource constraints are recognised features of social work agencies and it seems that we all have to learn to work with them. Our argument, knowingly repeated, is that to fail to recognise such essential staff resources makes the task impossible to manage, wasteful, and dull.

We would, therefore, endorse the three principles proposed by Richards *et al.* (1991) that permeate the work of a competent supervisor.

- to be more proactive *v* being purely reactive
- to attempt to become a good role model for practitioners
- to develop personal effectiveness.

SUSTAINING ASPIRATIONS THROUGH LEARNING

These three principles have the quality of aspirations, and to remain alive require sustenance. Each reflecting practitioner collects and refines an eclectic toolbag of workable practice theories which make the journey possible. Commonly quoted theoretical constructs which have potential relevance to supervision are *adult learning* models (Rogers 1969, Freire 1972, Knowles 1978, Reynolds 1965, Kolb and McIntyre 1979 and Haring 1978); transactional analysis (Berne 1964); and counselling and therapy models (Shohet and

Hawkins 1989, Heron 1975, 1990). Many of these are concisely summarised by Morrison (1993) and explored rigorously by Shohet and Hawkins (1989) for the enquiring reader. The former points up practical explanations and pragmatic strategies for the busy supervisor. The latter invites a deeper conceptual approach in examining process and developmental models of supervision, focusing particularly on those who supervise counsellors, psychotherapists and work with the other helping professions undertaking therapeutic activity. Our own particular journey has drawn significantly upon adult learning processes, notions of style, and reflective explorations of the helping role in terms of power, rights and perspectives on oppression. Such a journey with its language shaped by both liberal and radical trends in social work education may seem at first glance to be too distant and impractical for the hurly-burly 'real world' of organisational supervision. We shall aim therefore to make some connections.

As we have implied earlier, the first and most obvious connection made by writers in this field is that the health of the organisation and the quality of service delivered will depend considerably on the learning and development of its main resource: *the staff.*

Understanding how people learn, facilitating and indeed accelerating these processes, is critical and underpins the educative function of supervision. Knowles (1978) and Freire (1972) and before them Rogers (1969) invite us to challenge objective pedagogic models of teaching and to consider androgogy 'the art and science of enabling adults to learn'. The teacher/supervisor is seen as facilitator, joining the learner/supervisee in a process of enquiry, and mutual challenge rather than an expert transmitter of knowledge.

Knowles' concept of androgogy is based on four assumptions about the characteristics of adult learners. These are:

(1) as a person matures, his self concept moves from one of being a dependent personality towards self direction;

(2) he accumulates a growing reservoir of experience that becomes an increasing resource for learning;

(3) his readiness to learn becomes oriented increasingly to the developmental tasks of his social roles;

(4) his time perspective changes from one of postponed application of knowledge to immediacy of application, and accordingly his orientation towards learning shifts from one of subject centredness to one of problem centredness.

This model is student/supervisee centred, with an emphasis on problem-focussed learning which takes account of prior experience and developing needs. Such an apparently creative and open model of learning is clearly connected with Payne and Scott's desired 'democratic and egalitarian approach' (1982) and has been influential in developments in practice teaching and social work education in general.

Like all models, however, its credibility is not enhanced by claims to providing perfect solutions. Good service delivery cannot solely be attributable to creative learning climates and methods. Equally, as Humphries (1988) powerfully demonstrates, Knowles' concept of androgogy is offered in a political, social and historical vacuum. His white, male, middle class professional thesis is seen as essentially flawed by giving no account of black people's experience or class or gender differences within the educational system. Nor does he address the institutionalised context of learning which characteristically has 'hierarchical and bureaucratic structures which demand unilateral control of assessment and clarity of objectives' (Humphries 1988). Placing these criticisms in the context of staff supervision, we can readily recognise the recent additional bureaucratic structures, the demand for control, the desire for clear objectives, and the pursuit of narrow functional analysis.

We can also readily see the comparative absence of black and female perspectives as the push towards 'stronger' management tends to be identified with so-called 'masculine' characteristics. Eley (1986), for example, found clear gender differences in approaches to supervision. Most of the men in her research study emphasised the importance of ensuring that the statutory responsibilities are carried out along with practical advice-giving in managing cases. On the other hand, most of the women prioritised supporting staff in dealing with the stresses of the job, followed by help with workload organisation and then ensuring statutory responsibilities were met. The differences between male and female perceptions and styles is usefully explored by Marshall (1984) building on the work of Bakan (1966). We have found her exposition of the 'agency' (male) and 'communion' (female) styles most illuminating and invite the reader to consider her analysis later in this chapter.

It seems critical, however, to hold on to the positive directions of Knowles' thesis alongside Humphries' critique in order to recognise, sustain and maximise individual contributions, through mutually supportive relationships to the process of change. Within the debilitating current political climate, many organisations undergoing change exhibit low morale, and understandable flagging of energy and a passive lack of creativity. A real commitment to learning and a proactive attitude to developing staff individually and collectively can move things on considerably and provide the impetus to providing quality and quantity of service.

DEVELOPING SKILLS

John Heron's work (1975) offers one model for building in some practical analysis of what actually happens in supervision, and refining the core skills, language, and behaviour that contribute to effective practice. His counselling and psychotherapeutic perspectives may seem outmoded for some in the current organisational context of social services. Yet counselling outside social work would now appear to be a growth industry! In our view, such skills are directly transferable and can offer an important sense of stability within an apparent sea of chaos. Shohet and Hawkins (1989) indicate for example how workers who become supervisors may abandon initially their very useful practitioner skills, yet ultimately draw strength from revaluing them, albeit in a new context and role. Instead of rejecting these skills, there is a clear case for celebrating them.

Heron's thesis, put simply, is that all helping interventions can be divided or reduced to six categories. We thus have the possibility of a framework which can assist supervisors in becoming aware of the different interventions they use. Retrospective analysis of language and behaviour using the framework can reveal 'valid' and 'degenerate' intervention, with the prospect of applying this understanding towards skill improvement and a potentially wider repertoire of choice. Crucially, the categorisation also enables us to examine the dynamics of power and authority within the supervisory partnership. This dimension is central, whether one is concerned with issues of control, accountability and effectiveness, or personal learning and development. This can be expressed diagrammatically in Figure 1.1.

AUTHORITATIVE or DIRECTIVE INTERVENTIONS
Supervisor uses authority to be
       Prescriptive – Give advice, instruction
       Informative – Give information
       Confrontative – Give feedback, challenge

FACILITATIVE INTERVENTIONS
Supervisor values what supervisee brings and
       Cathartic – encourages expression of feeling
       Catalytic – encourages reflection and problem solving
       Supportive – confirms, validates the individual.

(John Heron 1975)

Figure 1.1.

These six types of intervention only have meaning if they are rooted in care and concern for the individual supervisee. Most of us manage to be both valid and degenerate. Occasionally, some supervisors may regrettably lapse into 'perverted' use which is to be deliberately manipulative or malicious. One final note of caution. Heron's counselling-specific terms can for some be off-putting. Jargon terms in this case are worth struggling with, as each reading seems to present further insight. Furthermore, one needs to remember to place this person centred approach within the context of a locally and nationally accountable context.

The effective supervisor does not deny her/his power and authority but uses it to ensure with the supervisee that s/he is clear about what is required and how they are meeting or not meeting those requirements together. The effective supervisor does not lean over backwards nor abrogate power and authority. S/he shares the responsibility for dealing with the pain and complexity of vulnerable life situations in a manner which promotes the supervisee's own sense of worth and personal authority. Anecdotal evidence from recent workshops for a significant sample of manager/supervisors at different levels suggests that it is the facilitative interventions which tend to be absent or poorly practised at the higher levels of hierarchical management structures. 'Moral patronage', 'smiling demolition', and 'sweet syrup' to use some of Heron's degenerate terms tend to evoke distrust, limited respect and downright suspicion, especially amongst potentially oppressed groups. Training to enhance the use of facilitative intervention skills tends not to be seen as a priority for senior management work. One result may be a vacuum or disparity between what most supervisees actually want and the prepared-ness or ability of some supervisors to deliver.

What seems to be important to recognise here is that individual skills are placed within context through the supervisory partnership. This can help to ensure that the wider functional needs of the agency do not deny that everyday social work is still about deploying those individual skills effectively on behalf of service users or clients. Opportunities to receive feedback on these skills in a relatively safe atmosphere of mutual respect should not be some-thing that ends with qualifying training. Like driving, we all slip into poor practice. Supervision should be the central reflective tool for us to remind ourselves of personal standards as individual 'professionals', as well as the agency's preference for monitored service delivery.

PROBLEM SOLVING

A keen thread extending through all the models put forward is the need and desire to solve problems. Andragogic approaches offer more perspectives through pooling, enquiry, and mutual challenge but Humphries (1988) warns us that traditional common sense ways of tackling problems may need to be unlearned rather than simply 'unfrozen'. She argues that a more radical concept of problem solving is necessary – one which allows a re-evaluation of past experience, and a preparedness to confront commonly held assump-tions, stereotypes, and the view that 'one's values are one's own private affair'. This argument seems more than pertinent in relation to the continuing 'po-litical correctness' debate, and the progress towards a reality rather than just a rhetoric of anti-oppressive practice. Confronting the bias and prejudice which support the 'isms', as Jean Kantambu Latting (1990) demonstrates, requires more than exhortation and information, 'Only those who already agree with the values expressed are likely to be influenced by the arguments presented' (Latting 1990). It is also a myth that social workers and their employing agencies are critical exponents of anti-racist, anti-discriminatory, anti-oppressive practice. Any sample of older people in residential care, or people with disabilities using day care, or black people with mental health problems would quickly dispel any such myth. Although many grass roots workers aspire to improved practice in these areas, the evidence of senior management support is far less available.

Addressing such wider issues should be part of the stuff of supervision. They tend, however, to be rapidly sidelined by the pressure to focus on the micro detail of cases. The time for interactive debate and the development of 'cognitive sophistication' (Gabelko and Michaelis 1981) or critical thinking skills is rarely deemed to be available. Such skills, first promoted in education and training contexts, enable us to be free to question our own and other's immediate reactive thinking processes. Whilst acknowledging the time factor and the felt pressure, we would ask what other opportunities for critical questioning and reflection-in-action (Schon 1987) actually exist outside supervision? The occasional quality training programme and/or the pursuit of post qualifying credits (eg. Approved Social Worker, Child Protection, or Accredited Practice Teacher Training) may well trigger and help to consolidate new awareness and knowledge. Quality is variable, however, and any learning derived usually requires agency commitment, reinforcement and support. Regular effective supervision offers opportunities for both supervisor and supervisee to draw on such experiences, build on them and sustain a critical approach to practice.

It may be helpful at this point to move from exhortation ourselves, and to identify some practical approaches to problem solving which can give some shape to the activity. De Bono (1981) and others have written accessibly about the use of the right hand side of the brain, which enables us to think in terms of images, whole patterns, and undefined feelings. By encouraging and enriching our perceptual maps, we can add an alternative dimension to the left hand side of the brain's contribution of logic and language. Many problems can be addressed just by finding the right information and subsequently processing this through a computer.

There are many situations, however, particularly in social services work where information alone will not do our thinking for us. Information by itself will not generate ideas. 'Ideas are organisations of information that the human mind chooses to put together in a particular way' (De Bono 1981). Both information and ideas are regularly required for effective problem solving. De Bono suggests that problem solvers tend to polarise into two groups: the information gatherers who are not very comfortable with ideas, and the ideas people who think they do not need information. Our view is that this may be a little extreme, preferring to see most people placed along a continuum. Nevertheless, the implications for supervisory partnerships, groups, team meetings and other learning and decision-making arrangements seem worth considering.

Another model which supervisors in our experience have found attractive is the 'Problem Solving Tree' (Figure 1.2). This model, whilst apparently fitting into the school of systematic, rational approaches, incorporates free thinking right brain activity. The visual organic image of the tree takes us through a process but acknowledges a variety of potential dynamic routes to a workable solution. A common flaw in much of this activity is that we do not always define the real problem, but rather address one or more symptoms. Using the tree image, we may place a given presenting problem in the 'trunk' box, but when pressed to generate a range of perceptions of the 'root' causes, we may well discover the 'real' problem or, indeed, several others which merit earlier attention. The solutions to that 'real' problem can be many and varied. We can thus generate both creatively and rationally lots of 'branches' to our tree. We then need to look closely at the consequences ('twigs') of these solutions and evaluate with a positive/negative rating ('fruit or blossom'). The possible best solution is the one with the highest positive rating.

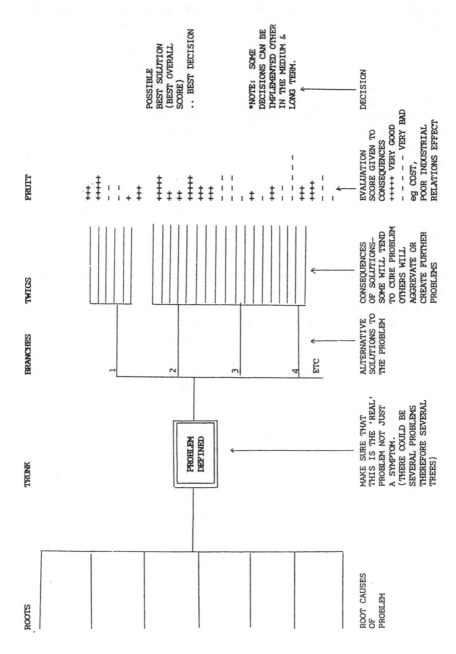

Figure 1.2 Problem Solving Tree

Such an activity is often most productive in a group supervision/team meeting context, but can be equally valuable in one-to-one discussions. It appears to allow for that magical but controversial quality of 'intuition', and also for 'operacy' (De Bono 1981) – the thinking that gets things done. They key issue here for us is that, in dealing with the detail of problem solving, care is necessary not to obscure the wider context of the work. The supervisory partnership can help to ensure that the focused and wide angle lens are both part of the practitioner's equipment.

MANAGING SELF

One of the recurring 'problems' in relation to being a supervisor is the business of self-care when arguably most time is spent giving out to or being alongside others. We all know most of the strategies for dealing with stress and self-care, at least at an intellectual level, but at one time or another most of us fail to follow our own good advice. Much has been written of the areas of stress and burnout (eg. McDerment 1988, Dainow and Bailey 1988) and the concerned reader will either have addressed this area already or will be able to pursue these and other sources.

Given the child protection focus of much social work practice, the contribution of Richards *et al.* (1991) seems particularly accessible and useful for both members of the supervisory partnership. They remind us how situations faced by social workers can evoke quite primitive and painful feelings, and that 'the most ordinary and natural response to pain is to try and avoid it'. Strategies for avoiding pain, previously outlined by Kadushin (1976) are cited again so that most of us can recognise when we have been in 'denial' or 'professionally distant' or become 'obsessive' about adherence to laid-down policies or procedures. We can ultimately spend more time and energy avoiding pain and conflict than may be necessary to deal with it direct. The image of a head swathed in bandages to block the senses is very powerful. As always, care must be taken not to polarise the causes for stress as either solely extrinsic - 'it's them' – or internalise the reasons and accept oppressive pathologising.

Morrison (1993) has usefully built upon these notions with the theory of the 'Professional Accommodation Syndrome' (Figure 1.3). His thesis is that workers expect to experience some primary stress arising from their work with complex situations, but they are 'far more distressed by the secondary stress arising from the agency's response to them when this happens'. The five stages of this model are an adaption of earlier work by Summit (1983) connected to child sexual abuse. Supervision in this type of context will often represent the agency's first response to the worker's stress. It can either relieve or exacerbate the stages predicted. Whatever the context 'advanced empathy' (or reading accurately between the lines) by the supervisor would appear to be an important factor in helping to prevent the common incidence of stress related aggressive behaviour, resignation and sickness. We would argue that this recognition and untangling of causative factors can enable a worker to emerge from very real pressures with some clarity and a sense of acknow-

The five stages of the Professional Accommodation Syndrome:

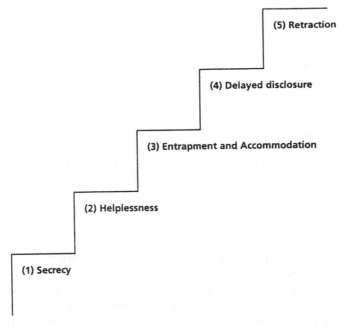

Morrison, T. (1993)

Figure 1.3 The five stages of the Professional Accommodation Syndrome

ledgement, rather than the label of victim or inadequate. This feels like a non-patronising notion of empowerment within a working partnership.

A third set of ideas which help in this context is the range of adaptions to the original work of Blake and Mouton (1964). We have found in particular the work of Thomas and Kilman (1974), as described by Ross (1982), on styles of coping with conflict, to offer a useful perspective. As with many similar learning and self-awareness packages, the completion of a questionnaire and associated reading enable us to identify preferences for five coping styles – Competing, Collaborating, Compromising, Avoiding and Accommodating. These are based upon two behavioural dimensions in a conflict situation:

(1) Assertiveness, the extent to which the individual attempts to satisfy her/his own concerns and

(2) Co-operativeness, the extent to which the individual attempts to satisfy the others' concerns.

Many of us within the 'helping professions' appear to rely more heavily on one or two (eg: Collaborating or Compromising), often to the relative exclusion of others (eg. Avoiding). Ross invites us to consider the relative merits of all five. He asks us not to place individual, cultural or indeed political values on any, so that we can increase our repertoire of skills for coping with conflict.

Is this possible, we wonder? The capacity to employ all of these styles in the context of supervision is clearly desirable. Raised awareness of our own preferred styles can help us to try out less favoured ones. As we attempt these changes, the supervisory partnership can suggest, through recognition of our individual experiences of oppression, a way forward to assist personal survival. This, we believe, is an ART not a technical science and the skill lies in choosing and matching the style to the needs of the situation.

Such frameworks may offer the 'clarity of violence' referred to by Hesse, but cannot simulate the complexity and apparent chaos which many situations bring. Their value is often as retrospective analytic tools for explaining process and outcomes and for development of learning. We all seek clarifying 'guidelines' or 'formulae' but equally recognise that the human dimension to our work precludes such reductionism. The positive supervisory partnership with its emphasis on respect for difference and recognition of power can help us to develop alternative individualised strategies.

THE WHOLE IS GREATER THAN THE SUM OF THE PARTS

> 'To that piece of each of us that refuses to be silent...' (Audre Lorde 1988)

If such frameworks can be useful as analytic tools, are there also guiding principles which can be derived from them to help us in supervision? Shohet and Hawkins (1989) having offered us understanding, maps, and techniques, conclude that 'good supervision, like love, cannot be taught... How we personally relate to our supervisees is far more important than mere skills, for all techniques need to be embedded in a good relationship. 'We imagine that many hard pressed supervisors beset by pressures to be competent, in control, consistent and to produce measurable outcomes may afford a wry smile or even scoff at such a conclusion. The familiar lesson to be learned here, however, is that these pressures can take the form of self-perpetuating beliefs which may block personal learning and hinder the development of good open relationships. Dearnley (1985) helpfully exposes the difficulties of getting the relationship right when she says:

> 'I have come to learn that looking in detail at supervisory practice is widely experienced as a very exposing affair, much more so than discussing one's own difficult cases. It is as if the public confirmation that one is sufficiently experienced to supervise leads to persecutory personal expectations that supervisors should say and do no wrong.'

Each member of the partnership therefore has to recognise their own vulnerability and capacity to make mistakes as human beings still needing to and being open to learn. The process of engaging and setting a mutually beneficial working contract or agreement, whilst sounding formal, cannot be overestimated here. Morrison (1993) also suggests the development of a Staff Care Statement and a Self Care Plan for supervisors and supervisees which many teams might usefully adopt. The difficulty with such 'plans', valuable as they are as statements of good intent, is that they often represent a counsel of perfection. In other words, we rarely achieve the high and demanding standards that they set, and in trying and failing, we run the risk of injury or increasing the stress they were designed to prevent. Thus, Morrison's tenth point - 'Accept that you cannot anticipate all stress' – is timely, as is the selected quote from Erica Jong (1978), urging us to:

> 'Renounce useless guilt
> Don't make a cult of suffering
> Live in the now, or at least in the soon...' (*How to Save Your Own Life*)

Self care extends to supervisors as well. Their needs for stimulation, support and development as well as being accountable are equally valid.

These ideas ultimately lead us to more fundamental philosophies and strategies for living, and responding to complex, sometimes life-threatening situations. Our own different perspectives as a white man and woman find some complementarity within our partnership, but as training consultants, supervisors and practitioners we have different styles which rest significantly upon differences of gender, class and other socially constructed characteristics. As stated earlier, the work of Judi Marshall (1984), amongst others, is illuminating in exploring this difference. We shall seek to conclude this chapter by connecting these ideas with the practice of supervision.

Marshall draws upon the work of Bakan (1966) in defining two fundamental tendencies, or principles of human functioning. These are the 'agency' and the 'communion' styles which Bakan claims all individuals use to resolve core dilemmas of existence: those of being and not being; and of independence *versus* interdependence. In essence, they are basic coping strategies for dealing with the uncertainties and anxieties of being alive. 'Agency is the expression of independence through self-protection, self assertion and self expansion; communion is the sense of being "at one" with other organisms' Marshall (1984). Thus the main aim of the agency style or strategy is to reduce the tension by changing the world about it; the communion style seeks union and cooperation as its way of coming to terms with uncertainty. The aims, dominant strategies, and core characteristics of the two styles are effectively summarised in Figure 1.4 below.

Key words to hold on to are 'being' (communion), and 'doing' (agency), and Marshall argues that 'at the level of aggregates or groups communion can be broadly identified as a female and agency as a male principle'. She illustrates eloquently how these differences have emerged and are apparent in the relationship between the two sexes. She also usefully draws together how each style can contribute to the other, pointing to the example of sports training (Gallwey 1979) where a balance of communion with agency is advocated through the paradoxical state of 'relaxed concentration'. This leads naturally to a discussion of androgyny, which is based on the assumption that everyone has some feminine and some masculine characteristics, but that these two sides are more or less developed in different individuals.

The relevance to supervision is to be found in the extent to which we are aware of the interaction, separation and blending of these two sets of coping strategies in the world of social work practice. There is much to indicate that 'agency' characteristics remain dominant and tend to be expressed through control and formal organisation – men predominantly hold the power. 'Com-

	Agency	Communion
Main aim	Control	Union
	Independence	Interdependence
Dominant	Assertiveness	Cooperation
Strategies	Control through: separation\splitting; projection; mastery; denial; encountering the projected threat. Change	Contact Openness Acceptance Personal adjustment
Characteristics	Doing Egoic Formal organisation Physical action Classifies, and projects classifications onto environment	Being Tolerance Trust Naturalistic perception of environment: emphasis on wholes, patterns, relationship, context
	Distance Contracts	Emotional tone Non-contractual cooperation; forgiveness.
	Change resisting Achievement oriented	Change accepting Contextually driven

Figure 1.4. Summarising the characteristics of communion and agency

munion' characteristics which help to maintain society through physical and emotional nurturing and valuing interdependence tend to be less appreciated. Effective supervision requires each to be available and recognises that they may be in tension. Each strategy or style, therefore, if used alone continually walks the tightrope between the possibilities of success and degeneration. Use of the two styles in combination or synthesis offers a broader base of potential coping. But what form should or could integration take? Do we see 'agency' mitigated or softened by 'communion' or 'communion' enhanced by agency? The balance of 'relaxed concentration' epitomised by Gallwey's tennis player may elude us quite frequently. It seems worth practising, and practising if we are to aspire to the slippery slogans or Equality and Quality in our attempts at supervision.

FINAL THOUGHTS...

The supervisory partnership is, in current jargon, good value for money. It is not a sort of liberal free thinking left over from the 1960s, but offers a radical opportunity for developing and monitoring good standards of practice. Crucially for those directly engaged and prepared to make the time, it opens up ways of working positively with power and difference in the context of unremitting change. We believe that it is a central part of the survival tool bag, and can ensure that front line practitioners experience positive role models for providing an effective service.

REFERENCES

Atherton, J.S. (1986) *Professional Supervision in Group Care*. London: Tavistock.

Bakan, D. (1966) *The Duality of Human Existence*. Boston: Beacon Press.

Berne, E. (1964) *Games People Play*. Harmondsworth: Penguin.

Blake, R. and Mouton, J.S. (1964) *Managing Intergroup Conflict in Industry*. Houston, Texas: Gulf.

Coulshed, V. (1990) *Management in Social Work*. London: MacMillan.

Dainow, S. and Bailey, C. (1988) *Developing Skills in People*. New York: Wiley.

De Bono, E. (1981) *An Atlas of Management Thinking*. London: Temple Smith.

Dearnley, B. (1985) 'A plain man's guide to supervision.' *Journal of Social Work Practice*.

D.H.S.S. (1978) *Social Services Teams: A Practitioner's View*. (Parsloe, P. and Hill, M.) London: H.M.S.O.

Eley, R. (1986) 'An examination of the role of the senior social worker analysed from a gender perspective.' Unpublished dissertation University of Liverpool.

Evans, D. (1990) *Assessing Students Competence to Practise*. London: CCETSW.

Fontana, D. (1989) *Managing Stress*. London: Routledge.

Freire, P. (1972) *Pedagogy of the Oppressed*. Harmondsworth: Penguin.

Gabelko, N.H. and Michaelis, J.U. (1981) *Reducing adolescent prejudice: A handbook*. New York: Teachers College Press.

Gallwey, W.T. (1979) *The Inner Game of Tennis*. New York: Bantam.

Grimwood, C. and Popplestone, R. (1993) *Women, Management and Care*. London: MacMillan.

Hanmer, J. and Statham, D. (1988) *Women and Social Work*. London: MacMillan.

Haring, N. *et al.* (1978) *The Fourth R*. Columbus, Ohio: Merrill.

Harrison, R. (1988) *Training and Development*.

Heron, J. (1975) *Six Category Intervention Analysis*. University of Surrey.

Heron, J. (1990) *Helping the Client*. London: Sage.

Hooks, B. (1991) *Yearnings. Race, gender and cultural politics*. London:Turnaround.

Humphries, B. (1988) 'Adult learning in social work education: towards liberation or domestication?' Critical Social Policy.

Kadushin, A. (1976) *Supervision in Social Work*. Columbia University Press.

Knowles, M. (1978) *The Adult Learner: A Neglected Species*. Englewood, N.J.: Prentice Hall.

Kolb, D. and McIntyre, J.M. (1979) *Organisational Psychology: An Experiential Approach*. Englewood Cliffs, New Jersey: Prentice Hall.

Latting, J.K. (1990) 'Identifying the "Isms": Enabling social work students to confront their biases.' *Journal of Social Work Education*.

Lorde, A. (1988) *A Burst of Light*. London: Sheba.

Marshall, J. (1984) *Women Managers: Travellers in a Male World*. New York: Wiley.

McDerment, L. (1988) *Stress Care*. Social Care Association.

Morrison, T. (1990) 'The emotional effects of child protection work on the worker.' Practice 4.4.

Morrison, T. (1993) *Staff Supervision in Social Care*. Harlow: Longman.

Payne, C. and Scott, T. (1982) *Developing Supervision of Teams in Field and Residential Work*. National Institute for Social Work.

Pettes, D. (1967) *Supervision in Social Work*. London: Allen and Unwin.

Reynolds, B.C. (1965) *Learning and Teaching in the Practice of Social Work*. New York: Farrar and Rinehart.

Richards, M. *et al.* (1991) *Staff Supervision in Child Protection Work*. London: NISW.

Rogers, C.R. (1969) *Freedom to Learn*. Columbus, Ohio: Merrill.

Ross, M.B. (1982) 'Coping with conflict.' Annual Handbook for Facilitators.

Sawdon, D.T. and Sawdon, C. (1991) *Developing Staff Supervision and Appraisal in the Probation Service*. Humberside Probation Service.

Shohet, P. and Hawkins, R. (1989) *Supervision in Helping Professions*. Buckingham: Open University Press.

Schon, D.A. (1987) *Educating the Reflective Practitioner*. San Francisco: Jossey Bass.

Stewart, V. and Stewart, A. (1977) *Practice Performance Appraisal*. Aldershot: Gower.

Summit, R. (1983) 'The child sexual abuse accommodation syndrome.' *Child Abuse and Neglect 7, 2*.

Thomas, K.W. and Kilman, R.H. (1974) *Conflict Mode Instrument*. Sterling Forest.

Towle, C. (1963) 'The Place of Help in Supervision' *The Social Service Review*. Vol 38 No 4

Webb, A. and Hobdell, M. (1980) 'Coordination and teamwork in the Health and Personal Social Services.' Manpower Monograph 14 P.S.S.C.

Westheimer, I. (1977) *The Practice of Supervision in Social Work*. London: Ward Lock.

CHAPTER 2

SUPERVISION – TAKING ACCOUNT OF FEELINGS

ELIZABETH ASH

Effective supervision, although an essential aspect of social work practice and training, often suffers from lack of resources, as others in this book have noted. Like many 'essentials' to good practice it frequently happens more in the intent than in the reality. In this, social work does not differ a great deal from other fields of endeavour where, despite written manuals, guidelines, expectations and even contracts, supervision of the individual is often sacrificed to the more 'pressing needs' for urgent action on the part of managers. Since we understand, in principle, how important good supervision is to effective work, particularly in the personal social services, we must ask ourselves why it can so readily be diminished in practice. I think the answer lies in that aspect of supervision for which it is most difficult to legislate, which exists outside procedural frameworks and which centres on the actual interchange between supervisor and supervisee.

This exchange takes place at both professional and personal levels, since we each bring the whole of ourselves to any face-to-face communication with others, and this inevitably involves *feelings*. Feelings, about ourselves, about others and about the 'raw material' of the supervisory dynamic – clients and colleagues and *their* situations and emotional states – provide the ever-present but ever-changing climate of supervision. This climate may enhance the supervisory process, or undermine it. It cannot, or should not, be ignored. This chapter, then, is especially concerned with how to take account of 'feelings' in the processes of supervision. It will explore some of the impediments to effective practice, and make suggestions about overcoming them. In doing this, it recognises the value of written procedures and guidelines to supervision, whether at work or in training, so that expectations for both supervisor and supervisee remain clear and negotiable.

THE IDEAL SUPERVISOR

- a warm wall – to give me support and firmness and to bounce off ideas
- a deep well from which I can draw strength and wisdom

- a helicopter ready to winch me out of danger
- a pilot to make sure I steer the right course through difficult waters
- a harbour master to ensure that I have safe haven in times of storm and stress.

These were the metaphors of expectations of a supervisor, produced by highly experienced practitioners and trainers, who advised on the making of *Acceptable Risk?*, a video-based training package on supervision in child abuse cases (Ash 1988). It was based on the premis that decisions in these complex cases could be distorted if the emotional and attitudinal responses to them were not taken into account and that supervision had an important part to play in this.

This ideal is not limited only to supervision in childcare. The images are shorthand for a considerable range of skills which an 'ideal supervisor' in any setting should have available. Supervision of practice, as in training, should not only provide advice and support but also maintain an element of learning.

Supervisors should be able:

- to offer insights into working within a particular system, and information about the legislative and procedural framework
- to provide support in relation to senior management and a communications link
- to be sensitive to the frustrations of social workers occasioned by scarce resources
- to recognise and take account of the effect on their supervisees of a stressful environment and workload
- to be alert to situations of emergency
- to be reliable and accessible.

In addition, thought the advisory group to *Acceptable Risk?*, supervisors should be sensitively aware of their supervisees as individuals with personal lives which might impinge upon the work, while not intervening inappropriately. They should, in their role as 'facilitators of learning' and staff development, be skilled in helping practitioners make the link between current work and previous experience, drawing out 'what you don't know you know'. While having been competent practitioners themselves, they should be sufficiently distant from the particular situation under discussion to probe the complexities with illuminating questions, and to challenge accepted practice 'wisdom'. This demands awareness of developments in current practice and its legislative framework.

In short, the ideal supervisor requires a constellation of abilities which assist in the integration of the social worker's knowledge, understanding, sensitivies and existing competencies, while facilitating a learning process which both illuminates present and past experience and enables competent professional judgements. A fulcrum of the supervisory process, then, should be an exploration of the conflicts and contradictions between the espoused theory of practice and its reality (Argyris and Schon 1974). Do we do what we think or say we do? if not, why not? and what should we do about it?

IMPEDIMENTS TO EFFECTIVE SUPERVISION

The current context of the provision of social work and its supervision is the emerging system of community care. Recent legislative changes in the general delivery of personal social services and health care and in the specialist areas of mental health, child care and the justice system are still being absorbed and implemented in practice. The adaptations required of social workers and their supervisors are still in process in terms of the organisation of services. Anxiety and uncertainty are high. Questions of identity, statutory responsibility and 'what is social work?' abound. Inter-professional working, required by the new community care systems, introduces additional stresses in the already complex arena of service delivery. Scarce resources exacerbate the situation. The boundaries between service provision and purchase are blurred. All sectors – public, voluntary, private and individual/volunteer – are affected. Who is supervising who doing what and why?

While acknowledging the impact of this context, my concern is to suggest that *wherever it takes place, in whatever mix 'n' match of services and professions, for whichever client groups, in whatever resource scenario, the same basic principles apply, the same opportunities and hazards exist in the process of supervision. Contexts may change with the prevailing political, socio-economic and professional climates; the essence of effective supervision remains the same.*

The vision of the 'ideal supervisor' outlined above perhaps represents an unattainable goal in reality. Whether supervising students or workers, supervisors usually face enormous demands upon their skills and time with very little opportunity for input or training for themselves. Supervision cannot easily be a task in and of itself because, to be effective, it must retain links with practice and management. Indeed, most supervisors in the personal social services are also line managers with other responsibilities. Some may have the apparent luxury of holding posts as senior practitioners without direct management responsibility, although they invariably carry heavy caseloads. Practice teachers and supervisors on courses usually have additional 'normal' workloads and in some areas so little support from their agencies for this teaching role that they are in very short supply, to the great detriment of social work training. Social work supervisors often feel torn between the demands of management and those of their social workers, while, isolated and Janus-faced, they attempt to look in two directions at once. The conjunction of organisational pressures and the stresses of the supervisory process itself can act as a powerful inhibitor to effective supervision. The emotional impact of the distressing circumstances of many clients, exacerbated by lack of resources and support, can set off resonances which may distort supervision and, therefore, practice, in social work.

MIRRORING

This is the term given to the dynamic which attempts to mop up the anxiety produced by stressful aspects of work within organisations at different levels of responsibility. In the supervision of social workers or students, it can operate in a sort of unconscious contagion, whereby stress-related anxiety, arising from a particular source, which may well be distressing 'case content', gets passed on from client to social worker to supervisor to manager, obscuring the decision making process and affecting outcomes. It seems to work particularly virulently in cases where the organisation has statutory responsibilities, and therefore anxieties, as in mental health and child care. It is not a new concept, being based in the psycho-dynamic theory of transference and projection, and was illuminated years ago in psycho-analytic studies (Searles 1965), later applied to social work (Mattinson 1975) and more recently to collaboration in multi-disciplinary work (Woodhouse and Pengelly 1991).

The stress resulting from a particularly painful client situation, for example the actual or suspected physical abuse of a child, or severe neglect of an older person or a person with developmental disability, may be too upsetting to contemplate fully when other work is also making pressing demands on time and energy. This can set up an avoidance strategy which conceals the reality, so that the facts remain unexamined and the (often unadmitted) emotional response – outrage, anger, sadness or frustration – takes over, impeding clear thinking and decision making.

The evidence may also trigger painful individual experience, either personal or professional, arising from the past or the present, in either social worker or supervisor, which is too risky to express. How safe does it feel to be aware of such connections? How supportive is the structure in allowing the expression of such feelings? How much does 'being a professional' demand a stiff upper lip and denial of emotional response? How unconscious, anyway, are such 'feelings connections' and do we trust existing mechanisms to bring them to expression? This dynamic is not only set in motion by the situations of clients. It may be initiated by competition and hostility between different sections or levels of an organisation; by a sense of being undervalued and overworked; or by rivalry between professional groups. Whatever the roots of this mirroring process, it is fed by lack of acknowledgement and expression of authentic feelings, nurtured by the felt need to keep up some sort of front, and encouraged by a working context which promotes anxiety. Supervision has an obviously crucial role in short-circuiting such a potentially destructive force. In agencies which contend with statutory demands, inadequate resources, confusion about role, competing needs, potentially adverse publicity, and the resultant 'cover your back' defensive culture, what hope do supervisors have in preventing this dynamic? What do they need to support them in the process?

THE SUPPORT OF SUPERVISORS

If mirroring, stemming from the stressful content or context of work, is taking place, supervisors are also likely to be caught up in the process and need to resort to defensive denial or collusive behaviour to spare themselves. So, before discussing their role in limiting the damage, it is important to emphasise that they too need consultation and support in unravelling the process and that the face they turn to management should also be demanding this. The government is now encouraging industry to pursue a policy of 'investing in people'; how much more necessary this is in people-centred services, and how crucial for the 'piggy in the middle' whose role has so often been seen as pivotal in the effective provision of service to the most vulnerable groups in society. Poor supervision has been cited in several reports of the failure of the childcare system to protect a child at risk, for example. If supervisors are to be able to do their job effectively, the mirroring must work in reverse – they must feel valued, in order to value their social workers and enable them to value their clients by providing, directly or through purchase, the best service available. Financial resources and procedural guidelines alone are not sufficient to achieve this. Even in the present situation of scarce resource, the *manner* of support and consultation can go a long way to ameliorating the pressures under which supervisors and their staff are working.

It is impossible to discuss the role of supervisors without also touching on that of their managers and the hierarchy in which they work. Much of what comes later in this chapter, particularly the 'reflective questions' at the end, is applicable to the responsibilities of senior managers in the supervision of social workers. Their capacity to grasp the emotional impact of much of the work and to recognise the effects of stress on themselves and their staff is central to providing adequate support for the supervisory role. They must develop mechanisms to ensure that they are informed of and respond to these aspects of work. Their availability and accessibility to supervisors should be guaranteed as a part of the *sine qua non* of the supervision of social workers. I hesitate to denote actual levels within the hierarchy as this will depend upon the different structures in the range of public, voluntary and private organisations. Indeed, in some cases, the supervision of volunteers may fall within the responsibilities of basic social workers, who themselves will be receiving supervision. In essence, I mean 'supervision' to apply to the *process*, at whatever level it takes place, and assume that in a truly aware organisation it will occur at various levels in the hierarchy in different but appropriate ways. It may not even be called by that term; perhaps 'consultation' would fit better in some circumstances. Wherever it happens, whatever it is called, however it is structured, a key aspect to explore is the '*personal in the professional*'.

THE PERSONAL IN THE PROFESSIONAL

Admitting to vulnerability, expressing feelings, or helping others to do so, may seem to cross boundaries which take one outside 'professionalism'. The essence of the following discussion is extracted from an article written for the *Journal of Interprofessional Care* (Ash 1992). Trying to answer the questions *what is personal? what is professional? where do they overlap?* leads into murky waters; the more one seeks clarity of definition, the more confused become the boundaries. Yet, in common parlance, reference to 'professional' implies elements of specific knowledge, expertise, experience and training, and a certain reliable objectivity and replicability in action. Professions vary in their prescriptiveness to practitioners. Codes of practice and ethics commonly exhort professionals to ideals of attitude and behaviour towards clients and colleagues, implying that 'personal' and 'professional' matters should be quite separate. Being 'professional' seems to mean monitoring and restraining expression of feelings and, in particular, suppressing the 'subjective' experiences which may be part of the current moment or triggered by it, in behaviour which emphasises head rather than heart. Being 'personal', on the other hand, suggests the possibility of expressing (perhaps spontaneously) a whole range of feelings, arising from the present or any previous situation, and emphasising heart rather than head.

This may seem a simplistic and artificial divide, but it applies to many who regard themselves as 'professionals' and, in so doing, disregard their personal agenda in interactions with clients or colleagues. Obviously, there would be little benefit to clients in sharing personal concerns inappropriately. But trying to ignore or suppress part of our experience can result in an impoverishment in the interaction between practitioners and clients, supervisors and social workers. It is both wasteful and perilous to ignore feelings and life experiences in the belief that there is some unsulliable 'professional' mode of being.

We know, from the contrasting viewpoints of depth psychology and quantum mechanics, that there is, in reality, no neat divide between the 'objective' (professional) and the 'subjective' (personal). Whether or not it is acknowledged or utilised, we, willy-nilly, bring all of us to each encounter and aspects of our personal selves inevitably leak into our professional activities. How we dress, for instance, provides an enormous amount of 'personal' information and says something individual. How we stand, speak, compose our faces, use makeup, cut our hair, all tell a huge amount of our personal story. But, more important, our feelings, either the left-over emotion from recent encounters or from past experience, resonate in every present interaction, however 'professional' its context. 'Objective professional' and 'subjective personal' constantly overlap and the less aware we are of this the less effective we are in practice.

We tend to get drawn into either work or life experiences that relate to our individual internal issues. We are influenced by, often unacknowledged, forces springing from our personal/individual experience which, if brought into the open, could fuel and energise our contribution. We cannot afford to miss this rich resource by hiding within the armour of 'professionalism'. The family therapist, Robin Skynner, commenting on his work with a married couple, in which his personal life unexpectedly but helpfully intruded, put it like this in a *Guardian* article (Feb 1992) – 'This kind of discovery – that many successes in one's chosen work are brought about by very simple factors, easily understood by anyone, rather than through painfully acquired professional knowledge – probably has to wait until one is old enough not to be worried about playing a humbler role than one envisaged at medical school.'

How, then, can this personal/professional overlap become transparent and useful in the supervision of social work practice? The route seems to be through a reflective and critical process, which acknowledges the part that feelings, whatever their source, play in responses to others.

REFLECTIVE SUPERVISION

Using supervision *appropriately* – to examine when personal issues are unhelpfully triggered by work; to become more aware of when projections might be colouring perceptions of others; to own the feelings that are aroused by present or dredged up from past experience; to rehearse authentic practice – may sound difficult and as though confusing the roles of supervisor and counsellor. But such reflection can happen at any level of engagement and is, quite simply, admitting that there is more of oneself in every interaction than meets the eye.

Reflective supervision produces reflective practice. This is significant because it can take into account and both value and evaluate *any* response to a given situation. Feelings are as important as facts, gut reactions as valuable as theory. Only by allowing and exploring them can those that distort or promote defensive practice be discarded. There are various ways of achieving this.

Supervisors can be compared to educators or facilitators of learning, in the way they are described by Donald Schon in his book *The Reflective Practitioner*. He comments 'If educators hope to contribute to the development of reflective practitioners, they must become adept at such reflection on their own teaching (*supervision*) practice' (Schon 1991). A later paper (Schon 1992) refers to some

> 'rare individuals (who) are not so much 'teachers' as 'coaches' of reflection-in-action. Their artistry consists in an ability to have on the tip of their tongue, or to invent on-the-spot, the method peculiarly suited to the difficulties experienced by the student (*or social worker*) before them... The development of forms of professional education (*or supervision*) conducive to reflection-in-action requires reflection on the artistry of coaching...' (my parentheses)

The very notion of 'artistry' leads directly into territory which smacks of the esoteric – the 'mastery–mystery' of professional knowing, which seems to deny its groundedness in everyday experience. But the reflective process does recognise the need for mutuality between supervisor and practitioner, for self-criticism and for the ability to operate simultaneously at different levels of awareness.

Working with social workers, their supervisors and managers and colleagues from other disciplines on preparation for applying the changed childcare legislation, we discovered the value as well as the difficulty of addressing feelings aroused by practice issues. These were triggered by client scenes from *Acceptable Risk?* (*op.cit.*) chosen by the training officers for their appropriateness and the fact that they were typical in interpreting legislation and procedures in the decisions about children at risk.

It would have been easier to have focused only on the legal and procedural framework. The 'reality' of troubled clients introduced another dimension to the responses and stimulated some heated and conflicting views, often based on past experience or the acknowledgement of personal and professional dilemmas. Yet the workshops were enlivened and enriched by these expressions, and understanding about applying the procedures deepened. The immediate 'gut' responses to the clients' predicaments included a range of feelings – anger, exasperation, frustration, guilt, sadness, inadequacy – and led to the conclusion that there is no 'right' emotional response and that each person brings their own constellation of experience from all aspects of their lives to bear on each client encounter. The exercise illuminated the importance of accepting this variety, acknowledging and expressing the feelings which could have impeded clarity of thought about the social work task in each case. It was particularly interesting to see how members of the different professions present became more aware of the particular stresses of each professional role when emotional as well as procedural responses were examined.

These multi-professional training events emphasised that, whatever our role and work responsibility, we share a common humanity and that the individual expression of this determines our impact on others and theirs on us. Writing in quite another context, although concerned with the connections and contradictions between 'rational thought' and 'irrational feeling', Mary Catherine Bateson (Bateson and Bateson 1988) offers an insight into how we make sense of each other and the world around us, by using the self as a metaphor. She writes:

> 'Of all available metaphors, the most central and salient, available to all human beings, is the self. Here I mean not only the psychological construct of the 'self' but the entire being, psyche and soma... Central to the net of metaphor through which we recognize and respond to the world is the experience of self and the possibility of reference to it. The evocation of self knowledge as a model for understanding another, because of similarities or congruences that make knowing possible, is properly called sympathy, but the current usage that seems to come closest is the term empathy... Empathy is a discipline.' (p.194)

EMPATHY IS A DISCIPLINE – SOME PRACTICAL SUGGESTIONS

Feeling undermined and undervalued, reflecting the low self-esteem of many clients, is a common complaint in social services. It is exacerbated by systems which honour structure and procedure before people, paperwork before inter-personal exchange. Researching *Acceptable Risk? (op.cit.)* also revealed how feeling undervalued could lead to the misuse of authority, or to lack of confidence in being appropriately authoritative, in the case of both supervisors and social workers. Stereotyped attitudes and responses to colleagues and clients can also result from the frustrations of feeling inadequate to the demands of the work, when the prevailing climate does not 'allow' people to say 'I don't know' or 'I can't' or 'I have too much to do already'.

In these cases, illness is often the get-out, as sick leave is often the only 'acceptable' reason for not performing well. To admit, even to oneself, to feeling overwhelmed, or needing personal time for family matters when others are battling on does not fit the work ethos of many social service organisations. Sickness is a well-documented response to stress; stress is usually the result of an overload of *distress* in some aspect of life. Distress, as noted above, may often be based in the impact of client situations on social workers and supervisors. Horrific abuse and neglect of the elderly and children, abandonment to the vagaries of community care provision for the mentally ill or handicapped, inadequate discharge arrangements for the chronic sick, lack of adequate housing for young families...the list could go on.

These situations, at the sharp end of social provision, are the daily diet of most social workers and, therefore of their supervisors. To meet clients in such circumstances day after day with heart as well as head makes huge demands, particularly if some of their problems resonate with our own. The following suggestions outline an approach to supervising couched in terms of the sort of questions that both supervisor and social worker might ask of themselves and of each other to promote the 'reflection in action' that Schon describes as the hallmark of professional practice (*op.cit.*). They are both general – that is, relevant to supervision in any sector and setting, and specific – that is, related to the process and dynamic of the supervisory encounter. They acknowledge the exploration of feelings as a legitimate aspect of the supervisory process.

The following are addressed to *both supervisors and supervisees*. Given the differences in organisations and the varying demands of the range of sectors and settings, they are in the first person, to emphasise that each individual should take responsibility for their own part in the supervision process. They should promote a reflective approach.

PURPOSES

General

- Am I aware of the organisation's expectations about the purposes to be achieved by supervision? How do I feel about the organisation's espoused purposes? Do I regard them as trouble-shooting? supporting? developmental? other?
- Am I clear about the *general* purpose of my supervisory sessions? Are they to reflect and advise on professional relationships and practice: with clients? with colleagues within the agency? with colleagues outwith the agency? with students and tutors?
- Are they an essential to the procedural framework of decision making? Is a line management function involved? Are statutory responsibilities involved?
- Are they an essential of resource management related to: finance? contracting out to other services? prioritising or rationalising staff assignment and workloads?
- What other *general* purposes does supervision serve?

For each session

- Am I clear which purposes are being served by each session? Is there a format which helps to clarify the agenda and distinguish between its different aspects? Do I have access to a mechanism for introducing unexpected concerns? Do I feel comfortable about challenging the 'given' purposes?
- If more than one other person is involved, are there arrangements for agreeing on main concerns beforehand? Or during the session?

Frameworks

- Are supervision sessions: regularly timetabled? on an *ad hoc* basis? a mixture of these? Does the prevailing arrangement suit: me and the rhythm and demands of my work? the culture of the organisation?
- Is the timetable adhered to? is it negotiable? Is time protected or is it vulnerable to other demands?
- Am I invariably available as arranged?

Environment

- Are supervision sessions held in a place where privacy can be respected? How important is this to me in relation to confidentiality re: myself or clients and colleagues? What might need to be changed in this respect?
- Is the environment conducive to reflection and considered thought? Is it quiet and comfortable? How do I feel about the 'supervisory space'? If I wanted to, could I do anything about it?

Process

- Is an agenda set at the beginning of each meeting? Do I feel free to introduce other concerns?
- Is the time available sufficient to deal with the matters of concern? How are priorities decided? Is the time extendable if necessary?
- Do I and others provide relevant material (papers, case notes, memos etc) beforehand? in sufficient time for reading and reflection? with suggestions as to the major issues?
- Do I prepare myself beforehand by reflecting on what I most need to achieve in the session? Do I make this intention clear to others involved?
- Are outcomes and decisions clearly noted? Are points for action agreed and noted?
- Are follow-up discussions arranged when necessary?

Dynamics

- Do I check out how the other person(s) is feeling on starting?
- Do I express how I am feeling? Do I look for clues in terms of stance, expression etc.? If I suspect that someone is feeling unwell do I comment? If I feel strongly about something, do I express this? Are there some feelings which are more difficult to express or to receive? Do I avoid these? Is confrontation a problem for me? Can I be assertive while valuing others' views? Do I feel valued in and by the process of supervision? Are there personal problems or concerns which are making work difficult? Do I feel free to express these? Do I recognise when I or others are unhelpfully 'mirroring' clients' attitudes and feelings? Is there an accepted way of exploring this appropriately without prejudice? Do I feel secure in questions to the

organisation or senior management? Can I admit that: I don't know? can't cope? need extra input? need a break? Do I feel assured that other resources or support would be available if the supervision becomes stuck or breaks down? Am I clear about the boundaries of confidentiality in supervision?

CONCLUSION

There may be aspects of supervision, additional to those implied above, specific to particular settings or sectors, which also need to be examined. However, I suggest that many of the above questions would provide a useful starting point for exploration between supervisors and supervisees and their senior managers of just what supervision means, entails and achieves. Expectations may vary and even conflict, but differences can only be addressed and, perhaps, resolved if they are expressed. Concealed conflicts can breed bad feeling which undermines the supervisory purpose and process. Openness and the security which comes from feeling valued at whatever level in an organisation is the only path to the sort of reflection and constructive criticism which entails speaking one's mind and voicing one's feelings, even when feeling foolish or vulnerable. Silence is the enemy of effective supervision wherever it takes place.

REFERENCES

Argyris, C. and Schon, D. (1974) *Theory in Practice: Increasing Professional Effectiveness*. San Francisco: Jossey-Bass.

Ash, E. (1988) *Acceptable Risk?: Supervision in Child Abuse Cases Video and Training Guide*. London: CCETSW.

Ash, E. (1992) Towards Reflective Education. *Journal of Interprofessional Care*, 6, 3.

Bateson, G. and M.C. (1988) *Angels Fear*. London: Century Hutchinson.

Mattinson, J. (1975) *The Reflection Process in Casework Supervision*. London: Institute of marital Studies.

Schon, D. (1983, 1991) *The Reflective Practitioner – How Professionals Think in Action*. England: Avebury Academic Publishing Group.

Schon, D. (1992) The crisis of professional knowledge and the pursuit of an epistemology of practice. *Journal of Interprofessional Care*, 6, 1.

Searles, H.F. (1965) *Collected Papers on Schizophrenia and Related Subjects*. London: The Hogarth Press, Institute of Psychoanalysis.

Skynner, R. (1992) Article in *Weekend Guardian* Feb 8/9.

Woodhouse, D. and Pengelly, P. (1991) *Anxiety and the Dynamics of Collaboration*. Aberdeen University Press.

CHAPTER 3

SUPERVISION IN A STATUTORY AGENCY

PAUL BORLAND

'The supervisor-worker relationship is the key encounter where the influence of organisational authority and professional identity collide, collude or connect.' (Middleman and Rhodes 1980)

This chapter explores the tension that can exist in a statutory agency when practitioners' experience of supervision is at variance with what they say they need to help them do their job. The unacknowledged complexity and potential conflict of what is on offer and what is looked for can have a demoralising effect upon both the practitioner and manager – if the expectations of both parties, which may at times be different, are not made explicit, then neither the needs of the practitioner nor the expectations of the agency are met. The focus of this chapter will be on individual supervision by the line manager – the usual, but not the only way in which the work of practitioners is supervised.

During the 1960s and 1970s, when practitioners were promoted to be team leaders and supervisors, the term 'management' did not feature prominently, either in the interview for the job or in the initial training for the new role. There appeared to be a consensus about what constituted the key tasks of the role, with little written specifically about the elements of being a manager in a social work agency. Lawrence (1986) defines management as:

- getting things done
- setting objectives
- taking decisions about the means by which objectives will be reached
- solving problems which frustrate the achievement of objectives.

Staff who became supervisors were promoted because of their ability to act as senior practitioners – they might be people who were thought to be able to assist staff deal with the complexity of the work with cases. The assumption implicit in this process supported the idea that the practitioner had the authority to make decisions about cases, prioritise their own schedule and resources (usually the practitioner's own time). The practitioner consulted the supervisor whenever it was felt appropriate. A discussion about a particular issue was, and often still is, initiated by the practitioner and not by the supervisor. This was based on social workers being seen as professionally trained and therefore as enjoying a degree of autonomy over their particular approach or style of intervention, and subscribing to a set of ethical principles which determined how they behaved when they were with service users. However uneasy we might be about the accuracy of the terminology, the practitioner had a 'professional' relationship with the agency client, often referred to as 'my client'. It was assumed that the practitioner, and only the practitioner, would know when to bring a case for discussion in supervision. The team leader had the task of making herself available to discuss cases or issues that the practitioner brought.

There seemed to be a degree of consensus, about what were the key areas of the work with clients. Social work as a profession appeared to have a cohesion and contained an optimism about its efficacy. The sense of confidence which grew from this may in fact have been little more than an illusion, as few researchers had looked at the outcomes for clients from contact with social work agencies. The theoretical framework used by a significant number of practitioners could loosely be described as psychodynamic counselling or 'rehabilitation through casework' (Vanstone 1990) – this laid great emphasis on the relationship between the client and the worker. There was a tacit agreement between managers and practitioners that managers did not have the right to inspect work and that the agenda for the supervision of work was generated by the practitioner alone. Supervision might attempt to concentrate on the difficulties brought by the practitioner, or where the case was 'stuck', by focussing on the dynamics of the interaction between worker and client. Much of the literature supporting this approach came from the world of psychotherapy, a key text being Janet Mattinson's book *The Reflection Process in Casework Supervision* (1975).

How social workers behaved started to be scrutinised much more in the 1970s and 1980s. The enquiry into the death of Maria Colwell in 1973 was the start of a series of significant public, and often painful, examinations of what had happened in cases where practitioners had the responsibility of helping vulnerable children who had subsequently died (DHSS 1974, London Borough of Brent 1985). Whilst these enquiries also seemed to serve other purposes as society looked to find scapegoats there is no doubt that they created an increasingly hostile climate for social workers. Marguerite Valentine has explored this theme in an interesting essay 'The Social Worker as "Bad Object"' (Valentine 1994). But, significantly, the enquiries created anxiety for agency senior managers who began to prescribe the type of oversight that was expected from team leaders – most, if not all, social work agencies in England and Wales have clear guide-lines for the supervision of practitioners involved in child protection cases.

Local Area Child Protection Committees have produced detailed sets of procedures for any worker likely to encounter child abuse. Some agencies, for example the Probation Service, have policy statements about their expectations of supervisors (South Yorkshire Probation Service 1992), Blom-Cooper (London Borough of Brent 1985) goes so far as to describe what the public have the right to expect from the supervision of staff, in his enquiry report on the death of Jasmine Beckford:

'He (sic) must compel the front line worker to examine their judgements in a critical way. If it is felt that the judgement of the front line worker is faulty it would be the duty of the supervisor to make a visit with the front line worker to see for himself or herself what the true situation is. The loss of objectivity is a common factor in the management of high risk cases.' (p.217)

Blom-Cooper also describes the optimistic approach which social workers regularly adopt in their work and suggests that the supervisor has a particular task:

'The supervisor must constantly apply the suppressor to the unbridled rule of optimism.' (p.217)

During the same period a radical appraisal of social work was developing as sociologists questioned many of the assumptions and values that had been prevalent for two decades or more (Pearson 1975). Social work practitioners were faced with real dilemmas as they went about their work – people on statutory caseloads were from socio-economic groups that were marginalised in society and seemingly had little power. The behaviour of statutory agency clients could only be understood in the context of the pressures the clients were experiencing. The casework approach, relying as it did on a medical model of seeing problems brought by service users as symptomatic of individual pathology, was criticised comprehensively (Walker and Beaumont 1981).

This led to a crisis of confidence among many practitioners as they felt they were dealing with intractable difficulties caused by a complex series of events, not least of which is the way society is structured. They might, like myself, have also been painfully aware the failure of their clients' lives. It was also a failure that practitioners were in danger of internalising – it could become their failure to bring about change. They were caught between the articulate critique of radical social work commentators and an increasingly impatient and judgmental public. The self-image of practitioners and supervisors was easily undermined.

The other major influence on team leaders was the rise of managerialism during the 1980s, prompted by the reforms generated by the new right under Margaret Thatcher. Public sector organisations became more cost conscious and were compelled to think about budgets as funding was cut back. The political decisions made about funding the public sector were accompanied by generalised criticisms in the press about the standard of service offered. The liberal ideals upon which social work has been built – that society has a responsibility towards those experiencing difficulties, that a penal policy in any democracy should reflect a need to care as well as punish and so forth – were called into question. This increased the uncertainty within the social work profession about its place in society and what it could accomplish.

The development of policies and guide-lines within agencies, whilst sorely needed in a number of important areas of practice, are sometimes perceived by practitioners as a restriction on their autonomy. Greater controls were being exercised about what practitioners did and how resources were used. The Audit Commission has emphasised the importance of developing management expertise within social work agencies (Audit Commission 1986, Audit Commission 1989). Managers became more aware that they needed to manage their resources carefully and were expected to exercise a greater degree of oversight of the work taking place in their teams (Department of Health 1990). Policies were also being developed within agencies, sometimes in line with legislation and best practice (Equal Opportunities, Anti-Racism, Health and Safety etc.), or practice procedures determined by public and professional concerns (the development of guide-lines within probation services on the handling and review of, for example, dangerous clients, and the Area Child Protection Committee policy documents which have an impact on any manager supervising staff). The effect is to prescribe what should happen when managers and staff meet and supervision is experienced in many instances as not being practitioner-led. Elsewhere in this book the impact of the Community Care Act is examined (see Chapter 6). Modern technology can give managers rapid and, sometimes, accurate information about resources and demands for service and the decentralisation of budgets means that the ability to read a balance sheet and cope with technological change can be a required skill for team leaders. The 'purchaser/provider' split within social services departments has moved many middle managers into unfamiliar territory. These changes have a profound effect on the relationship between them and their staff.

Middle managers in social work needed to be more explicit with staff about the employer/employee context of supervision. Team leaders now have an expectation placed upon them that they will monitor work and inspect what is happening in cases – usually those cases covered by policy directives. Those cases are ones which give rise to agency anxiety where checks are required to avoid mistakes and where there is the likelihood of public scrutiny. This anxiety can be generated by the type of media coverage of cases where a tragedy has occurred, but it might also be more than simply a pragmatic 'back covering' exercise.

Managers may genuinely wish to assist staff over such matters as assessing risk and dealing with the complex cases where clients' behaviour poses problems for the public or for staff. The difficulty arises when staff see the purpose of supervision primarily as a way of checking that difficult cases are being handled properly. The notion of 'accountability', defined as making staff answerable for their decisions and actions, can be an overriding feature of supervision. Parsloe (1981) has described an important confusion that exists in social work between 'accountability' and 'responsibility'. She sees accountability as 'the formal line of decision-making, and control and authority of the position from the Director, through the line-manager/supervisors, to the practitioner'. Responsibility is 'the practitioner's feelings of personal responsibility for the quality of the work with clients and for the judgements informing that work' (Parsloe 1981).

The Beckford Report is unambiguous – supervision is about the formal structure of accountability within an agency – and it has had a strong influence on our understanding of the supervisor's role.

Supervisors have the difficult task of encompassing the whole experience of the work in supervision and meet the staff member in a number of ways:

Figure 3.1

Supervision of social work staff is more than the simple oversight of employees to ensure that they are conforming to agency guidelines. It must take account of the whole person; it has to model what is good practice with clients. It has to acknowledge that staff have discretion and should exercise their own judgement as they are best placed to make assessments about needs of service users and any other matters connected with their lives and behaviour. Staff do need to be held accountable for their judgements but not in a manner which diminishes their sense of themselves as professional people trying to empower service users. Some of the judgements that workers make have profound social implications for people and those judgements need to be tested – sometimes in the context of supervision with the line manager, sometimes in a case discussion with colleagues or a multi-agency group. Many workers bring difficult cases for examination and are open about their need to have that judgement tested and to be held accountable.

In a statutory agency there is an expectation that the line manager will instigate case reviews as part of the agency procedure in complex cases. The supervisor can easily be seen by members of the team as a representative of the employing authority and supervision becomes drawn more towards the employer/employee setting, with demoralising consequences for staff. Managing the tension between offering a safe reflective environment within which staff can develop and be supported on the one hand, and ensuring that agency requirements are met on the other, is possibly the most important task for supervisors.

Managers need to share with teams something of the dilemma of the role – being open with staff and exploring what those tensions might mean for them individually or as a group. Motivating staff and helping them deal with the conflicts that face them demand a versatility and an openness from managers. That process can be initiated during team meetings. The illustration in Figure 3.2 might be a useful starting point for a discussion about expectations of supervision as it reminds everyone of the numerous nuts and bolts that go to make up the whole. Conducting the discussion within the group might empower staff to talk more freely about their hopes and expectations. This can be a useful stage before any discussion about a supervision contract. The illustration in Figure 3.2 is taken from an appendix to the South Yorkshire Probation Service Supervision Policy.

Is supervision simply about exercising a degree of oversight of the work of staff, as Blom-Cooper would have us believe? Supervision is talked about by social work practitioners and managers in a manner which suggests that it is central to how people understand, and cope with, the job they are asked to do. Supervision cannot be understood solely in the managerial context of exercising oversight to ensure that the right things have been done.

Staff in statutory agencies work with marginalised and troubled people and the maintenance of morale becomes central as workers need to sustain themselves emotionally and remain motivated to provide a service of high quality. There are matters which are implicit in supervision which can create a tension between supervisor and supervisee. What motivated someone to join a social work agency? What understandings have people developed about a range of issues such as good-enough parenting, delinquency, race, gender, violence? It is primarily in supervision that the exploration of the values we hold and the prejudices we have grown up with can be explored in a way that helps us learn and move forward.

Can staff trust the supervisory relationship enough to share their thinking about their work? Because of the interpersonal nature of social work, its assessments and interventions, sharing your thinking does not remain a cerebral activity – you describe in that process something of yourself and your belief system. Supervision touches on questions about power and authority – the worker's power in a case and the legitimate exercise of authority; the supervisor's power over the worker and the authority of a line management structure in an organisation where staff, rightly, exercise a professional judgement and have a personal responsibility for the quality of the work.

The supervisor will be bound up with the personal as well as the professional and the managerial. When work is being examined, supervisors need to be keenly aware of the process issues as well as the content of what is being said. What is the real meaning of what the client has said or done? What does it mean to the worker? How are we to make sense of it? How does the service user make sense of what is happening in their lives and the agency's role? The complex dynamics of the interaction between service-users and agency staff is not a straightforward business and developing an understanding of how best to help or intervene requires careful reflection (see Chapter 2).

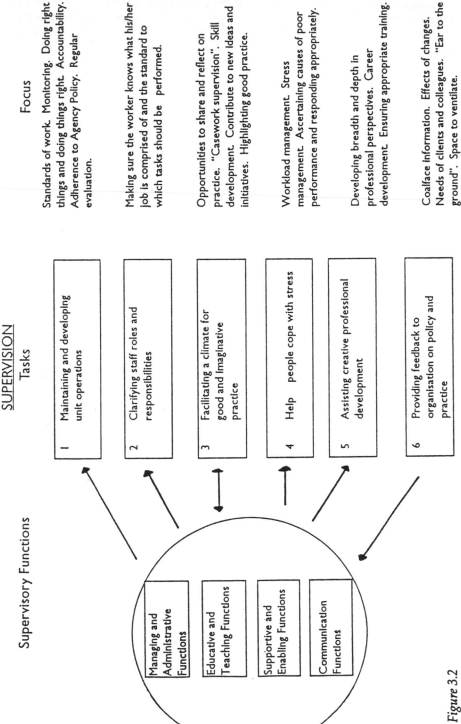

Figure 3.2

SUPERVISION
Tasks

1 Maintaining and developing unit operations

2 Clarifying staff roles and responsibilities

3 Facilitating a climate for good and imaginative practice

4 Help people cope with stress

5 Assisting creative professional development

6 Providing feedback to organisation on policy and practice

Supervisory Functions

Managing and Administrative Functions

Educative and Teaching Functions

Supportive and Enabling Functions

Communication Functions

Focus

Standards of work. Monitoring. Doing right things and doing things right. Accountability. Adherence to Agency Policy. Regular evaluation.

Making sure the worker knows what his/her job is comprised of and the standard to which tasks should be performed.

Opportunities to share and reflect on practice. "Casework supervision". Skill development. Contribute to new ideas and initiatives. Highlighting good practice.

Workload management. Stress management. Ascertaining causes of poor performance and responding appropriately.

Developing breadth and depth in professional perspectives. Career development. Ensuring appropriate training.

Coalface information. Effects of changes. Needs of clients and colleagues. "Ear to the ground". Space to ventilate.

The sensitivity that the work requires means that workers are open to a range of feelings that they have to manage. It can be a distressing occupation and the optimism of staff, so regularly criticised as naive by child abuse enquiries, is a fundamental approach that brings many into the job in the first place. Challenging that 'optimism' during supervision has to be done with sensitivity and care. The straightforward exercise of applying tighter controls through supervision will have a demoralising effect. Not to acknowledge the underlying complexity of the work is to ignore how human beings behave and the feelings that they have. If supervisors are not able, or are disinclined to enter into a reflective discussion of the work, and its impact, staff may feel that they are not being given the experience of being heard in a way which has meaning for them. Despite our best efforts, supervision may be viewed by staff as a bureaucratic exercise within which the agency seeks to ensure, through the supervisor, that the collective 'back has been covered'.

REFERENCES

Audit Commission (1986) *Making a Reality of Community Care*. London: H.M.S.O.

Audit Commission (1989) *The Value for Money Audit Guide*. London: H.M.S.O.

Department of Health (1990) *Management Development: Guidance For Local Authority Social Service Departments*. London: Social Services Inspectorate.

D.H.S.S. (1974) *Report of the Committee of Inquiry into the Care and Supervision Provided in Relation to Maria Colwell*. London: H.M.S.O.

Lawrence, P. (1986) *Invitation to Management*. Oxford: Blackwell.

London Borough of Brent (1985) '*A Child in Trust*' – the Report of the Panel of Enquiry into the Circumstances surrounding the Death of Jasmine Beckford. London: London Borough of Brent.

Mattinson, J. (1975) *The reflection process in casework supervision*. London: Institute of Marital Studies.

Middleman, R. and Rhodes, G. (1980) Teaching the Practice of Supervision, *Journal of Education for Social Work*, 16, pp.51–59.

Parsloe, P. (1981) *Social Services Area Teams*. London: George Allen and Unwin.

Pearson, G. (1975) *The Deviant Imagination*. London: Macmillan.

South Yorkshire Probation Service (1992) *Child Protection Procedures*. Sheffield.

Valentine, M. (1994) 'The Social Worker as Bad Object' *British Journal of Social Work* 24, 71–86.

Vanstone M. (1988) 'Values, Leadership,and the Future of the Probation Service'. *Probation Journal*, 35: 4, pp.131-134.

Walker, H. and Beaumont, B. (1981) *Probation Work – Critical Theory and Socialist Practice*. Oxford: Basil Blackwell.

CHAPTER 4

SUPERVISION OF SOCIAL SERVICES MANAGERS

PATRICIA RILEY

INTRODUCTION

Guidance on supervision of social services staff has, in the past, tended to concentrate on support for front-line staff only. Much less attention has been paid to the need for skilled supervision of social services middle and senior managers. Yet if the management of staff and services is incompetent, or underfunded and too thin on the ground, front-line staff get no support and cannot deliver a quality service. The consequences of such service failures can be tragic and irreversible, both for users of social services and for staff.

This chapter will attempt to redress that balance. First, the environment in which such social services managers have to operate will be described. Second, a model for supervision will be proposed which has been devised to provide support for the complex and very challenging role fulfilled by social services managers. This model will embrace both the need for individual supervision of social services managers and for team development. Some examples of training exercises which can be used for management development are included in an Appendix at the end of the chapter.

MANAGEMENT IN SOCIAL SERVICES

The work of a manager in social services, if it is thought of at all by the wider public, is generally misunderstood. The role of the social services department itself is frequently confused with that of the Department of Social Security, or is seen as an agency concerned primarily with the welfare of children. If a government minister can, with a naiveté that would be touching if it were not so dangerous, suggest that social services departments should recruit 'street-wise grannies' to work in child protection, what hope have we that members of the general public are aware of the complexity of the task, or the need for high levels of professionalism in social services management? This dismissive attitude is further encouraged when trade unions, Councillors and the media simplistically demand more resources for front-line services, conveniently forgetting that someone has to manage these services properly if they are to be effective.

Social services managers are required to ensure the implementation of the huge variety of social services legislation affecting children and families, older people, people with physical disabilities, people with learning disabilities, and people with a mental health problem. Social services managers, at coal-face and at a more senior level, are also required to manage a bewildering variety of services set up under the discretionary powers of local authorities to meet actual or perceived local needs – day centres, nurseries, outreach schemes, welfare rights advice services, provision for post-disaster counsel-ling, and so forth. All demand different levels of professional and technical knowledge and, depending on systems of delegation, different levels of sophistication in managerial skill. Thorough knowledge of the geographical area covered by the department, levels of local service demand, social pat-terns, needs of minority groups, and resources provided by the council and other agencies, are just the foundation on which other more sophisticated managerial skills must be built.

The higher up the promotional ladder a manager climbs, the greater and more diverse become the demands of his/her legal knowledge, and profes-sional and technical skills. In more senior posts, managers find themselves involved less and less with the routine work of the department. Instead, they concentrate on decisions in situations of significant risk, politically sensitive issues, industrial relations and personnel problems, policy development, negotiations with other agencies (especially the NHS, housing, schools and the police), and investigations into complaints of poor service standards. Good interpersonal skills, alongside the development of a much broader range of professional and technical knowledge, become essential. At the most senior level (apart from where exceptionally difficult cases arise), managers will concentrate on strategic planning, working with elected councillors, budget control, the management of change, and on the maintenance of service quality through middle and front-line managers and specialist senior practi-tioners.

Social services departments are the second-largest consumers of council funds, their annual budgets being exceeded only by those of education departments. The largest social services departments have budgets well in excess of £100m and employ upwards of 8000 staff. Despite this, the social services managerial task is under-estimated by the department's own staff, officers from other departments, and councillors. Decisions may be made by other council departments without considering the consequences for social services (e.g. changes in council rents, priorities in housing allocation, or education provision for children with special needs). Or the council may decide to adopt a new monitoring system well-suited to a small department such as Trading Standards, but quite unsuited to a department the size of social services. (Cross-authority comparisons of staff sickness levels taken from computerised payroll data are a good example of this. Such data fre-quently fail to differentiate between part-time and full-time staff, thus artifi-cially inflating sickness levels in any department such as social services with a high proportion of part-time staff.)

Senior social services managers need to be adept at interpreting statistics and accounts, and effective at negotiating with colleagues from across the Authority, as well as being able to stand back from sectional interests to take a corporate, council-wide view. They do not, of course, need to be qualified accountants, statisticians, or personnel managers, since specialists will be employed in those roles. But without a significant working knowledge of statistics, budgets and employment law, Social Services managers will be over-dependant on those specialists, and unable to fulfil properly their responsibilities for planning, monitoring, line-management, and control of service quality.

White collar trades union membership is particularly strong among social services staff, especially those employed in fieldwork, while manual unions have many members among residential and domiciliary care staff. Manual and white collar unions do not always agree in their approach to employment issues, which can create problems for managers. However, with the trends towards amalgamation of unions (e.g. the amalgamation of NALGO, NUPE and COHSE in 1993 to form a new super-union, UNISON), such inter-union clashes may occur less often in future. One aspect of industrial relations in social services is unlikely to change, however, whatever changes parliament may make to trades union law. Social services staff, whether qualified or not, interact on a daily basis with the most disadvantaged members of society, for whose welfare they care passionately and for whom they are frequently called upon to act as advocates. That same passion and those same advocacacy skills can very easily be used in negotiating with managers about their own needs as employees – and frequently are! Social services managers need to accept the reality of this, and to be committed to working constructively with trades unions. In a highly politicised industrial relations climate such as social services, the management of change will always prove particularly challenging: careful planning, an honest approach, a sense of humour, and excellent negotiating skills are required. If cuts in services are the issue, a real appreciation among managers and councillors of what will mean *on the ground* for service-users and staff is essential.

Latterly, as a result of legislation, the rise of consumerism, and changing fashions in management training, there has been a welcome rise in emphasis placed in social services departments on proactive methods of managing service quality. To carry this out effectively, managers must study structure (inputs such as buildings, equipment and staff), process (what is done with the inputs), and outcomes (Donabedian 1990). Outcome cannot be assessed unless standards are set. Standards should be high – if minimum standards are set, those are what will be interpreted as being acceptable. An element of inspection and policing is an inevitable part of quality management. Some is statutory, for example the operation of inspections under the Registration Act 1984, and scrutiny of complaints. Other systems are discretionary, for example the monitoring of statistics on the employment of people from disadvantaged groups.

Quality assurance, with its emphasis on ownership of service quality by the whole staff-group, is the other imperative. Managers must not regard the management of quality as an optional extra, or as something that would be 'very nice to do if we only had the time'. The lives of vulnerable people depend on the commitment of managers and staff to the achievement of high quality service standards and to their determination to tackle shortcomings when these are found – even if a few feathers get ruffled in the process of problem solving.

Finally, there is the political dimension underlying all work in local government, and the need to understand the role of councillors, both collectively and individually. The council's policies and level of member involvement in the work of the social services department will be heavily affected by ideology. Broadly speaking, the further towards the political Left the council moves, the deeper will be the active interest of councillors in the work of its social workers and care staff.

Whatever its political colour, however, the council is accountable through Acts of Parliament for a whole range of Social Services functions. It is inevitable, too, that many such functions will be viewed warily by local politicians of all political parties – that is, as potential vote-losers if mishandled and subjected to adverse media attention. Home help services, the care of juvenile offenders in the community, and the protection of abused children are examples of issues regarded very understandably by councillors as having particular political sensitivity. Councillors may deal with these potential problems by working in partnership with managers to prevent problems arising. They may deal with tensions by becoming increasingly personally involved with particular cases, or by developing systems with enable them to monitor social work activity very closely (e.g. by involvement in staff selection to quite a low level of seniority, or by regular attendance at management meetings). At the other extreme, councillors may decide to distance themselves as much as possible from the department's activities, thus enabling them to blame front-line staff and/or senior officers with impunity when anything goes publicly wrong.

The approach of councillors to the media will reflect the prevailing political view of council accountability for service quality, and the rightful role of councillors as advocates for members of the local population. It will also reflect the politicians' need to keep one eye firmly focussed on the ballot box. Councillors will be preoccupied to some extent with the implications of internal battles for power between prominent councillors, and media attention will be sought from time to time to focus attention on both rising and waning stars. This will sometimes be advantageous for the department: at other times, it will be detrimental. A wise local government manager keeps abreast of internal political developments and teaches colleagues to do likewise, or much time will be wasted on initiatives that will not receive council support for reasons that have little to do with the merit of the proposal concerned.

The political challenge presented by management of local personal social services provisions is a fact of life. It cannot be avoided, as to intervene in society by the provision of social services is to undertake a political act. The UK has an adversarial political system: hence, some groups will applaud an intervention, and others will condemn it as a matter of principle. In view of this, it is a naive manager who views councillors as a source of interference in the exercise of his/her managerial and professional responsibilities.

Certainly, the relationship between councillors and social services managers can be frustrating, especially at the senior level, but if local democracy is to mean anything at all it must be made to work through a partnership of understanding and mutual respect. Relationships between councillors and managers should never be allowed to degenerate into a bitter civil war between opposing power-blocks. Social services staff and middle-managers often underestimate the influence of councillors, or fail to take into account the pressures councillors face. If a real partnership is to be achieved, social services managers must become more politically aware, and must educate their staff in political awareness. If they fail in this, the department's clients and staff will suffer.

> Nothing is more guaranteed to undermine morale and energies than constantly putting up proposals for change which are doomed to fail, either because they are presented in ways which are totally out of tune with the prevailing political viewpoint or because they are not fed into the political process in the appropriate manner. (Daniel and Wheeler 1989)

Summary

It is ironic that public sector managers are constantly being exhorted to look to the private sector for models of managerial expertise and professionalism. Social services managers daily manage much larger budgets, more complex operations, and greater numbers of employees on more widely dispersed sites than the vast majority of managers in the private sector are ever expected to do. They generally do this very effectively, but with little public appreciation or knowledge of their work.

The business social services managers are in is externally defined and re-defined, both by the Government of the day and local politicians, not by market forces or the personal vision of gifted groups of entrepreneurial manager. As such, the task changes constantly. It can be influenced by its senior managers but not controlled by them. Media exposure and political pressures are a way of life, and customers in the social service's 'business' consist of the most vulnerable or unpredictable groups in society. Social services managers work in a highly stressful environment, do not enjoy high status, and are not recognised for the skills they have either by politicians or by members of the public. Without the often spectacular financial rewards paid to senior managers of large organisations in the private sector, it is doubtful whether private sector managers would queue up to take on the challenge of running a social services department, let alone enjoy success and personal fulfilment if appointed! The managerial task is very different from that faced by a private sector manager, demands different skills, and attracts different people.

To fulfil their increasingly complex role effectively, social services managers must develop expertise in the following areas:

Professional

- Social services legislation (current and planned)
- Needs of different client-groups and service settings
- Roles of professionals from other agencies

- Research findings
- Government reports
- Codes of professional practice.

Knowledge of the geographical area

- Social structure
- Minority groups and cultural issues
- Local factors (e.g. unemployment, poverty, urban or rural environment)
- Resources (council, other public agencies, the private and voluntary sector).

Technical

- Information technology and interpretation of statistics
- Accounts and budgeting
- Employment law and industrial relations
- Cross-council relationships
- Corporate management techniques.

Line-management

- Communication and interpersonal skills
- Equal opportunities issues
- Quality assurance
- Stress management
- Personnel management
- Performance review.

Political awareness

- Understanding of the role of elected councillors, in power and in opposition
- Local party political structures (formal and informal)
- Committee work
- Knowledge of the manifesto, beliefs and 'culture' of the local party group in power
- Links between groups (e.g. links between unions and Labour members, local employers and Conservative members, voluntary organisations and councillors, family links, etc.)
- Contracts with the voluntary and private sectors
- Media management.

SUPERVISION OF INDIVIDUAL MANAGERS

Content of supervision sessions

Supervision of social services managers must be a semi-structured, two-way process through which a supervisor

- provides information, gives support and feedback, and helps to improve the level of competence of a manager in his/her work
- monitors the effectiveness of that work
- identifies training needs and potential of managers for career development
- encourages and channels new ideas, while advising on departmental realities and political strategy
- monitors manageability and equity of workload between managers
- acts, as far as possible, to minimise stress and avoid burn-out among managers and staff.

Supervision should take place in regular timetabled sessions (e.g. one hour monthly, or more frequently if local circumstances warrant this), but supervisors should also operate an 'open door' policy, being available when needed. *Ad hoc* sessions can be used

- if urgent guidance or support is needed
- where a serious incident or breach of good practice has occurred
- where a high level of risk means that accountability for a particular decision should be shared
- over an issue which has become politically sensitive, or where there is media interest.

The higher the level of responsibility of the managers concerned within the social services department, the more the content of supervision sessions will become strategic, and the less concentration there will be on cases or issues of individual professional practice.

Development of managers through individual supervision sessions should focus on their skills in those areas of expertise identified previously in this chapter.

Supervision should not be confused with annual appraisal, through which job descriptions should be reviewed, achievements formally considered against objectives jointly set the year before, and training needs identified.

Practice of supervision

If managerial decisions made during supervision sessions are to be effective, the process must involve a two-way exchange of ideas and information. It must be based on a relationship of trust, honest feedback, and mutual respect. This is best achieved by discussion and agreement, at the start of the supervisor/supervisee relationship, of what supervision is and what it is intended to achieve.

Social services managers, especially at a senior level, often have to supervise people from managerial backgrounds or professions different from their own (e.g. accountants, administrative officers, transport or personnel managers, or ex-NHS staff). Some of these managers are unlikely to have the same understanding of the supervision process or its potential benefits as managers from a social work background. If the supervisory relationship is not based on a shared understanding of supervision as a positive and supportive process, the arrangement of regular supervision sessions may be misinterpreted and seen as indicating a lack of trust in the work of the supervisee. Managers with a 'macho' attitude to their task and managers who are particularly ambitious may find it difficult to accept support, or even to admit their need of it. Managers scarred by reorganisation, or drowning in the face of complex new demands, will require particularly patient handling.

Both supervisors and supervisees have the responsibility of seeing that supervision is constructive, and that appropriate issues are brought for discussion at supervision sessions. Both also have a responsibility to see that agreements reached are carried out, and their outcomes monitored in subsequent sessions.

Senior managers are responsible for familiarising themselves with the work of the managers who report to them, and the settings in which they work. If they fail to do this they will be seen as remote, and their advice will lack credibility. (This is particularly so when managers from a field social work background manage residential staff, and *vice versa*.)

Senior managers should provide regular information to middle-managers about political developments within the department, the financial position, and the progress of strategic plans, both for the department and the council as a corporate body. Senior managers should discuss new developments and the implications of new legislation with middle-managers at the first opportunity, so that the results of such consultations can be fed into top-level planning as soon as possible. In this way, decision-making at the senior level will remain focused and relevant, and the contribution of middle-managers to the work of the department will be enhanced.

Supervisees have a responsibility to warn senior managers immediately of impending problems, especially if a breach of professional practice has occurred, or if there is likely to be trade union, councillor or media involvement. A joint approach to resolving the problem should be adopted, and no time wasted in rhetoric or recrimination. In this way, mistakes (which are inevitable, because staff and managers are all human), will be reported early and, it is the be hoped, rectified before serious damage has occurred.

General advice on management of the grievance and disciplinary processes, and issues to do with regrading claims, may be discussed in supervision if they concern staff under the line-management of the supervisee. However, if such formal issues are arising out of the work of the supervisee him/herself, these should always be considered *outside* the supervision session, or operation of the department's formal procedures may be compromised.

Managers should be actively encouraged to implement this focused, two-way model of supervision with managers and staff who report to them – if necessary, by the adoption of a written policy on individual supervision. Some managers may see the adoption of a written supervision policy as bureaucratic or unduly restrictive. This objection, if voiced, warrants closer examination. It may the last-ditch defence of a manager who is afraid he/she will be held accountable for the first time, instead of having the freedom to escape responsibility, take the credit for others' ideas, scapegoat subordinates in times of trouble, or be unavailable whenever decisions are needed. (Characters such as these exist in all walks of life. Sometimes, sadly, they reach very high levels of influence by operating this 'non-stick' approach to management accountability. In a high-risk, high-stress environment such as social services, staff reporting to such a manager pay a very high price for their manager's personal ambitions, and it is up to senior managers to put a stop to such managerial behaviour when they discover it.)

If an effective model of individual supervision is successfully implemented, stress levels will be reduced, decision-making will improve, morale will rise and higher standards of service quality will be achieved.

THE BUILDING OF MANAGEMENT TEAMS

The need for teamwork

Much has been written about the changing of corporate culture, organisational development, and the achievement of management excellence. Writers and researchers such as Belbin (1981), Kanter (1983), Handy (1976), Babington Smith and Sharp (1990), and Peters and Waterman (1982) have analysed the characteristics of successful management teams, and an industry has grown up to promote the ideas of these different thinkers on management. Some social services departments have enthusiastically embraced these developments in management thought, especially at a senior level. Consultants have been brought in, training provided, and the technical skill levels of senior managers have been raised to meet the demands of the contract culture. Teamwork has also been enhanced, sometimes as an end in itself, and sometimes as a by-product of other initiatives in training of managers in groups.

But what of departments where this has not happened? How can they cope with the twin demands of the contract culture and an ever-increasing workload, when public funding for directly-provided social services is being reduced? The answer has to be by improved teamwork, including ensuring that the work of each section combines seamlessly with the work of others to make a coherent whole.

A good team is always greater than the sum of its individual parts. Previously untapped creativity is released when staff and managers come together in an atmosphere of trust to discuss policy, raise service standards and improve employment practice. People feel their views are important, and that they can have greater control over their work environment.

The members of a good team feel more secure: stress and sickness levels, and staff turnover, reduce. A dysfunctional team adds significantly to the stress levels already experienced by undertaking the difficult work done in a social services department. In a dysfunctional team, staff turnover will increase, as will sickness levels, grievances, breaches of discipline and small local labour disputes. Social services departments cannot afford dysfunctional teams at any level of the organisation but, if the dysfunction occurs at Directorate level, the consequences for the department will be particularly damaging.

Despite the importance of teamwork at all levels in social services, competing priorities render it unlikely that significant funds will be made available in many social services departments to bring in outside trainers and
facilitators to assist the bulk of its managers with team development. Even in
the era of performance review and the contract culture, management training
is often seen as a low priority in comparison with service maintenance and
development, or funding for training of professional staff. In addition, those
social services managers most likely to miss out on any initiatives in management training that do come to fruition are groups of managers at the 'coal-face'
in field or residential social work. This is precisely where the absence of good
teamwork will cause the most immediate damage to service standards, and
to the quality of life of vulnerable people.

What is needed, therefore, is a practical model for largely in-house team
development. The model needs to be easily understood, and to be able to be
put in place either by teams themselves or with the active involvement of their
line-managers. It is suggested that the following principles be adopted (Sharp
and Babington Smith 1980):

'1. Teamwork needs to be seen not as an end in itself but as a very
     valuable means for *tackling situations and getting things done.*

2.   The focus in reviewing and planning to improve performance must
     be on learning to use both the task skills and knowledge and the
     interpersonal skills available within the group *in order to get things
     done.'*

(The words in italics are important. Busy managers will give this work no
priority if teamwork is seen as self-indulgent 'navel contemplation' by managers who should have better things to do.)

Development of teamwork at all levels

STAGE 1

Senior managers should determine priorities for team development among
the many different groups of managers requiring this in the department. In
weighing up priorities, consideration should be given to current levels of
management skill, to service standards, to cost factors, to staffing problems,
and to the best way in which managers can be freed up to make proper use
of the training offered.

Groups of managers who regularly work together, but could do so more
effectively, may be brought together for team development, on their own with
clear tasks or with line-management support. Alternatively, groups of managers who do not normally work together may be brought together in mixed
groups with line-management support, with the objective of integrating the
work of all sections into a cohesive whole.

Teams known to be dysfunctional will require special support. Dysfunction is often focused on individuals who are seen as 'the problem', or outside
factors such as 'management' or 'staffing establishment' may be blamed.
These may be contributory factors, but the picture is rarely this simple, and
the dynamics of the group will have a great deal to do with whether or not
the culture is supportive or destructive. Such teams will need active involve-

ment from line-management if their problems are to be overcome but they may, if they have a long history of dysfunction, need an independant facilitator to help them to improve communication and to decide once and for all time to leave their painful history behind. Examples of ways in which such problems can be tackled are given in the appendix at the end of this chapter.

Once the general teamwork development initiative has been discussed thoroughly with all teams of managers in the department, and decisions on priorities have been made by senior management, an *achievable* programme for team development throughout the department should be drawn up. The phasing of the programme and the reasons for decisions on priorities must be explained to all managers, to avoid raising expectations too soon and discrediting the whole initiative.

STAGE 2

A group of managers (ideally not more than 12) should be brought together on one day a week for four weeks to consider and agree on:

(1) Team rules (confidentiality, the corporate approach to decision-making, honest communication, no destructive 'deals' behind the scenes, etc)

(2) The departmental role of each manager in the group, and how his/her specialist skills can best be utilised in the team

(3) Their values and beliefs as a group of managers (on staff management, service standards, etc)

(4) Priorities for problem-solving (staff care, recruitment, selection and retention of staff, client advocacy, industrial relations, equal opportunities, etc) and, where appropriate, the setting-up of small groups to put ideas together locally to tackle these issues

(5) Stress management

(6) Budgetary constraints and political reality

(7) New ideas and developments, including the setting-up of small project groups where appropriate

(8) Future action, including monitoring the continued health of their team, and the effectiveness of the processes they use '*in getting things done'*.

If project groups are set up, such groups must have a time-limit and clear terms of reference. They must liaise regularly with a member of senior management to obtain a 'political steer' for their work. There is nothing more time-wasting or demoralising for a department than to have project groups duplicating the work of others, or developing ideas doomed from the start through political or financial constraints unknown outside senior management.

Teamwork can be further enhanced, and individual or pairs of middle-managers be helped to grasp political realities, by spending a week 'shadowing' a senior manager. This is a time-consuming process of parallel team development, but well worth the investment of time and energy involved.

Middle- and coal-face managers see for the first time the breadth of the department's work, where their sector fits, how decisions are actually made (as opposed to their fantasies), and the constraints on senior management and political power.

STAGE 3

The model should be evaluated, modified and repeated for the next group of managers.

CONCLUSION

Social services managers often feel unsupported and that existing systems cause them problems, rather than making their working lives easier. In addition, collectively, they feel overwhelmed by the unrealistic expectations society has of what social services departments should be able to achieve. To protect children at risk without infringing the rights of parents, to ensure that juvenile offenders behave well at all times, to provide home help for everyone who needs it, to ensure that people with mental health problems never become ill again when they are in the community, to deal with every referral immediately – the list of such expectations sometimes seems endless, and the media pressure unremitting.

There are some very talented managers and staff at all levels in social services departments up and down the country. To work with many of them is a delight and a privilege, and they deserve far more public recognition than they get. But managers who are a cross between King Midas, King Solomon and Mother Teresa of Calcutta are likely to remain a scarce commodity. For the sake of service-users and staff, not to mention the managers themselves, we have a duty to enable all our managers to do the job to the best of their abilities.

The management task in social services is difficult, but it is not impossible. It can also be exciting, creative, interesting and deeply satisfying. It can be done well and, when it is, social services managers should be praised, and shown how much they are valued for the work they do for their department and employing council

To assist social services managers to achieve the best they can from other managers and staff, the nature of the management task in social services has been described, and practical models both for individual supervision and for team development have been outlined. In the short appendix that follows this chapter, some practical training exercises in management development are set out.

REFERENCES

Adair, J. (1986) *Effective Teambuilding*. Aldershot: Gower.

Babington Smith, B., and Sharp, A. (1990) *Manager and Team Development*. London: Butterworth Heinemann.

Belbin, R. M. (1981) *Management Teams – Why They Succeed or Fail*. London: Heinemann Professional Publishing.

Daniel, P. and Wheeler, J. (1989) *Social Work and Local Politics.* London: MacMillan.

Donabedian, A. (1980) *The Definition of Quality and Approaches to its Assessment.* Health Administration Press.

Handy, C.B. (1976) *Understanding Organisations.* Harmondsworth: Penguin.

Kanter, R.M. (1983) *The Change Masters: Corporate Entrepreneurs at Work.* London: Allen and Unwin.

Peters, T., and Waterman, R.H. (1982) *In Search of Excellence – Lessons from America's Best-run Companies.* New York: Harper and Row.

Suggestions for further reading

Harris, T.A. (1970) *I'm OK – You're OK.* London: Jonathan Cape.

Kilman, R.H., Saxton, M.J. and Serpa, R. (1985) *Gaining Control of the Corporate Culture.* San Francisco: Jossey-Bass.

Lee, R., and Lawrence, P. (1991) *Politics at Work.* Cheltenham, Glos: Stanley Thornes Publishing.

Pollitt, C. (1990) *Managerialism and the Public Services.* Oxford: Blackwell.

Small, N. (1989) *Politics and Planning in the National Health Service.* Oxford: Oxford University Press.

APPENDIX 4A

Some Training Exercises for Use in a Phased Programme of Management and Team Development

MANAGING DYSFUNCTIONAL TEAMS

Four short case studies are set out below. These can be discussed by small groups of middle-managers, or used as the basis of role-play followed by discussion.

Objective: (1) For managers to gain greater insight into the way in which group dynamics can jeopardise standards of service

(2) To improve co-operation between different sections of the social services department

(3) To teach managers to devise strategies that enable them to work with dysfunctional teams to achieve change.

Case Study A

Following the retirement of a principal social worker who had been in post for ten years, a new principal has been appointed to manage a fieldwork team of ten staff. The new manager is anxious to improve what she sees as poor standards of child care practice and out-dated systems of workload allocation and monitoring. The longer-established members of the team resent what they see as criticism of their former principal, and are resisting these changes. The situation is further complicated by the fact that one of the two most influential senior social workers in the team was an unsuccessful candidate for the post of principal. All the staff are very tense, sickness is increasing, and there is trouble in filling vacancies, so a backlog of unallocated work is building up.

Case Study B

The social services personnel section has been run by the same manager for 15 years. He is very experienced and knowledgeable, and believes that the personnel function must always be tightly controlled so that line-managers do not take decisions that breach procedures. He has a large team of staff, but delegates little authority to them, so work builds up in his in-tray and he is constantly under stress. The section has a very poor reputation among social services managers, who find it slow and inefficient, and regard the manager as obstructive. Recruitment, re-grading, disciplinary and grievance cases are all affected, and the manager never has time to work on policy development.

Case Study C

A child care residential establishment has been without a manager for six months, following the resignation of the former manager. The unit has gained significant notoriety in the locality, and has featured several times in the local Press because of misbehaviour by its adolescent residents. The previous manager had a strong personality, and imposed rigid systems of control on children and staff. The acting manager has tried to make the regime more therapeutic and less controlling, supported by his line-manager, but half the staff think this is the wrong philosophy and wish to return to the old systems. The regime varies daily, depending on who is on duty.

Case Study D

A home for elderly people is faced with closure in six months' time because of budget cuts and competition from the private sector. The staff, residents and their relatives were told of this decision two months ago. Many of the staff, including the manager, feel that closure is inevitable and there is no point in resisting. Other staff, however, are campaigning against the closure and encouraging residents and relatives to do the same. This small group is openly hostile to the manager, accusing her of 'selling the residents out'. Standards of care are declining, and councillors are becoming very annoyed at the media attention the campaigners are getting. Fieldworkers are frustrated at the lack of co-operation they are experiencing when trying to arrange alternative placements for the residents.

Working with Councillors

Objective: (1)   To improve managers' understanding of the political interface in local government.

                 (2)   To improve their effectiveness as middle- and future senior managers.

(i) Arrange for a senior councillor (preferably the Chair or Deputy Chair of Social Services) to come to speak to groups of middle-managers about the role of councillors and how accountability is viewed in the Authority.

(ii) Encourage managers *always* to consider the political perspective of any new policy or proposed development being considered. Ensure their committee reports are drafted in language that is in sympathy with the manifesto of the party in power, without being overtly party-political. (This is a fine balance, and only regular practice in report-writing under the supervision of a senior manager will enable middle-managers to learn this skill.)

(iii) Arrange for middle-managers to attend a meeting of the social services committee, or its sub-committee, and discuss the proceedings afterwards with a senior manager.

(iv) Encourage middle-managers to liaise effectively with the local councillors for the areas in which they work, so that members become familiar with the range of services available for local people.

Shadowing a Senior Manager

Objective: (1)   For middle-managers to see where their work fits in with others in the wider department.

                 (2)   For middle-managers to see how decisions are made at senior management level, and to gain greater knowledge of the political interface of the department.

Arrange for a middle-manager to spend a week accompanying a senior manager throughout each working day. The middle-manager must understand that, if he/she obtains information that is not yet public, confidentiality must be observed. If individual interviews or meetings with people from outside the department occur during the week, it is courteous to ask them if they mind the middle-manager being present as an observer. Permission is rarely refused.

STRESS MANAGEMENT

Objectives   (1)   To enable managers and staff to gain greater control over their own working environment.

(2)   To reduce sickness absence and staff turnover, and improve morale.

Set aside a two-hour staff meeting for staff who regularly work together to discuss the causes of the stress they experience, and what they can do *themselves* to reduce this. (They will be surprised at how much is within their own power to change.)

CHAPTER 5

CHILD PROTECTION – SUPERVISION IN SOCIAL SERVICE DEPARTMENTS

JEAN MOORE

To allow a social worker to carry a case of child abuse without sensitive, structured and scheduled supervision is not only risky but downright dangerous. This is because abusive families 'beam out' powerful forces that can entrap and immobilise a worker, as a result of which children can become endangered. Supervision in cases of child protection is vital. This chapter will therefore look at *why*. It will also look at *what* work supervisors have to do to offer effective help and *how* they can tackle their task.

WHY

Inquiry reports have not shown social workers to be uncaring but only recently have we acknowledged that workers are influenced by the powerful forces emanating from the abusive family itself. It is these phenomena which skew professional performance and can immobilise workers, which can lead to some of the errors that have figured prominently in reports.

The first of these is the *pick up* of omnipotent and impotent feelings. Omnipotence felt by abusing parents passes right through the worker to the agency, so the whole agency begins to feel, 'if you follow the procedures you can protect all children in the country'.

Looking a second time at this statement one can see how ridiculous it is. Yet countless executives have assured the lay public after an abuse scandal that all will be will now procedures have been tightened up. Supervisors may have to reassure workers that they *have* correctly followed the guidelines, but sadly the child has been killed. A death does not automatically imply that someone has done something wrong. So many ghastly things may have happened to abusive parents that even 24-hours surveillance would not prevent them damaging their children.

The other side of the coin is the impotence. Child-abusive families make even qualified and experienced workers feel helpless. We start to doubt our skills and feel deskilled. This is when, if we are not careful, procedures, registers and conferences can become talismen.

Another pair of ambivalent feelings is guilt and anger: anger that the parent has let us down after so much work; anger at ourselves that we have been sucked in by the cry of the child inside the parent, so we have ignored the actual child's plight; the all pervasive anger that a caring and hardworking colleague has been put under the spotlight. It is easy, with hindsight, to see flaws in practice. It is not so easy when it is your last visit, at the end of a very long day, when the alsatian is growling, the cohabitee is threatening and there is nowhere to sit down. There is also the genuine anger ricocheting around a case that the very people who should have been the caring protectors of a small child are the very people who have inflicted dreadful injuries.

At the same time there is the feeling of guilt. Why couldn't we hear the child's first comment 'Daddy did it' before she changes the story to 'I fell down the stairs'? We feel guilt that the most obvious things were not followed up. This is the sort of guilt that encourages criticism even to the point where the worker is seen as the murderer.

There are two other ambivalent feelings: depression and accusation. Abusing families can drag us down and we feel depressed. Facing extreme hostility on a daily basis can cause too much adrenalin to circulate in the body, leading to a flat, depressed feeling. The difficulty in working in child protection in the 1990s is that so much more is known that higher standards are expected while there are fewer resources available. Abusing families suck us dry so we feel drained. Even if there were all the resources in the world we would still accuse our agencies of lack of support. Figure 5.1 attempts to explain the phenomenon of the petrified stance.

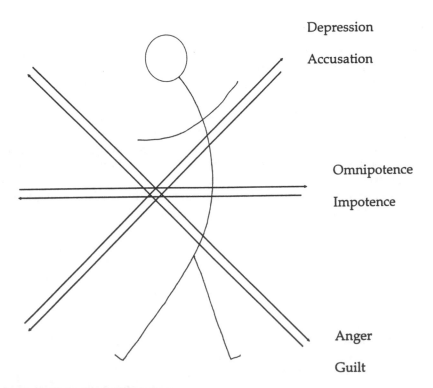

Depression

Accusation

Omnipotence

Impotence

Anger

Guilt

Figure 5.1 Stuck in the petrified stance

Feelings of omnipotence/impotence, anger/guilt, depression/accusation go through the worker and we become like a rabbit caught at night in the headlights of a car (Moore 1992). So we, like the animal, remain stuck and immobile. The case drifts and many cases drift towards disaster.

The second reason why supervision is so essential is because of the phenomenon of *learned helplessness*. Seligman (1975) observed animals and human beings and came up with the theory that if experiences are feared to be inescapable our desire to initiate action and solve problems declines. The ability to recognise success is undermined and we fear we are losing control. We then experience an awful cocktail of helplessness, depression, anger and anxiety. Families become stuck in learned helplessness and workers appear to catch the same complaint. Challenging supervision is needed to confront the defensiveness of workers locked in ineptitude. Supervisors have to invigorate workers who have become overwhelmed by tedium and failure.

Contrary to the impression given by the press, it is not always easy to discover that children are being abused. This is because of the power of the *victim/victimiser syndrome*. This was originally discovered when Olssen, a bank robber, escaped from prison, found two of his mates and broke into the Kreditbank in Stockholm (Strenz 1980). They failed to get to the money but took the bank clerks hostage instead. A visiting American psychiatrist advised the police that within 72 hours a powerful bond would be struck up between victim and victimiser. This arises from the helplessness of the captives, who develop a powerful desire to breathe human qualities and moral values into their captors which will make their own survival more likely. Moreover, if you can identify with your oppressors it relieves some of your own helplessness. This also happens to abused children. In order to survive mentally and physically they see their parents as all good. They cling to their abusers and this clinging can often be interpreted as affection by workers.

The classic response to violence is that for a few seconds we cannot believe that we are being mugged. If our attacker stays, we appease. When the incident is over, we blame ourselves, (e.g., we should not have been in that part of town). All this is mirrored in child protection social work. There is the denial. We deny the signs of abuse. How could such a charming mother abuse? The second stage is psychological infantilism and is reflected in our professional contact with families 'Let's monitor the case' which often means 'Let's do nothing'. The family starts to pull our strings and we lose the initiative and any sense of direction. The last stage is depression, with workers taking all the blame for what went wrong.

The next reason why supervision is so essential is that often , about two and a half years after qualification, the best workers become *burnt out*. They begin to have negative self concepts and job attitudes. They lose concern for clients. It is only through stimulating and proactive supervision that workers can use their burnout to become more sensitive and better workers. Without supervision they become empty, cynical, time-servers.

Staff can get caught up in *dominant ideas*, which may be good in themselves. The trouble is that dominant ideas drown out everything else and skew practice.

Classification is useful but not if it leads to other matters being overlooked. For instance the Lester Chapman case was classified as a housing matter and child abuse was not even considered *(Lester Chapman Inquiry Report 1979)*. Frozen watchfulness can become a dominant idea so that aggressive children are seen as problem children and *not* as abused children. Rehabilitation can become so dominant that clues to abuse are ignored. There can be positive stereotyping. As Mrs Henry was a woman she would cope. As Mrs Henry was black she would cope. Because Mrs Henry was a grandmother she would cope. So Mrs Henry (Tyra Henry Report 1987) was expected to cope in impossible situations in which no one could be expected to cope. Love can become a dominant idea. Because parents love their children they could not possibly injure them. This is, of course, false. Supervision must continually challenge dominant ideas.

The last reason why supervision is so essential is the phenomenon of *Terminal closure* (Reder *et al.* 1993). Parents who fear their dependence begin to feel desperately out of control. Their frustration increases. Workers rightly diagnose the case as becoming dangerous. The spiral begins. The more workers sense the danger the more interventionalist (rightly) they become. The parents make a false act of compliance and if the workers fall for it and withdraw, the child is in considerable danger. As Reder *et al.* (1993) put it:

> Taking a little control may be more dangerous than taking none at all. The intervention needs to be authoritative and decisive so that the situation is assessed and the child protected before any vicious circle can spiral out of control ... If professionals decide to take control they should take a lot of it. (p. 132)

The complexity of child protection work can immobilise professionals. Proactive supervision that challenges and refreshes is necessary to protect children.

In order to be open enough to provide such sensitive structured supervision the next section will look at what self work supervisors need to undertake.

SELF WORK FOR SUPERVISORS

Children

Supervisors are two degrees removed. It is therefore important that they keep in touch with what it means to be an abused child, perhaps using guided fantasy and experiencing the feelings – not just the physical and emotional pain, but the confusion. On Monday you are beaten. On Tuesday these same parents expect love from you and you feel guilty about the anger you felt yesterday. On Wednesday you are beaten again!

Every supervisor should have readily to hand some material about social, emotional, intellectual and physical milestones children should reach at certain ages (DOH 1988). It is so easy for workers' standards to drop when they are handling so many borderline situations.

Supervisors must also know their child protection legislation. They must know not what people say the Acts say but what they actually do say; they must be ready to help staff learn key phrases for use when cross examined in court.

Finally, supervisors must believe that direct work with abused children is a top priority and must encourage face-to-face work with the abused child and when necessary the siblings as well.

Authority

Supervisors must work with their own feelings about authority and its use with clients and staff and be clear where the authority emanates from, to work with abusing parents. Parents who abuse need that special combination of care and authority. Because they feel so empty and of such low esteem, battering parents will lie and cheat. Workers and supervisors have to be alive to parental ruses (Jasmine Beckford Report 1985). Sexually abusing parents, particularly, need caring confrontation as they deny and minimalise.

The Tyra Henry Report (1987) stated:

> 'The striking of the right balance between friendliness and authority is a perennial difficulty of the job. It can be taught in the abstract but it is only on the job that it can really be learnt and the learning process can only be fruitful if it is accompanied by meticulous supervision.' (p. 110)

Risk

Supervisors must continually update themselves about risk theory as they are the managers at the cutting edge. Perhaps we need a new word, as usually the event has occurred when we describe the child as 'at risk'. There are 'here now risks' like a bleeding wound which requires *immediate action*. Then there is 'accumulated risk'. One incident by itself would not be sufficient to take action, but a series of incidents of neglect would provide evidence. So it becomes a question of *when*. Then there is 'potential risk'. A mother is mentally ill – *what* would make us take action? Elsewhere I have drawn up lists to help predict a poor prognosis (Moore 1992) always remembering the predisposing factors must be seen in the light of current interactions and interventions.

Reder *et al.* (1993) also remind us that there are risky situations. Weekends and public holidays are often violent times for abusive families. Professionals can become risky if they are part of a closed system or trapped in polarisation playing games. The non-sharing of information or of bits of information seen in isolation are both dangerous. Reder *et al.* also warn us about allowing one thing to become an indicator of success or lack of it and ignoring all the other issues.

Violence

Supervisors have to help staff work with violent and hostile clients. Methods of doing this cannot be worked out if supervisors do not create a safe atmosphere in which workers can share their fears and anxieties. Supervisors need to be able to teach staff to recognise the stages through which people progress before becoming violent (Kaplan and Wheeler 1983). Staff need to feel safe to ask for joint visits.

Supervisors particularly need to know the long term after effects upon staff, be it violence of the tongue or the fist. When attacked, staff lose their sense of security and professional distance. They need to describe as soon as possible what went on and analyse what they did well and not so well, otherwise they will turn everything against themselves and feel they did nothing right. It may take the body many months to come to terms with what happened. A person in Tesco's wearing the same jacket as the assailant may trigger a crying or anxiety attack.

Gender Issues

Gender issues must be openly discussed in supervision. Sexual abuse particularly highlights this need. Without stereotyping, it must be remembered there is a tendency for men to put out painful feelings and woman to take them into themselves. Thus a male supervisor has to recognise that if the worker is a woman, not only is the power balance mirrored but it is easy for the female worker to see him as cold-hearted by focusing on solutions while he sees her as making a meal of the situation. The male supervisor who supervises a male worker must watch out for 'all boys together' and seeing women as 'asking for it'. Women supervisors must be alert for 'all men are bastards'. A female supervisor with a male worker must be aware of the game of 'little boy lost' and 'mother knows best' – both used to cover his hostility at being supervised by a woman.

Every supervisor must be sensitive to the effects of racism, sexism, homophobia, classism, disabilityism, ageism and adultism on child abuse issues.

Exercise 5.1

Aim
To look at how bad dominant ideas can skew supervision.

Participants
This is an exercise that can be undertaken during group supervision or as part of a training course on supervision (up to 18 participants maximum). Break a large group into smaller groups of three or four.

Equipment
Paper and pens.

The exercise

Ask group 1: to look at how racism can skew practice in child protection work.

Ask group 2: to look at how sexism and homophobia can skew practice in child protection work.

Ask group 3: to look at how classism can skew practice in child protection work.

Ask group 4: to look at how diabilityism can skew practice in child protection work.

Ask group 5: to look at how ageism can skew practice in child protection work.

Ask group 6: to look at how adultism can skew practice in child protection work.

Feedback to large group.

Area Child Protection Committees (ACPCs)

Finally, supervisors must be familiar with guidelines and departmental procedures produced by the local A.C.P.C. However, having guidelines does not mean we suspend our critical and imaginative faculties.

HOW TO SUPERVISE

Exercise 5.2

Aim
To spell out the range of feeling that is around when a supervisee and supervisor meet.

Participants
This exercise can be undertaken in one-to-one supervision sessions or in group supervision.

Equipment
Paper and pens.

The exercise
Ask the following questions and write down responses:
   (1) What feelings well up in a supervisor before s/he starts to supervise a child protection case?
   (2) What feelings well up in a worker when s/he arrives to have supervision on a child protection case?

Compare the two sheets.

What conclusions can be drawn?

CONTRACTS

Supervisors should always draw up a contract with staff. This makes issues explicit and shows up immediately any mismatch of expectations and where further negotiations need to take place – always remembering the responsibility the supervisor has as the manager. Ground rules must be laid down and the system used if a problem cannot be resolved. If this is clearly stated at the beginning it saves a great deal of pain at what could be a very sensitive time (See Owen & Pritchard 1993 and Morrison 1993).

A MODEL

A useful way of looking at Supervision is shown in Figure 5.2

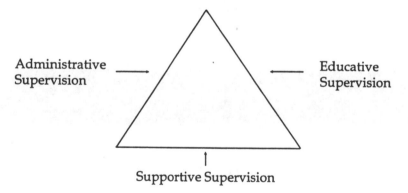

Administrative Supervision ⟶   ⟵ Educative Supervision

Supportive Supervision

Figure 5.2 (based on Kadushin 1976)

The relationship is shown as a triangle because if one side is missing the whole construct collapses. Supervision has to be sensitive to the needs of the worker and the needs of the case; structured so that both sides have worked out what they want to cover; scheduled so that dates and times and length of session are agreed; flexible but not so flexible that either side can be blown off course. The aims and objectives of supervision must be jointly shared. The supervisor cannot shed his/her responsibility to the agency. The agency has the responsibility to provide effective supervision and as the Kimberley Carlile Report (1987) made clear, the workers also have the responsibility to get the supervision they need. Both supervisor and supervisee must make notes after the session and put notes on the case file as to the decisions for action – why, when, where, how, what and by whom action is to be taken. Unless there are real emergencies there should be no interruptions. This means planning and giving instructions about alternative times for callers.

Both supervisors and supervisees have the responsibility to create an atmosphere, which is very important in child protection situations, in which it is possible to question and challenge and where issues are not ducked. There must be an atmosphere in which workers can grow and develop – but not at the expense of clients.

There is a danger in abuse work that supervision can drift into therapy. A manager cannot be a therapist. The job of the supervisor is to help the supervisees with their work. If sessions help with personal issues that is a bonus but it should never be the aim. If supervisors start becoming the supervisee's social worker it will only breed resentment later on and will change the whole focus, to the detriment of the case.

SUPERVISION ON THE HOOF

There are a few – but very few – occasions when supervisors have to give supervision on the hoof. The danger is that 'Have you got a few seconds?' can be a way of avoiding a proper discussion – or a way of getting what the supervisee wants from a harassed and hurried supervisor. Supervisors have to develop the consummate skill of knowing what is truly an emergency and what should wait for the supervision session.

SUPERVISORY SKILLS (Shulman 1982)

(1) Supervisors have to learn the skill of 'tuning in' – giving themselves a brief time to clear the head and become open to cues the next worker may be giving as to what needs to be put on the agenda.

(2) An agenda needs to be set. The worker may not yet be in touch with what needs to be discussed so the supervisor may need to 'reach out' picking up the verbal and non-verbal clues. Workers are often ambivalent about sharing problems lest they be seen as incompetent. It is the job of the supervisor to clarify and to develop what is brought by the supervisees. Focused listening is demanded and an understanding of the significance of silences (see exercise 5.3).

Exercise 5.3

Aim
To help supervisors handle silences in supervision more easily.

Participants
This exercise can be undertaken alone, in pairs or small groups.

Equipment
Paper and pens.

The exercise
Ask the following questions and chart the answers:

   (1) What may be some of the reasons why supervisees become silent in supervision?

   (2) How should a supervisor handle silences?

Feedback and discuss.

(3) Supervisors must be empathetic to enable supervisees to cope and not be swamped. They must work with the feelings that child protection evokes in pursuit of the purpose – to get the job done. They should not rush in too quickly to reassure but let the workers articulate for themselves the feelings they have not so far been able to put into words.

(4) Supervisors must also be human as Shulman (1982) said: 'A supervisor who appears to be always under control who has everything all worked out, who is never at a loss or flustered, would be an impossible person to relate to anyway' (p. 113).

(5) Supervisors have to be clear about the work that has to be done. It may help sometimes breaking the task into small surmountable bits, recognising that, although there is ambivalence, most workers want to complete the task.

(6) The ending of a supervision session is as important as the beginning, summarising what has been discussed, noting what has been agreed, generalising from the content, spelling out what needs further discussion and perhaps even role playing what are the next steps.

ADMINISTRATIVE SUPERVISION

It is the supervisor who protects the reputation, policies, philosophies and priorities of the agency. Metcalf and Curtis (1992) describe the supervisor as 'the fulcrum between the individual and the organisation'. It is administrative supervision that ensures the rules and procedures of the department are carried out. But more than that, imaginative administrative supervision can discover quicker than the other types of supervision what is really going on between worker and user. Inflexibility in carrying out procedures shows that a worker has an acute fear about a case. Rules that are ignored may show the worker has got sucked in by a hostile client. Slack administration may reveal that the victim inside the worker is colluding with the victim part of the parent. Unwillingness to operate guidelines may reveal that the worker is afraid to confront the client. The supervisor may have to watch out for whether the worker's battles about departmental memoranda may have more to do with their own battles with authority than the client's welfare. Supervisors also have the management responsibility to ensure that the worker has the necessary resources to do the job and if necessary to represent their needs energetically to higher management.

EDUCATIVE SUPERVISION

Supervision is also an educative process. Supervisors must discover how the individual supervisee learns. It is for the supervisor to adapt as far as possible *their* teaching style. Some supervisees are plodders. They learn by going from

Exercise 5.4

Aim
To enhance supervisors' understanding that supervision is a learning activity and supervisors must adapt *their* approach to meet the learning needs of supervisees.

Participants
This exercise can be undertaken alone, with a supervisee or as part of a training programme. If there is a large group participants should break into smaller groups of three or four.

The exercise
Ask each individual supervisor to consider how s/he thinks each staff member learns. The supervisor can write this down if undertaking the exercise alone or with a supervisee, or discuss within a group.
Then ask each supervisor what are the implications for their practice of their discoveries.

point one to two to three. Others are inspirational leapers. Imagine the boredom if the worker is the latter, and the supervisor like the former. Other workers need time to digest. Some are good thieves, stealing ideas. Some workers need to fight the supervisor every inch of the way before they can accept an idea. There are also workers who take on board everything, only later spitting out what they do not want. Fitters would be a good word for those who can only learn if they fit everything into their own shape. There are those who learn by seeing things and those who learn by hearing them. Some learn best on their own while others learn best in groups. Thus, there is need for group supervision as well as individual sessions.

Consider how each member of your staff learns. Staff learn best if they are highly motivated so it is for supervisors to show the relevance of new learning in an article by relating it to an aspect of the case. This means supervisors have to find a painless way of keeping up to date. One way might be by asking staff on a rota basis to read the key professional journals and feedback at staff meetings.

To do the job of a supervisor well we need to know what motivates and what dissatisfies each member of staff in order to help them find their own solutions. The aim is to be a mentor, not a tormentor and to make demands out of a desire to help not to hurt. Because of their tasks of challenging errors, calling attention to ignorance and pointing out mistakes, supervisors may never be popular but they should aim to be respected.

Unfortunately, people do not learn in even curves. There will always be plateaux and occasional slipbacks. Adults learn in stages (Westheimer 1977). There is the first realisation that they do not know something. They may cover it up by over talking or cracking jokes. Supervisors can feel very frustrated with the worker who talks well but performs badly. It is at this stage the supervisor must discover something relevant the worker does know and use it as a raft to drift towards what needs to be learnt. The second stage of learning is when the worker understands without the power to control his/her own activity. Workers think they have mastered the art but practice often lags behind understanding. Then comes the time of relative mastery in which the worker understands and controls the activity. The supervisee has welded his/her old and new skills together. Conscious intelligence and unconscious responses are working together. This is a delightful time for supervisor and supervisee alike, a time of professional growth. But lurking in the wings is burnout. It is essential that burnout is seen as a natural and normal process, if the worker is responsive to clients. It is for the supervisor who knows about burnout to give at this stage stimulating and relevant supervision and advise about self care, so that the worker can develop and grow through the burnout to greater sensitivity (Moore 1992).

Supervisors need to know what specific skills are required to undertake child protection work and, if missing, to teach them.

SUPPORTIVE SUPERVISION

The last side of the triangle is supportive supervision. This is not support against the agency but within the agency. The supervisor needs to discern

---

Exercise 5.5

Aim
To help supervisors become more aware of what specific skills
workers need and to accept the challenge that as part of their
supervision they need to encourage staff to develop their skills.

Participants
This exercise can be undertaken alone or in small groups of three or four.

Equipment
Paper and pens.

The exercise
Ask each individual or group to chart their responses to the
following questions:

(1) What specific skills do workers need to function adequately in
the child protection arena?

(2) How can supervision help staff develop these skills?

Feedback and discuss.

---

when a worker has given their all to a job and they need positively to move
on; when someone needs to be sent home, to have a good sleep or when
someone needs to be dragged kicking and screaming to do something new
and stimulating. In addition, every worker must be encouraged to find their
own support systems. It cannot be just one person or just people we like. Many
people should form an individual support system.

Feedback must be given by both sides as to the effectiveness of supervision.
Staff need to know what they are doing well and be valued for it, as child
protection work drains us dry, there is little positive feedback from clients and
in the case of neglect the pace is irritatingly slow.

SUPERVISION SABOTEURS

The worst saboteurs of supervision are the games that supervisees and
supervisors play. Here are a few:

(1) *Two versus the agency.* Workers use a throwaway line by the
supervisor and circumvent attempts to get a job done 'You don't
think this form is useful – you said so yourself', 'I'm sure you

would prefer me to spend the time with the client who is having a crisis'.

(2) *Let me do my own thing.* 'I'm a gifted worker if left alone,' which being interpreted means 'don't supervise me'.

(3) *You're wonderful Mr/Ms Supervisor.* Thus flattering the supervisor so that it is difficult to be critical of their work.

(4) *Treat me don't beat me.* The supervisee is so full of personal problems the supervisor feels bad about evaluating work or allocating new cases.

(5) *I know Kempe better than you know Kempe.* The worker undermines the supervisor by recounting their superior knowledge about child abuse. Supervisors have to remember the art of supervision is different from the knowledge of the subject.

There are so many more (Moore 1992).

Supervisors play games too

(1) *I'm so busy – keep things brief today.* The worker then has to adapt to the needs of the supervisor.

(2) *I would do it but its them 'up there' who won't let me.* But the supervisor never does test out or challenge higher management.

(3) *I was only trying to help* (Hawkins and Shohet 1990). The supervisor defends against criticism from the supervisee by pleading altruism.

Supervisors have to remember it takes 'two to tango'. Games lead to an avoidance of responsibility and poor decision making. Supervisors have to unmask the game and refuse to play. As Kadushin (1976) said: 'Supervisors have to give up the sweet fruits of flattery, the joys of omniscience, the pleasure of acting as therapist and the gratification of being liked' (p. 252).

CONCLUSION

The child protection setting is not only a complex arena to work in but it is also professionally dangerous. There are two reasons for this. First, it is too painful for the community to face up to the horror of abuse so the rage is often projected onto the messenger, the social worker. Second, there is something deep and primitive in all of us that victimises those who work with victims. Supervisors have to create as much safety at work for their staff as possible. New staff have to be helped not to bay at the moon and angrily demand things should be different. Supervisors have to help them to survive by giving quality supervision and ensuring they have a good knowledge base and an array of skills. Supervisors also need to demand that social service departments have their own full-time, appropriately qualified press officer who can, all the year round, built up good relations with the local and national press, so that when there is a crisis, the press are aware of the issues and they are handled maturely. The voluntary agencies have known this for years and have therefore had a better press where there are problems.

The job of a supervisor is certainly not an easy one but it can be exciting and professionally satisfying. To see a member of staff developing new skills to ensure that an abusing family gets the quality service that will really protect a child, is truly rewarding. But supervisors also need to be regularly supervised by their managers in a structured and sensitive way. The supervisor's notes need to be read by the executive manager to ensure the supervisor's skills are meeting the needs of the developing worker. These notes will also provide the manager with the necessary information to ensure that difficult or experienced staff are not being avoided.

Supervision supports staff working with the stress of child protection cases. Supervision develops professional practice provided it is rooted in an accepted departmental supervising policy which goes from first line worker to the top of the agency.

REFERENCES

DOH (1988) *Protecting Children – a guide for social workers undertaking a comprehensive assessment.* London: HMSO.

Hawkins, P. and Shohet, R. (1990) *Supervision in the Helping Professions.* Milton Keynes: Open University Press.

Kadushin, A. (1976) *Supervision in Social Work.* New York: Columbia University Press.

Kaplan, S. and Wheeler, E. (1983) 'Survival skills for working with potentially violent clients'. *Social Casework* 339–346.

Metcalf, J. and Curtis, C. (1992) Inside Staff Supervision *Insight* in *Community Care* 30 July, page vi.

Moore, J. (1985) *The ABC of Child Abuse Work.* Aldershot: Gower.

Moore, J. (1988) 'The Question the Carlile Report failed to answer'. *Community Care*, 14 January, 26–27.

Moore, J. (1992) *The ABC of Child Protection.* Aldershot: Ashgate.

Morrison, T. (1993) *Staff Supervision in Social Care.* Longman Group U.K.

Owen, H. and Pritchard, J. (1993) *Good Practice in Child Protection. A manual for professionals.* London: Jessica Kingsley Publishers.

Reder, P., Duncan, S., Gray, M. (1993) *Beyond Blame – child abuse tragedies revisited.* London: Routledge.

Seligman M.E.P. (1975) *Helplessness of Depression, Development and Death.* San Francisco: W. H. Freeman.

Shulman, L. (1982) *Skills of Supervision and Staff Management.* Illinois.

Strenz, T. (1980) 'The Stockholm Syndrome Law enforcement policy and ego defences of the hostage'. *Annals of the New York Sciences* No 347 137–150.

Westheimer, I. (1977) *The practice of supervision in social work. A guide for staff supervisors.* London: Ward Lock Educational.

REPORTS

Beckford, Jasmine (1985) A Child in Trust – the report of the Panel of Inquiry into the circumstances surrounding the death of Jasmine Beckford. London Borough of Brent.

Carlile, Kimberley (1987) The report of the Commission of Inquiry into the circumstances surrounding the death of Kimberley Carlile. London Borough of Greenwich.

Henry, Tyra (1987) Whole Child – a report of the public inquiry into the death of Tyra Henry. London Borough of Lambeth.

Lester Chapman Inquiry Report (October 1979) – Berkshire and Hampshire County Councils and Health Authorities.

CHAPTER 6

SUPERVISION AND WORK
WITH OLDER PEOPLE

CHERRY ROWLINGS

Supervision of social work and social care takes place within a political and a personal as well as a professional context. An understanding of this in relation to work with older people is essential if supervision is to be effective and this chapter therefore begins with a discussion of the political and then the personal context of work with older people, outlining some implications for the supervisor. It continues with three main sections. The first addresses setting up supervision and the use of group supervision; the second focusses on care management and the third explores risk assessment and management, including where abuse is known or suspected. Finally, there is a short conclusion.

THE POLITICAL CONTEXT OF WORK WITH OLDER PEOPLE

Probably the most prevailing and pervasive of influences upon work with older people is the negative stereotyping of older people and their marginalisation by society. Ageism is a strong, oppressive force which creates and supports systems and policies that deny older people the quality of life which more powerful people within social and political institutions aspire to and generally achieve. Indeed, as Walker (1980) and Townsend (1981) have shown, the dependent status of many older people can be directly attributed to the actions (and in some instances, the inactions) of successive governments whose economic policies have kept the state retirement pension amongst the lowest in Europe and whose social policies are increasing older people's dependency upon their adult children should care be needed.

An insidious consequence of oppression is the internalisation by those who are oppressed of the negative status ascribed to them, so that they, too, come to share the view of themselves as less important in society, less worthy as individuals and less entitled to full participation in social and economic life. An analysis of the history of women in our society or of black people offers powerful illustrations of this process and it is possible to see it also as contributing to older service users' tolerance of their difficult conditions and their generally low level of expectation as consumers of health and personal social services. The majority of the elderly population is, of course, female and a small but growing number, black. For them, ageism is likely to reinforce their existing minority status in society, becoming one of several 'jeopardies' to which they will be subject (Norman 1985).

The significance of this for supervision can be illustrated by the following example. A worker is proposing to close a case on the grounds that the older person seems to be coping and there does not seem a need for further intervention. Various explanations may account for the worker's view. The worker may be accurately reflecting and endorsing the older person's considered assessment of his or her position – in which case, closure does seem appropriate.

However, using a political perspective, an alternative explanation could be that the worker (and maybe the older person too) are accepting of a status quo because each adopts (or has had thrust upon them) an essentially pessimistic and minimalist approach to life in old age. The professional literature unfortunately contains many examples, over a sustained period, of social workers, care staff and managers adopting such an approach when faced with problems of older service users. It is characterised by remarks such as 'it's their age' (the implication being that therefore little can be done) or that older people 'have had their life' (so there is no need to bother so much) (Brearley 1975, Rowlings 1981, Marshall 1990). Amongst older people, fatalism and at times depression arising from low self-worth and the lack of purpose in their lives, can prevent even relatively simple medical and social problems from being remedied.

The task of the supervisor is to check out the accuracy of the worker's judgement and, using an understanding of the social construction of old age, to be alert to the possible influence of ageism upon worker, older person or both in the decision to cease contact. Challenging taken-for-granted assumptions about what is right, best, or even just acceptable in work with older service users has to be an integral part of the supervision process. Since both worker and supervisor are part of an ageist society and neither can therefore guarantee to avoid ageist assumptions and practice, the responsibility for delivering a positive, sensitive service must be a shared one. However, the supervisor, as the more powerful participant, may need to take the initiative in showing that challenge is not just permissible but also essential and two-way. There are other factors, also with their roots in the politics of old age, which are likely to affect supervision of service delivery to older people.

To summarise briefly, social work and social care practice with older people have a relatively weak professional base. This is not surprising given the long-standing failure by the social work profession and by employers to acknowledge the complexity of such work and the need for practitioners and managers in all settings to receive appropriate training. As a result, though, the supervisor is operating in a professional environment where the task is likely to be poorly conceptualised and where theory is under-developed. This throws the supervisor back on his or her own resources and especially upon the ability to make sensitive use of concepts and theory which have been developed in respect of other service users. Furthermore, workers may be unused to supervision which addresses professional practice and values, having experienced either minimal support and oversight in the past or an administrative 'checking up' form of supervision. Suspicion of or resistance to supervision may have to be overcome.

The repercussions of the NHS and Community Care Act, 1990, have done little to consolidate professional confidence or competence. Indeed, the early and convincing experiments in care management, which drew out the professional task and located the values and competences firmly within social work (Challis and Davies 1986), have not been replicated on a wider scale (Lewis 1994). Instead, the introduction of the purchaser/provider split, the imperative in England and Wales to purchase from the independent sector and the emphasis on the local authority as enabler have combined with resource constraints to produce a climate in which administrative procedures seem to dominate what once were professional domains. In Northern Ireland, the uncertain place of social work and social services, as health and social services Boards move toward trust status, exacerbates things further. The future of social work with older people seems itself under threat and, within social care, the role and the availability of publicly provided domiciliary and residential care have been drastically changed, especially in England and Wales.

Thus there is widespread uncertainty in the statutory sector but it is not confined there. Amongst independent agencies and residential and nursing homes, competitive tendering and contracts with specified service outcomes have introduced their own pressures, a primary one being to maximise efficiency and to keep costs down. True, there are opportunities for expansion into areas of work such as respite care or providing a bathing or a putting to bed service for people in the community, but there are risks involved in such development work. The financial one is obvious and for many ever-present, but professional risks are there, too, as independent agencies and their staff take on work which carries higher levels of responsibility and which may be unfamiliar to them as either practitioners or managers and supervisors.

Whatever the opportunities that the community care changes have offered or may come to, the supervisor can therefore expect to be working with staff many of whom are anxious about how their job may change, how they will cope, who will end up employing them and, for some, whether a properly paid job will exist. This will apply, almost irrespective of where the supervisor is based. Nor will supervisors be protected from such concerns for themselves and an aspect of their skill as supervisors will be to manage their supervisees' stress and anxiety whilst dealing with their own.

Such, then, are the major political and organisational issues that provide the context within which practice, service delivery and supervision take place and which will bring particular influences to bear upon how each is made operational. In a few years' time, the account may seem very much a product of the time at which this chapter was written. Nevertheless, whilst the precise examples may come to change, the question for the supervisor will always be there – what political factors may be impinging upon the quality of the service that is being provided and what is my role, as supervisor, to examine, challenge and influence what is happening?

The Personal Context

The other significant context within which the supervision of work with older service users takes place may be described as the 'personal context' – the feelings that workers bring to their practice and, in turn, the impact that their practice experience has upon them. The reasons why older people come to the attention of social workers and social care staff are often linked to disability, declining physical and mental capacity and chronic and perhaps terminal illness. Being with people who are coping with one or more of these challenges is painful and likely to arouse strong and ambivalent feelings: anxiety, fear and maybe even disgust along with compassion, protectiveness and caring (Menzies 1970, Stevenson 1989).

Since most workers with older people can themselves expect to live into old age, they are facing what could turn out to be their own future – an unusual situation in social work and social care, where workers mostly have either overcome the problems being experienced by their clients (a reinforcing experience for the worker) or are not likely to have a personal involvement. In working with older people there is a very real sense not just of 'this could be me in X years' time', but for many workers 'this could be my mother/father/aunt in a few years' time' and for some 'this is exactly like how my mother/father/aunt is now'.

This degree of personal relevance is not unique to work with older people (a social worker on an oncology unit, for example, would identify with a good deal of the above), but the experience of witnessing the ageing of parents, of taking on the role of carer for dependent elderly relatives and, ultimately, of becoming old oneself, is so much part of contemporary society that the *pervasiveness* of personal relevance throughout work with older people could be said to be its distinguishing feature. It is certainly an aspect that the supervisor cannot ignore, for it could result in workers avoiding the emotional and psychological needs of older clients because they, the workers, cannot face the pain such involvement could mean for them (Rowlings, 1981).

Setting up Supervision: Using Supervision Agreement
The value of group supervision

In the final page of their book on supervision, Hawkins and Shohet (1989) state 'a good supervisory relationship is the best way we know to ensure that we stay open to ourselves and our clients' (p. 157). Their book is an excellent testimony to the use and usefulness of supervision in helping workers help clients and service users. The potential of supervision to increase competence and confidence and thereby to empower the worker in his or her practice is very evident.

The significance of this last sentence for supervising workers with older people is not difficult to see. A significant proportion of workers with older people are women with few formal qualifications, occupying lowly positions in agency hierarchies and used to being left to get on with the job with little attention from others unless things went wrong. They have as a result developed their own ways of working and many have built up a practice wisdom, albeit one that was seldom accorded much recognition elsewhere in the organisation and therefore rarely called upon when assessments were made and decisions reached. Older people, and especially older women, could be described in almost identical terms, as we saw earlier in this chapter.

If workers are to feel safe to work with older people and to help them to make decisions and to value themselves, then workers have first to be and to feel validated in their professional roles. The way in which supervision is negotiated and carried out is of central importance in this process.

Good supervisory relationships do not simply exist. They are *working* relationships which develop over time and what is achieved is the result of the contributions of supervisor and supervisee. Both have responsibilities: the former to provide supervision which will enhance practice, the latter to bring material on which to be supervised. That both supervisor and supervisee have a responsibility for what happens is not always recognised and may indeed be a novel idea to the worker used to a 'top down' checking up approach. The process of clarifying and negotiating expectations of supervision contributes directly to an acceptance of respective responsibilities. It helps to avoid unproductive situations in which both parties deny the worth of the other – 'I am senior, so therefore I know the answers' from the supervisor as against 'I know my client, so my judgement is best' from the supervisee – both attitudes in effect taking on total responsibility for what should happen.

Alternatively, either party can abdicate responsibility – the supervisor who says 'He's your client, so you do what's best', the supervisee who sees supervision as a time for offloading, the equivalent of saying to the supervisor 'it's all yours, over to you, you deal with this'. Both the total assumption and the total abdication of responsibility in supervision have the same undesirable consequences, namely a supervisee who becomes professionally stunted, unable to develop as a worker or to be at ease with the authority inherent in the professional role.

Drawing up a supervision contract or agreement is one way of emphasising the joint nature of supervision. Agreements address questions such as mutual expectations, frequency, length and location of supervision, how it will be recorded and by whom and how its effectiveness will be reviewed. It is important to note that the agreement should make clear what happens if supervision has to be postponed (*note*, 'postponed' not 'cancelled', so as not to imply that supervision is easily dispensable). For staff unused to professional supervision, the negotiation of a supervision agreement is an acknowledgement of their importance in the activity and may also reassure them in that boundaries are made explicit, as are the requirements of them. Such an approach experienced in supervision, may subsequently be helpful if applied in situations where a newly referred older person or carer is uncertain, maybe suspicious or fearful, about what 'the Welfare' might do.

For the supervisor, negotiation of a supervision agreement should be preceded by consideration not just of the purpose of supervision for each worker, as an individual, but also of the intended outcomes of supervision more generally – as a purposeful activity which makes its own contribution to the enhancement of the quality of practice and of service delivery. Social work supervision has traditionally been an individual and rather private activity, mirroring the individual and private nature of the 'casework' carried out by fieldworkers. The appropriateness for other settings has been questioned (Payne and Scott 1982, Clough 1982).

The quality of service in day and residential centres is dependent not just on individual workers but also on how the staff group functions as a team. At the other extreme, home care workers, now frequently involved in more testing and high-risk situations than before in the traditional home help service, tend to be isolated – working on the client's territory, lacking the team office of fieldworkers or the staffroom of centre staff and maybe meeting colleagues only when handing in their worksheets. For both these groups of staff, some use of group supervision may be helpful and, indeed, for staff unused to professional supervision, a group can be less threatening (see Chapter 7).

In a centre, group supervision acknowledges the significance of the staff team *as a team* in the quality of care that is offered, for example by focussing on certain aspects of life in the establishment such as meal times, the provision of recreational activities or work with relatives. For home care workers, using group supervision to pursue common professional situations (for example responding to clients who have become sexually disinhibited or working with people who have been bereaved) fulfils the several functions of providing a shared learning environment in which practice wisdom can be acknowledged, encouraging group support, lessening individual isolation and establishing a baseline of recognised good practice in an area of work which is only just beginning to articulate standards.

Increasingly, though, the implementation of community care is creating situations where some form of group supervision is called for in fieldwork settings. One example would be where budgets have been devolved to team level. As team members' use and purchase of resources become more transparent and the implications of their decisions upon the total budget become more obvious, so it can be argued that there is a team as well as an individual responsibility for the service that is provided for a given geographical area.

This brings the fieldwork team closer to its residential counterpart, having its own budget of the aggregated working hours of all team members and having an income from the combination of charges and departmental grant. As in the residential centre, there is a responsibility to the individual service user, to the collective of service users and, arguably for the fieldwork team, to those in the community on the threshold of receiving help. Group supervision reinforces the corporate responsibility of the team for the community it serves.

SUPERVISION AND CARE MANAGEMENT: ASSESSMENT, MAINTENANCE AND REVIEW: PROBLEM SOLVING

The supervision of workers involved in care management does not require a different set of supervision skills. As in any aspect of work with older people in any setting, the supervisor has to apply skills in a way that is sensitive to the worker and appropriate for the issue under discussion.

It is, however, appropriate for the supervisor to ask of him or herself 'what do I know about care management which should inform my supervision of care managers?' In the previous section we saw that devolving budgets to team level arguably brings the field and residential work tasks closer together in that in both settings 'the team' has a corporate responsibility for the service provided to and for specific communities – in the former instance, older people and their carers who are living in a particular geographical area or 'patch', in the latter for the residents living in a residential centre. This understanding of care management might therefore lead the supervisor to consider some use of group supervision, instead of relying solely on the individual approach which is so strongly rooted in the fieldwork under-standing of supervision.

The literature on care management contains a wealth of information relevant to supervision. Here just three topics will be addressed. The first is in the area of assessment. It is clear that the transition from 'service led' to 'needs led' assessment is proving difficult (SSI 1991, Petch et al. 1994) and we are not as a general rule seeing the imaginative construction of care packages which were a feature of the original studies of case management (as it was then called) undertaken at the University of Kent (Challis and Davies 1986, Challis et al. 1989; Challis et al. 1990).

Given that most workers are probably not enjoying the protected caseloads or the resource levels of these earlier care managers, it is hardly surprising if traditional approaches and solutions are still prevailing. Nevertheless, irre-spective of resource levels, improvements in practice will be slow to come unless supervisors address workers' approach to assessment (Bland and Hudson 1994). Questions such as 'what does Mr X want?' or 'what outcome is everyone seeking?' can bring the service user and carer into higher promi-nence if the worker has been focussing on what can be provided before addressing what may be needed and who is articulating the need.

Research on discharge arrangements for older people in hospital suggests that more attention is likely to be given to relatives than to the older person (Neill et al. 1988); knowing this, the supervisor should be sure to check what contact the worker has had with the older person and how the older person is being and could be involved in the decision making process.

At the point of assessment, and indeed thereafter, it may well be that supervision provides the forum for disentangling conflicting needs and re-sponses. Carers and older service users will not always be in agreement over the nature of the problem, the desired solutions or both. This may be openly expressed and therefore there to be addressed. However, this will not always be the case. Sometimes the existence of differing views may surface through the supervisor who, in the course of listening to the worker's account of an interview, has become aware of feeling confused or bewildered.

This is only one example of the value of the supervisor voicing his or her response to the worker as a means of elucidating what the worker is dealing with and what the hidden currents are. The supervisor can help the worker to separate out the differing interests of carer and service user. In the course of so doing, the reasons for and sometimes, too, the reasonableness of the differences can be clarified, thereby helping to avoid situations where one party is seen as to blame and the other becomes the innocent victim.

Workers in hospitals and in residential centres are probably more exposed than others to the potential for polarising carers and users in this way, especially in those situations where relatives are involved in a more limited way than the service user would like (and maybe workers privately think is right).

Through exploring what is happening between carer and service user and what it is that both might be looking for from the worker, the supervisor can help the worker to avoid being sucked into the conflict or taking sides. Supervision is a means of ensuring that the worker remains on the outside and rooted in the here and now, rather than becoming part of a conflict which may itself be another re-enactment of a familiar theme in the relationship between family members.

A second message from care management research is the importance of maintenance and review. In current guidance on the implementation of community care, much attention has been paid to assessment and rather less to what happens afterwards. This is not unusual in social work nor indeed in the provision of domiciliary care, where there is a history of home help organisers sacrificing time to undertake review visits for the more pressing demands from new referrals.

The work of Challis and colleagues, in Kent and elsewhere, has shown the importance of actively sustaining support systems and services that are provided and of constantly reviewing their effectiveness. This is a reminder that the situation of older people is rarely static and that the older they are, the more likely it is that short or long-term needs will change through illness, worsening disability or a development in the circumstances of a significant carer. A deterioration in an old person's level of function may result in carers, involved when things were better, suddenly finding themselves carrying more responsibility than they had bargained for. Fear of being swamped by needs they feel they cannot meet may lead to panicked withdrawals of support or anger with the service user for 'being so demanding'.

Alternatively, service which stays at a level which is no longer adequate reduces the quality of care being provided and may result in anxiety and loss of confidence in the ability of support systems to maintain care. The level of dependency being sustained in the community is increasingly becoming one where services must be reliable and capable of ensuring survival and security. This requires flexibility and responsiveness from service providers and the worker who is the care manager must be sufficiently in touch with service users and formal and informal carers to keep a check on the appropriateness of the continuing care.

Particularly where the right resources have been difficult to obtain, it can be tempting to see the provision of services as itself constituting a successful outcome. In fact, of course, it is the improvement that those services bring to the life of the service user (and sometimes the carer) that is the indicator of success. It is this that the supervisor may need to help the worker keep in mind, through questions such as: What was the purpose of these services? Has this purpose been achieved? Could it be better achieved by viable alternative means? Is the original purpose still valid or have others emerged in addition to or instead of the original?

Cost factors will also need to be addressed – cost to the agency, to carers, to the service user and, increasingly, to those potential service users whose needs cannot yet be met. One service user receiving a high level of services may be absorbing resources which would relieve the situation of two people with slightly less need. Decisions about rationing (the most difficult part of targetting) should not always be left with the worker. The supervisor has to address the means by which there can be appropriate sharing, perhaps by undertaking joint visits or interviews or by writing an entry in the file which demonstrates that the supervisor is or has been party to the discussion and decisions about what should happen.

The third and final matter from the research on care management to be considered is about problem solving. Too often, albeit for understandable reasons, workers focus on the deficits of the service user's situation. What the older person *cannot* do takes precedence over what they *can* do and the positives of what they can manage and what they would like to achieve are lost (Barrowclough and Fleming 1986). Yet older people are survivors, with a history of problem solving behind them and practice in adapting and 'making do'.

Challis and Davies (1986) noted in their study that the involvement of the service user in problem definition and problem solving increased feelings of being in control and being able to influence what was to happen. Levin *et al.* (1989), in their research on community care by relatives for old people who were 'confused', describe the problem solving abilities of informal carers who were both realistic and at times imaginative about how the strain of caring could be eased.

These examples show that the resources of the service user and informal carers are there to be acknowledged and to be included in the planning of supportive services. Both parties may also have views about how priorities might be set and scarce resources best used.

However, the supervisor who wishes to see team members promoting more of a partnership with service users may have to deal first with workers' fears that they will be swamped by excessive and unrealistic demands. The reality, as is shown in the two studies referred to above and reiterated, in the residential setting, by Willcocks *et al.* (1987) is that service users and carers are more likely to be modest, even excessively so, in their desire for change.

SUPERVISION AND THE MANAGEMENT OF RISK

The assessment and management of risk is a feature of many aspects of work with older people. It may take the form of encouraging an older person to be more venturesome, when an unexpected fall or a stroke has undermined confidence. More frequently, it occurs when an older person is either unaware of the degree of risk in their situation or when they wish to live with the risk but others are anxious on their behalf. As services are increasingly targetted at those most in need, which will in many instances be related to the level of dependency, so one can expect higher levels of risk being maintained in the community and also in residential centres.

Concern for the physical safety of older service users has been a significant influence upon residential and community-based work with older people. This is not surprising, for the vulnerability of some older service users, exacerbated in the community if they are socially isolated, evokes strong responses from workers. Not only are there fears of being found to have been wanting if something were to go wrong, but the desire to care, protect and safeguard will be shared by informal and formal carers alike.

Consideration of the rights of the older person to take risks can be lost amidst concern about his or her capacity for understanding and the shortcomings of present legal remedies for situations where there is a tension between rights and capacity are likely to encourage caution and over-protection (Norman 1980). Yet we know that physical security alone is not sufficient to preserve individuality and a sense of purpose in life and the measures that may be taken to eliminate physical risk may in turn present a threat to emotional and psychological well-being as well as to civil rights.

As the person once removed from the immediacy of the situation, it may fall to the supervisor to help the worker to keep the balance: to maintain space for the older person, to offer reassurance to other carers (and often, too, other professionals) and to develop with the parties involved an arrangement which is based on least harm and least invasiveness. Sometimes, simple rearrangement of visiting times can provide protective cover for a longer part of the day and the sharing of the visiting rota with carers and neighbours can ease concerns. So also can clear advice and information about what to do if something happens and what contingency plan has been worked out. The supervisor can often be in the best position to help the worker deal directly and thoughtfully with other people's anxieties, taking the lead in problem-solving rather than being consumed by the prevailing·emotions.

It is essential for the supervisor to understand the nature and extent of the risk that is causing concern. Generalised anxiety needs to be translated into specifics. What is it that the worker and others are worried about? Is there agreement about this or where do the differences lie? Under what circumstances and when is the risk more severe? How real is the risk? What systems or mechanisms could diminish the risk? Or provide early warning that something is wrong? An older person who understands the risk can contribute to the discussion about how to make life more secure but where understanding is limited, the construction of a protective environment may be the task of the worker. Whatever the case, management rather than elimination of risk will often be the more attainable goal and the less harmful intervention. This is as true in residential settings as it is in the community.

Again, as with the earlier point about difficult resource allocation decisions, there will be occasions when the supervisor should record on a case file or care plan that the nature and degree of risk has been assessed and the following plan agreed. This is particularly appropriate where the main worker is inexperienced or without a relevant qualification or where various workers are involved and there needs to be a clear endorsement of the approach to be taken.

Since the mid 1980s, there has been a slow but growing recognition of the extent to which some older people are at risk of abuse by formal and informal carers. The abuse may be physical (hitting and striking), psychological (verbal abuse or rejection), financial (exploitation of income and possessions), sexual (enforced sexual activity) or medical (withholding or over-use of medication).

Problems of definition and detection abound (Rowlings, forthcoming) and legal protection for the abused is at present far from comprehensive. Unlike in cases of child abuse, the responsibility and the authority of the local authority worker to intervene on a protective basis is limited and often unclear. Yet the worker is faced with the private misery or the stoic acceptance of the abused who may be unable to articulate what is happening or reluctant to do anything because of the shame of admitting to being abused or fear of the consequences of so doing.

Here, as in other areas of risk assessment, the supervisor has the important role of clarifying and defining the nature of the concerns and pursuing, with the worker, different options for diminishing the likelihood of abuse occurring. The calling of a multi-disciplinary case conference is less part of the routine of work with older people and the supervisor may therefore have to take the inititiave in suggesting this to the worker.

In other circumstances, however, where the worker has not expressed a concern specifically about abuse, the supervisor may need to raise this possibility directly, as an explanation for changes in the older person's behaviour or appearance. The history of child protection contains several examples of workers reluctant or unable to acknowledge the presence of abuse – because of focussing on the parent(s) rather than the child, because of anxiety about whether they could cope with what they might uncover or because of a powerful wish to believe that such acts could not happen. There is no reason to suppose that the situation is any different in respect of workers facing the possibility of abuse of a dependent older person. Hence the need for the supervisor to keep the older person to the forefront of discussions and to be alert to the possibility of abuse as an explanation for what the worker is describing in supervision.

The acceptance by the supervisor of the possibility of abuse can model what may need to happen between worker and the suspected abuser. Again drawing from child protection experience, it is possible to see the importance of confronting the abuser and dispelling the secrecy which, if anything, is even more a feature of elder abuse (Gelles and Cornell 1985). Once the decision has been made to ask carers whether abuse has occurred, supervision can provide the forum for rehearsal work. How will the worker broach the subject? How do they think the carer(s) might respond? How would the worker follow up each of the different possibilites? What are they most worried about in undertaking the enquiry? What measures might be taken to diminish these worries?

Such preparation can increase the worker's ability to remain in control of his or her role in the interview. This in turn will increase the chances of the carer(s) feeling confident in the capacity of the worker to deal with whatever has to be said – something of particular importance where the abuse has been physical, psychological or medical (over-sedation) and a response to the stress of caring rather than the result of criminal intent.

Careful recording of observations, interviews and subsequent plans and discussions are essential. Endorsement by the supervisor is again both a protection and a support for the worker. A further part of the supervisor's responsibility may be to identify and to seek additional advice – from more senior colleagues or from other professionals with specialist medical or legal knowledge.

These aspects of good practice apply equally to supervisors in non-statutory agencies who currently are unlikely to be taking the responsibility for investigating and managing known or suspected abuse but who may be critical to the early identification of possibly abusive situations. Early rather than delayed contact with statutory colleagues is vital. So also is continuing support of their supervisee, who may have fears about what might happen following referral (will the family or the old person think I have betrayed them? Can I rely upon anyone who visits not to be clumsy and insensitive? What have I started?). Alternatively, given that some statutory agencies have not yet developed strategies for dealing with elder abuse, the supervisor may be supporting a worker who feels anxious and angry that so little attention is being paid to his or her concerns. In situations like this, however hard it may be, supervisor and supervisee cannot take responsibility for the inactivity of others, providing their own communications have been detailed, based on fact and not just supposition and clear about the assessment of risk.

CONCLUSION

This chapter has, of necessity, been selective in the areas of work with older people which have been addressed. The changing and varied nature of such work and the variety of agencies and settings in which it takes place did not permit comprehensive coverage. Yet the themes which have underpinned this chapter can be taken and applied to all supervisory situations. The first of these is the importance of the supervisor having an understanding of the external and internal influences upon the way the task is defined and addressed (the political and personal context). Second, the supervisor needs an understanding of the task of supervision, the responsibilities it contains and the potential it has to promote good practice. A third theme is that of *working with* the supervisee, to help him or her to learn, to increase his or her ability to help service users and to participate directly in questioning and clarifying. The supervisor needs to act as a 'critical friend', not as a rubber stamp or as an overseer. This is not, however, a cosy or collusive relationship but one in which there are mutual responsibilities and where there will be occasions when the supervisor must take the initiative or formally endorse what the worker is doing.

A fourth theme is that the work that takes place in supervision can sometimes reflect what is happening between worker and service user (Mattinson, 1975). It can also model what might happen or provide a safe environment for exploring possibilities (Collins and Bruce 1984).

The fifth and final theme is the importance of the supervisor keeping supervision client- or user-centred. This has a particular relevance where, as with older people, there is a history of a concern with services and practical tasks, rather than with the service user as a person with rights and feelings. Maintaining a user-centred approach with older people is not easy, because it challenges ageism and requires an attention to the personal and the particular as well as, increasingly, to the collective of service users and potential users.

However, unless supervisors and workers tussle with these issues and seek their resolution through various professional and political means, high standards of practice and service delivery for older people will never be achieved.

REFERENCES

Barrowclough, C and Fleming, I (1986). *Goal Planning with Elderly People,* Manchester: Manchester University Press.

Bland, R, Hudson B (1994). *Providing Home Support to Frail Elderly People,* Stirling: University of Stirling.

Brearley, C P (1975). *Social Work, Ageing and Society,* London: Routledge and Kegan Paul.

Challis, D and Davies, B (1986). *Case Management in Community Care.* Aldershot: Gower.

Challis, D, Darton, R A, Johnson, L, Stone, M, Traske, K and Wall, B (1989). *Darlington Community Care Project: Supporting Frail Elderly People at Home,* PSSRU, University of Kent at Canterbury.

Challis, D, Chessum, R, Chesterman, J, Luckett, R and Traske, K (1990). *The Gateshead Community Care Scheme: Case Management in Social and Health Care,* PSSRU, University of Kent at Canterbury.

Clough, R (1982). *Residential Work,* London: Macmillan.

Collins, T and Bruce, T (1984). *Staff Support and Staff Training,* London: Tavistock.

Gelles, R J and Cornell, C P (1985). *Intimate Violence in Families,* Beverly Hills, CA: Sage.

Hawkins, P and Shohet, R (1989). *Supervision in the Helping Professions,* Buckingham: Open University Press.

Levin, E, Sinclair, I and Gorbach, P (1989). *Families, Services and Confusion in Old Age,* Adlershot: Gower.

Lewis, J (1994). Care management and the social services: reconciling the irreconcilable, in: *Generations Review,* Vol. 4, No. 1, pp. 2–4.

Marshall, M (1990). *Social Work with Old People,* (2nd edition), London: Macmillan.

Mattinson, J (1975). *The Reflection Process in Casework Supervision,* London: Institute of Marital Studies.

Menzies, I (1970). *The Functioning of Social Systems as a Defence Against Anxiety,* London: Tavistock Institute of Human Relations.

Neill, J, Sinclair, I, Gorbach, P and Williams, J (1988). *A Need for Care: Elderly Applicants for Local Authority Homes,* Aldershot: Gower.

Norman, A J (1980). *Rights and Risks: a Discussion Document on Civil Liberty in Old Age,* London: National Corporation for the Care of Old People.

Norman, A J (1985). *Triple Jeopardy: Growing Old in a Second Homeland,* London: Centre for Policy on Ageing.

Payne, C and Scott, T (1982). *Developing Supervision of Teams in Field and Residential Work,* London: National Institute of Social Work.

Petch, A, Stalker, K, Taylor, C and Taylor, J (1994). *Assessment and Care Management Pilot Projects in Scotland: an Overview,* University of Stirling, Social Work Research Centre.

Rowlings, C (1981). *Social Work with Elderly People,* London: George Allen and Unwin.

Rowlings, C (forthcoming). 'Elder abuse in context', in: R. Clough (ed), *Elder Abuse and the Law.* London: Action on Elder Abuse/Age Concern England.

SSI (1991). *Assessment Systems and Community Care,* London, Department of Health.

Stevenson, O (1989). *Age and Vulnerability,* London: Edward Arnold.

Townsend, P (1981). 'The structured dependency of the elderly: creation of social policy in the twentieth century', in: *Ageing and Society,* Vol. 1, Part 1, pp. 5–28.

Walker, A (1980). 'The social creation of poverty and dependency in old age.' *Journal of Social Policy,* Vol. 9, No. 1, pp. 49–75.

Willcocks, D, Peace, S, Kellaher, L (1987). *Private Lives in Public Places,* London: Tavistock.

CHAPTER 7

Supervision of Home Care Staff

Jacki Pritchard

As a trainer I am very well aware that social services departments around the country organise their home care staff in a variety of ways. They all have various job titles (e.g. home help, warden, community carer) and perform different tasks. The purpose of this chapter is not to discuss the role of home care workers but to consider the importance of supervision for them. As a manager in a recently reorganised department I have come to realise just how important supervision for home care staff *should* be. Yet in the real world it is not always made a priority. I intend to consider why supervision for this group of staff is important and how it can be achieved. Throughout the chapter, attention will be given to key issues which have arisen from my own experience and which I am sure will be issues for other managers of home care staff in the future.

What is My Experience?

In my role as a trainer, I have trained home care staff in a number of specific areas, but my real lessons have been learnt from being a locality manager where I have witnessed staff in group meetings and through individual contact. I question whether home care organisers and their staff really think about what supervision means for them.

As locality manager I supervise social workers, home care organisers and a principal of a residential unit. All of them view supervision very differently and use supervision sessions in a variety of ways. The home care organisers who manage wardens and home helps felt 'at sea' to begin with because they did not know what to expect of me. I was an alien being because my background is field social work. Previously they had received supervision from a Senior Home Care Organiser, which involved discussing very practical matters related to workload.

I drew up written supervision contracts with *all* my workers and the agenda items for individual home care organisers covered a range of subject areas. An example of a contract made is given in Figure 7.1.

Figure 7.1: Example of Supervision Contract

STRICTLY CONFIDENTIAL

SUPERVISEE: Home Care Organiser (HCO)
SUPERVISOR: Team leader (TL)
Date contract agreed:

Supervision will take place every fortnight.
Time: 10.30–11.30 alternate Thursdays
Venue: TL's office

TL will take written notes, which will be shown to HCO, duly amended and agreed. The original notes will be kept in HCO's supervision file in TL's filing cabinet. A copy of the notes will be given to HCO.

The following items will be discussed during every supervision session, but additional items can be put on the agenda by both TL and HCO:

(1)   Workload/cases
(2)   Time management
(3)   Work/staff issues
(4)   Team issues
(5)   Training and development

This contract will be reviewed after 6 months.

Team Leader   Home Care Organiser

Similar contracts were made with other organisers. Examples of subjects/problems which came up for discussion under the agenda items are listed below:

Workload

- cover for long term sick leave
- recruitment
- handover book
- use of staff hours
- staff working in pairs
- group planning

- prioritising work
- discussion about particular cases/clients/problems arising.

Time management

- how to prioritise tasks
- use of diary
- planning in groups
- finding time to go on training courses
- allocating time for admin tasks
- taking lieu time.

Work/staff issues

- annual leave/lieu time
- recording overtime
- absence monitoring
- violence/alarms for staff
- health and safety
- duty system
- lack of admin support
- communication problems, for example with Housing Officers
- bathing clients – role of home care and district nurses
- administering medication
- use of hoists
- handling clients' monies/keys
- working with particular ethnic groups recently relocated in the locality (Somalians, Yemenis)
- use of interpreters
- placement of clients' pets
- dealing with complaints
- implementing disciplinary procedures
- gossiping amongst staff
- staff doing paid work for clients in their own time.

Team issues

- conflict with members of the team
- joint visits with social workers
- use of telephones within area office
- further discussion/feedback from team meetings
- team development meetings.

Training and development

- identifying training needs
- availability of courses within the department
- attendance at night school
- use of counselling courses/qualifications
- feedback from courses attended
- professional qualifications
- progression within the department
- career prospects
- changing jobs/getting stale/arranging work placements (with social workers, community psychiatric nurses, district nurses, police)
- day visits (e.g. to residential units, specialist wards, day centres, hospital wards).

A year on from reorganisation I have had positive feedback from my home care organisers about supervision:

'I feel relaxed now. It helps me to talk about how I am feeling.'

'The sessions help me to focus my mind, but I must come better prepared.'

'I never thought it would be like this. It's good. I'm not frightened now.'

At first the organisers found it difficult to think about specific topics for the agenda items. I often heard 'Well, there isn't much at the moment' or 'I've nothing to bring'. Sessions used to last no longer than half an hour. Now most sessions last an hour and full discussions take place. Organisers are broadening the topics they wish to discuss and feel the benefit of discussing issues rather than just practical work-related problems. Some specific issues which have been covered are:

- how to handle stress
- being assertive
- behaviour at case conferences
- role of and liaison with social workers (from different agencies, e.g. Family Service Unit, NSPCC)
- working with clients who have mental health problems
- schedule 1 offenders
- managing change/handling uncertainty
- assessment skills – differences in interviewing techniques (cf. home care organisers and social workers)
- joint working
- euthanasia
- ageism.

What Does Supervision Mean to Home Care Staff?

So far I have been discussing my experiences of supervising home care managers. It is clear that this group of staff were initially unsure about what supervision should involve, so one can assume that their staff (i.e. wardens and home helps) may also be unclear about what supervision means. As Payne and Scott (1982) have said:

> In some respects 'supervision' is an unfortunate term. For some it conjures an image of the production line and is associated with checking up, loss or lack of autonomy and strangulation by bureaucratic controls; thus being seen to destroy personal initiative and responsibility. But can a more acceptable word be found? Support? Too vague. Consultation? This excludes the vital element of accountability so essential to supervisory relationships. (p.8)

Many writers have tried to clarify the purpose of supervision for workers and there seems to be some basic agreement concerning the three major functions of supervision:

(1) accountability

(2) education

(3) support (see DHSS 1978, Kadushin 1976, Westheimer 1977).

All three functions are relevant to home care staff, but it is important at the outset to find out what the workers expect from supervision. This can be done very simply and in a non-threatening way on an individual basis or in a group situation.

Exercise 7.1: Expectations

Objective
To make home care staff think about what they expect from their line manager regarding supervision.

Participants
To work in pairs.

Equipment
Paper and pens.

Task
Staff are asked to discuss with each other what sort of practical advice/support they expect from their manager. They should think about things they do get, but also things that are missing, but they would like. As they talk they should write down their list of expectations.

Time

Ten minutes for discussion in pairs.

Each pair to take five minutes to feedback to the group.

GROUP SUPERVISION – THE EXPERIENCE

In most local authorities, home care organisers are managing large groups of staff (c. 35–60). It is unlikely that they will be able to undertake individual supervision sessions, unless a member of staff has a particular problem. Consequently, supervision such as it is will probably take place within a group meeting.

I have observed group meetings where wardens and home helps feedback on their work. The organiser usually checks the workload of the staff client by client from the mastersheets (e.g. 'Mrs Green – shopping, pension, cleaning') and if there are any problems with the client then these are discussed there and then. The nature of 'problems' can differ enormously, for example:

- a deterioration in mobility
- specific health problem
- use of medication
- difficulty in getting money from a relative for shopping
- the need to purchase clothes for the client
- asking workers to do jobs they are not allowed to do (e.g. clean outside windows)
- wanting to make a worker a beneficiary in a will
- the effects of a bereavement.

Accountability is a difficult issue, but it must be faced and most managers develop methods of monitoring what staff do. Yet these methods are not foolproof. Sometimes bad practices are discovered through clients. One client complained to an organiser that the warden had started putting her to bed at 3.30 in the afternoon. When an investigation took place, it came to light that this worker was working hours to suit herself.

Accountability of home care staff is greatly based on trust, in other words, staff contacting their managers when they have spare time (e.g. when a client has been admitted to hospital). Accountability is important because it is a way of home care organisers managing their staff, time and resources effectively.

Group meetings last for about one hour, but this is not long enough as there is never sufficient time to discuss issues in full. Consequently, the two other main purposes of supervision, namely education and support, cannot be addressed adequately. Yet this is a forum which could be used purposefully. Opportunities are often missed due to pressure of time. For example, workers make comments which should be confronted immediately because of the need to implement anti-discriminatory practice:

'There's nothing you can do about her feet. It's old age – what can you expect?'

'The old ones won't part with their money. It's pointless.'

'It's the coloured family ...'

'He's a Jehovah's Witness. You know what they're like.'

'I wouldn't send Phil [male home help] there, because Mr Evans is gay.'

Group meetings could be the place where training can be further developed. Home care organisers need training themselves (e.g. specific courses should be developed, for example, for training the trainers, or for group work skills) to help and develop skills to supervise in a group situation. Important issues could then be focused upon in order to promote good work practices. Two important subject areas are discussed below:

TRAINING ISSUE: PROFESSIONAL BOUNDARIES

When one uses the word 'professional' the image of doctors, solicitors, teachers and so forth is conjured up. However, many people do jobs which require them to be 'professional'. Some definitions of professional are given below:

- extremely competent in a job
- a piece of work or anything performed produced with competence or skill
- having or showing the skill of a professional
- engaged in a specified activity as one's paid occupation.

Other words which may be used instead of 'professional' would include:

adept, efficient, experienced, masterly, polished, practised, proficient, skilled.

The concept of being professional needs to be discussed with home care staff because otherwise they may engage in activities which are not appropriate and which may intrude into their private lives. Some examples are:

- A home help felt very sorry for some of her clients who had no family and were going to be alone at Christmas, so she invited them to her house for Christmas dinner.
- A client only liked a certain brand of coffee which was not available at the local shops. The new home help, who had started the job two weeks ago, said she would get the coffee from her local supermarket when she did her own weekly shopping. After a few weeks the client started asking for other things from the supermarket.
- A warden's husband started doing painting and decorating for clients.

There is a need to emphasise to home care staff that they are doing an important job but there have to be boundaries. They should not be seen 'as a friend'. Therefore, it is important that techniques are developed to ensure that staff can 'cut off' from work once they are at home. This is often very difficult for staff who live in the area where they work. These workers are sometimes approached in the street when they are off duty and asked to do things. It is difficult for them to say 'no' and because of this some assertiveness training in the staff group could be useful and beneficial. Other situations may arise for workers during their working hours. Exercises 7.2 and 7.3 will help staff think about how they may handle certain dilemmas.

Exercise 7.2: What would you do if?

Objective
To make home care staff think about what they would do if faced with a certain situation.

Participants
Exercise can be done in pairs or groups, whichever is more comfortable for the staff concerned.

Equipment/preparation
Cards need to be prepared beforehand. Each person/pair should be given a card which says:

What would you do if a client ...

followed by a simple short sentence presenting a dilemma e.g.

- asked you to lend him £5 until pension day so he could buy some cigarettes?
- asked you how your sex life is?
- said another home help had hit her?
- asked why a neighbour had been admitted to hospital?
- asked you to take care of her savings while she went away for a week
- enquired if you knew anyone who wanted to buy some jewellery?
- knew it was your birthday and said she wanted to give you a valuable tea set which she had had for years?
- asked you to act as a guarantor for his son to get a bank loan to buy a car, so they can go out for days?
- asked you how much you get paid a week?
- asked you to go on holiday as a companion and all your expenses would be paid?

- asked you to get your daughter, who is a hairdresser, to do a perm for her?
- wants to tell you something private but first makes you swear on the Bible to keep it a secret?

Exercise 7.3: Would you?

Objective
Another exercise to find out how home care staff would react in certain situations.

Participants
To be done individually.

Equipment
A short questionnaire needs to be designed.

Task
To complete the questionnaire and then use responses as a basis for discussion.

Sample Questionnaire

Please answer the following questions by ticking YES or NO.

Would you …

	YES	NO
Smoke in a client's house whilst working?		
Lend money to a client?		
Give a client a birthday card?		
Accept a present from a client?		
Borrow money from a client?		
Talk about your family?		
Talk about something that was bothering you at home or at work?		
Take a client out for a drink in the local pub?		
Let a client meet a member of your family?		
Sell something for a client?		

TRAINING ISSUE: CONFIDENTIALITY

The crucial issue of confidentiality leads on from professional boundaries. Confidentiality means different things to different people and no consensus about definition or practice has ever been reached. I have been horrified on occasions at how confidentiality has been breached by staff, but this is mainly due to lack of training and supervision.

Staff need to be given examples of bad practice, for example

- talking to another home help about a client whilst standing at the bus stop
- discussing a client with another client
- talking about another home help's illness with a client.

It is therefore important to help staff think about the real meaning of 'confidentiality', which can be achieved by using Exercises 7.4 and 7.5.

Exercise 7.4: Confidentiality – what does it mean?

Objective
To make home care staff think about the word 'confidential'.

Participants
To work individually, then in a group.

Equipment
Paper and pens.

Task
Staff are asked to write down (either in a sentence or separate words) what the word 'confidential' means to them in their work.

Each participant will read out to the group what they have written down. Discussion will then follow about whether there are any areas of agreement or disagreement about the definitions presented.

Each person will then be asked to think of something they have had to keep confidential during the course of their work.

Time
Five minutes for individual work.

Twenty-five minutes for groupwork (depending on size of group).

Exercise 7.5: Confidentiality at work

Objective
To think about what confidentiality actually means in day-to-day work.

Participants
To sit in a circle.

Equipment
Flipchart and pens.

Task
The first stage of the exercise is to ask staff to brainstorm what they think 'Confidential' means. The leader of the group will write contributions on the flipchart paper.

The second stage is to ask the question:
'What sort of things should be kept confidential?'

The third stage is to present staff with a scenario and ask them what they would do, for example

- Confused Mrs Hughes tells you that her son hits her but she does not want you to do anything about it
- Mr Elland says he thinks your home help partner is stealing money from him. He says that money has gone missing from the sideboard on several occasions and last week the shopping seemed much dearer than usual.

Supervision sessions, no matter what form they take, could be a way of increasing knowledge about particular subject areas which again would promote good work practices. Most staff groups do not like sitting still for very long and certainly many of them feel uncomfortable having prolonged discussions in front of a large group of people. It is therefore important to make the sessions interesting and worthwhile. As with any supervision session, the supervisor needs to find out the best method for learning. There are an infinite number of issues/topics which could be addressed in supervision. Some suggestions follow:

- Anti-discriminatory practices
  (FOR CONSIDERATION: what does ageism, racism, sexism etc. really mean?)

- Knowledge about different ethnic groups, cultures, religions (FOR CONSIDERATION: how do these things affect working with clients?)
- Knowledge about specific illnesses, diseases and their effects (FOR CONSIDERATION: diabetes, Alzheimer's disease, multiple sclerosis).

The home care organiser is responsible for supporting members of staff, but this can only be to a limited degree when managing such large numbers of staff. As with other staff within social services departments they need the opportunity to talk about their feelings and anxieties. Newly appointed staff may be feeling very vulnerable and unsure about situations they are facing. More experienced staff may find themselves working with extremely stressful situations. Some examples are:

- working with a terminally ill client who has chosen to die at home
- finding a dead body
- witnessing violence towards a client
- experiencing loss/death of a client known for years
- working with a family whose children are on the Child Protection Register.

It is very important for staff to be encouraged to talk about their feelings and Exercise 7.6. is designed to facilitate the process.

Exercise 7.6: Talk about when

Objective
To help home care staff vent their feelings.

Participants
To be done in a group.

Equipment
Prepare cards with one word written on expressing an emotion, for example:

- angry
- upset
- frustrated
- sad
- alone
- confused
- frightened
- worried
- nervous.

Task

Each member of the group is given a card. They are asked to think of something that has happened whilst they have been at work which has made them feel the emotion expressed on the card. Each person then has to talk to the group about how they felt by answering the following questions:

- what happened to make you feel this way?
- why do you think you felt like this?
- do you think you were right to feel this way?
- who did you talk to about the situation/how you felt?

Time

Five minutes for staff to think of a situation related to the card.

Five to ten minutes for each participant to talk about the situation they were in.

Finally, staff need to know that they must talk about how they are feeling but this must happen in an appropriate way, in other words, to their line manager or within the group, where there is confidentiality. It has to be stressed that it is not appropriate to talk to neighbours or friends about clients and their situations. It is also important that staff know who to go to when they are faced with a difficult situation. They need to be reminded about departmental policies and procedures on a regular basis. Building good support networks is vital and again this could be facilitated in group supervision by using Exercise 7.7.

Exercise 7.7: Safe house/community

Objective

To make home care staff think about who is important to them in their work, i.e., who they need to liaise with and who they would go to for help.

Participants

The first stage of the exercise is done in small groups (4–5 people). The second stage is done individually.

Equipment

Flipchart paper and lots of coloured pens.

Task

First stage: staff are asked to make a list of all the people they talk to during their working day. They are then asked to draw a village which represents their local community and place all the people on their list in the village.

Second stage: individual participants are asked to draw a 'Safe House'. In this house staff will put people they would go to for help/advice in different rooms in the house (e.g. if a client was ill the home help would call the doctor).

REFERENCES

Department of Health and Social Security (1978). *Social services teams: the practitioners' view*. London: HMSO.

Kadushin, Alfred (1976). *Supervision in Social Work*. New York: Columbia University Press.

Payne, Chris and Scott, Tony (1982). *Developing supervision of teams in field and residential social work*. London: National Institute for Social Work – Papers No 12.

Westheimer, I. (1977). *The Practice of Supervision in Social Work*. London: Ward Lock Educational.

CHAPTER 8

MAKING SUPERVISION WORK

ROGER CLOUGH

OVERVIEW

The people who live in residential homes and attend day centres are dependent on staff for the quality of services which are fundamental to their everyday lives. For some, life in the home or centre* will provide, in part, good physical care, a change from a difficult environment, an opportunity to feel safe, cared for and valued, and a place where, alongside friends, new perspectives on life are developed. The reality for many users is that, prior to life in the centre, they were despairing, defeated or despaired of by others. Life in the home or centre will not be able to put these things right nor make everyone happy or grateful. One of the most telling illustrations of this is someone who said that she ought not to have to live in a residential home: if only her fiancé had not been killed in the First World War she would be living with family and children (Clough, 1981, p. 178).

Work in these establishments may be immensely satisfying, giving the opportunity to demonstrate in the detail of everyday life the values inherent in good care. Indeed, one of the enjoyments of day and residential work is the frequency of informal contacts with people which allow real 'care' to be demonstrated. Yet the work is often physically heavy; further, it may be demanding and stressful in that so many emotions of user and worker are brought to the surface.

It needs no imagination to be aware of the deficiencies in day and residential care. Report follows report (Clough 1988) in cataloguing the shortfalls in practice: too often users are dissatisfied with the service which they get; the staff who work in these establishments feel overwhelmed and isolated; managers are aware that the quality of the work at times is not good enough. Nearly all these reports will stress the importance of supervision. In some ways this is not surprising. Around 80 per cent of the budget of a home or day centre will be spent on staff. The product of the service is in most cases staff providing a service. So, the argument would run, if you want to make basic improvements in the way in which staff work, you must influence their

---

*   To avoid repetition of 'home or centre' and 'resident or attender', at times I shall use words such as 'user', 'centre' and 'establishment'.

practice. Probably supervision is cited most often as the way to improve performance.

Yet, in spite of the rhetoric, my contention is that supervision is not an activity which will of necessity produce results leading to better provision. Guidelines for supervision are valuable. But a supervisor who follows the recognised guidelines will not necessarily affect the quality of work. The fact that supervisor and supervisee meet will not bring about improved performance. Everything may be carried out in accordance with set procedures: supervision sessions set up in advance, the agenda negotiated, the time protected from interruptions, the setting comfortable, and a record kept by both parties of what took place and what action is to follow. And yet all the endeavour may be sterile. Given the emphasis which so many organisations place on supervision as a prime means of improving the quality of residential and day care, we have to establish what are the values, objectives and skills of supervision.

We have all sat through too many meetings which were supposed to be aiding communication but were in fact a frustrating waste of time in which people's views were not sought or taken account of, to believe that *the carrying out of the event necessarily will result in the objective for which, supposedly, it was established*. Precisely the same is true of supervision. The supervisee will only feel that she or he is listened to if the supervisor does take note and think about what is said, and works out what to do drawing on this new information. Of course this is obvious stuff. Yet, we have a plethora of procedures for supervision and not enough good supervision.

Indeed, the way in which supervision is carried out will influence the life of the establishment and must tie in to the objectives of the establishment. If a centre claims to be empowering users, then supervision must empower staff. Stevenson and Parsloe (1993) make the point:

> We see supervision as a major process in the development of staff towards empowering practice. It is the channel for the new organisational climate to flow to management and to workers, users and carers. However, this will only occur if departmental policies make clear what is expected of the process: who is to supervise who; what are supervision sessions for and how does the supervisor acquire the skill for the job? (p. 57)

As with all other activities which require skills in relating to people, supervisors are not born fully fledged. The task for establishments (and for this chapter) is to help the supervisor learn and develop skills, including that of evaluating supervision. Tash (1967) describes a project to train supervisors of youth leaders. The book is valuable in that she analyses what happens in supervision, the different techniques used by supervisors, the feelings of supervisors and supervisees and sets out criteria for evaluation. Supervision has to be measured by outcome.

OBJECTIVES OF SUPERVISION

Supervision has three main objectives: accountability, support and development.

Accountability

Of the objectives listed by Payne and Scott (1982) two come under the heading of accountability: ensuring that 'the operation of the ... unit ... [is] consistent with the primary functions of the agency'; 'to ensure that workers are clear, individually and collectively, about their roles and responsibilities' (p. 15). The task of management differs from supervision. It is possible to carry out the task of management without supervising staff. But it is not possible to supervise properly without ensuring that the functions of management are embedded into supervision.

Supervision is designed to ensure the quality of the product, that is, the delivery of a service. An agency needs to be assured that staff are working in accordance with the values, practices and procedures which have been specified. Supervision is a mechanism to help achieve that. Managers, whether or not they are the supervisors, need to know that staff understand the requirements of the organisation and the nature of their responsibility as employees.

However, in addition, managers *being accountable for their own work*, will want to have a means for examining whether staff practice is in conformity with specified values and objectives. If as a manager I am accountable for the work of others, then I wish to be in a position to know how they are working.

There is a further aspect. Supervision is a means (though not the only one) by which some other functions of management may be carried out. Managers have a responsibility to ensure that staff know their employment rights, understand health and safety regulations and are informed of the action to take if they are dissatisfied with the service. They also have to undertake functions such as monitoring sickness, and supervision may be used to raise questions and concerns, as well as to inform supervisees of where their work is good and where it is poor.

Douglas and Payne (1988) state:

> As a basic value position we would state that people who are given responsibility and power over other people's lives should be prepared, equipped and *supervised* to discharge these responsibilities adequately. (p. 23, my italics)

Accountability describes a state in which a person is liable to be called to account for actions taken. It also encompasses aspects of responsibility. Accountability should not be seen only as being owed by junior to senior staff, or by a senior staff to a management body. In fact 'the organisation', however that is described, should expect to be accountable to those for whom the service is provided, to the public and to their employees. Supervision should be seen as a way in which *some aspects of accountability* may be considered.

Support

The supervisor has responsibility to support and motivate staff. Supervision is an act of intervention. It creates a setting in which the supervisee accounts for her or his work to the supervisor. An obvious danger is that by checking on how the staff member has been working, the supervisee's capacity for independent action is undermined. The next section on development will examine this issue. The focus here is on the importance of support for staff.

Staff in residential and day centres have a complex and demanding task. Writing about homes for older people I have set out elsewhere some of the issues:

> Staff ... are at the centre of society's uncertainty about the purpose of such institutions. They are left to carry out a confused task in the way they think best; in addition they are left to carry a mass of feelings from a multitude of people (relatives, social workers, doctors, residents and others). They will be seen as saints ('However do you do such a job?') and as sinners ('Fancy treating her like that'). They have to live with their own frustrations when the job does not work out as they would wish. (Clough 1981, p. 139)

Further, staff are often close to the pain and despair of the people with whom they are working; some of the physical care is heavy and unpleasant; the work is often done in public and semi-public situations, seen by others, whether users, staff or visitors. In the study quoted above, I found that many staff got their satisfaction from the gratitude of residents. 'I hope we can make them happy', one staff member said to me. Yet the reality is that however good the work of staff, some people will never be happy or say 'Thank you'. Staff need other measures of their performance.

There was a time when some people argued that professionalism meant distance from the concerns of users and it is well known that some establishments developed systems to prevent staff from acknowledging the feelings that accompanied their work. For example, Menzies (1960) wrote of the functioning of social systems as a defence against anxiety. Fortunately, such notions of professional distance have mostly been left behind. Not only is the worker to be open to some of the feelings of the user, it is inevitable that the worker will have feelings aroused by the work: joy, anger, despair are all closer to the surface when providing care for people who would not want to be dependent.

Such work also touches concerns about self of *both supervisor and supervisee*: how have I cared for people whom I love? How do I, or would I, manage being dependent or depressed? What does my life hold in store? The supervisor has provided a framework in which staff may live with these feelings without being overwhelmed by them and in which staff find ways to assess the quality of their day-to-day work which are not dependent on gratitude.

The stresses of residential work have been catalogued frequently. The stresses of day care work may be less intense because users' lives are shared with other carers, but remain substantial. There is evidence in much day and residential work of high levels of staff turnover and sickness. Supervision may be set up to fail if it is assumed that without other structures changing, all of these matters will be rectified.

To support staff, a supervisor should assume that staff wish to perform to the best of their ability, until there is evidence to the contrary. Such support should help the worker in the following ways: by acknowledging that it is appropriate to have feelings and by looking for ways to live with or draw on those feelings in the work; by helping staff assess whether or not they have done a good day's work; by encouraging the initiative of staff and responding to it; by promoting independent functioning; and by providing feedback on performance.

Development

There are two important parts to this aspect of supervision. The first is linked to factors which are often covered in appraisal: from a consideration of the supervisee's present performance, ability and interests to construct a list of developmental targets and how they are to be achieved. The second characteristic, which I term education, is frequently neglected. Given the importance of accountability, together with the stated responsibility of the supervisor to be checking on practice, there is a tendency for supervision to concentrate on considering a list of current activities of the supervisee. There are limitations in this approach. The supervisee has too great a control of what is discussed, both in terms of topic and often of the material. In addition, the session becomes largely reactive. Thus, at its simplest (and acknowledging the parody) supervision takes the form of the supervisee saying: 'This is the situation; I did this; I plan to do that; is that OK?'

To undertake the educative function of supervision, supervisors require knowledge of the ways adults learn so that they do not rely solely on their own preferred learning methods and skills. Indeed, a further subtlety relates to awareness by the supervisor of the supervisee's readiness for certain learning. A supervisor may be too wise or protective, drawing on her/his experience to give supervisees the answers to problems which they have not encountered (Tilley 1971). Perhaps more important, they have to develop skills in the *process* of supervising: in understanding, planning and using techniques. What processes are at work in the supervision session? What are the best ways to help the supervisee to develop? How do I challenge and question? What approach will encourage the supervisee to consider alternative reasons for the behaviour they report and alternative options for action? As educator, the supervisor should be willing to propose ways of expanding knowledge and skills along the lines of asking for an article to be read for discussion or suggesting a way to study the behaviour of someone whom the worker is saying 'keeps throwing temper tantrums'.

DISTINCTIVE CHARACTERISTICS OF DAY AND RESIDENTIAL WORK

Supervision is not an activity which is the same whatever the context. There are significant differences in residential and day care from the settings about which most people have written on supervision. The difference in the nature of the job affects the knowledge of the supervisor about the supervisee and the supervisory relationship.

First, is the public nature of life and work: people who use the centre see each other in formal events such as group meetings, semi-formal events (for example meal times) and informal times, as when people are sitting in a lounge. Staff share in the intimacies of others' daily lives, and for much of the time have their own work seen by other users and staff.

Second, there is the task itself, a significant part of which is related to help with daily living. Beyond this with younger people (and to a lesser extent with others) staff have to encourage, and at times ensure that people to certain things: get up, go to bed, behave properly towards other users and so on. Staff have to exercise control; they have significant power which they must use properly, but there is also the potential for them to fail *in the eyes of others* to be able to exert their authority to get the task done.

A third factor is that it is less easy than in field social work to define the boundaries of the job, in particular to specify the 'social work role'.

Fourth, much of the work of one person is carried on by another. Thus, one member of staff coming on duty, may meet users who have become tense, angry or excited over something which has to do with a member of staff who has just stopped work.

Finally, as important as any of the above, the manner in which staff work has a direct bearing on the well being of users, evidenced by the way in which someone is bathed or is served with a meal.

Thus, day and residential work involves sharing of life space (Beedell 1970), sharing in primary experiences and as does parenting, having to get things done (whether meals prepared, washing up completed or people to bed).

The significance for supervision is that the supervisor has a perception of the work of the supervisee, indeed may have seen the supervisee directly or heard from others above what happened. The supervisor does not rely solely on the supervisee *reporting* what happened. The supervisor in the day and residential setting is likely *without setting up special events* to have various sources of information.

Workers have degrees of closeness to users. The same will be the case with the supervisory relationship, I think to a greater extent than in field work.

There is a tendency in day and residential work for staff to be reactive: too often there is little planning as to what staff will do. The result is that people turn up to work and deal with what happens. A key task for supervision is to promote forward thinking.

A final aspect is that residents are stigmatised from the fact of moving into a residential home (as are day care users, although to a lesser extent). Staff will attract some of the stigma (Clough 1981 pp. 7–15). It becomes apparent that self-worth (of staff or residents) is a further topic for supervision.

SUPERVISION SYSTEMS

The size and organisation of day and residential centres varies hugely. Supervision systems must be congruent with the style and structure of the place.

Therefore, there is no one way of setting up supervision systems: there are objectives that the supervision system must be designed to achieve; there are the mechanics, as discussed in the next section, of what has to happen to achieve them. This section focuses on different systems of supervision.

Any system of supervision must establish the terms of the supervision. What happens to the information that is discussed? Who else sees the record? How far is someone free to talk about problems or skills which they want to develop? Might information from a supervision session later be used as part of disciplinary proceedings setting out someone's inability to perform the task adequately? *Accountability* has to be established. Clarity about the nature of supervision is essential because there is a temptation, in particular with long established or older staff members, to emphasise the developmental aspect of supervision and to conceal the management component.

However, if the line manager is the supervisor, all information must be regarded as management knowledge. You cannot know something as a supervisor and not know it as manager. It is useful in understanding supervision to distinguish it from appraisal and consultancy.

Appraisal includes: a review of the performance of an individual, including the work that has been undertaken and its quality, the factors that might improve performance, the work and training interests of the person being appraised and, where possible, an agreed plan. Appraisal may be carried out by a supervisor, a colleague who is not a line manager or someone from outside the establishment. The task is usually intended to be carried out at regular intervals to ensure that sufficient focus is given to the work practice of an individual. If the supervisor is both line manager and appraisor, the activity of the appraisal is incorporated into supervision in a straightforward way: the carrying out of appraisal ensures that the regular pattern of supervision is broken so that a focus is given to a systematic review of performance. When appraisal is carried out by others, there has to be clarity as to what is passed to the appraisee's line manager. Often, it is only matters agreed by appraisor and appraisee that are forwarded. There has to be similar decision as to who sets the agenda: is it set solely by the appraisee?

Second, supervision must be distinguished from consultancy. A consultant is a person from outside the establishment who is available by agreement with line managers for staff as individuals or in groups. Again, the terms have to be worked out carefully but the basis of consultancy is that someone without direct involvement or responsibility may be able to help staff review aspects of their work. Some establishments allow staff to see a consultant without informing their line management and regard everything that is said as confidential; or consultancy may be a regular feature of life in the centre; and there may be an agreement that, in certain circumstances, the consultant will convey information to a line manager. The consultant does not have oversight of the work of another.

It is possible for staff colleagues who are not line managers to be supervisors. This type of peer supervision requires clarity about boundaries. Thus the same activity may be called 'peer supervision' or 'mentoring' or something else. The words do not really matter: what is essential is that there is, in advance, clarity as to the nature of the relationship, and the responsibility for determining the agenda and action. I think that the activity of supervision must include the formal oversight of the work of another, *and* accountability. Thus, peer supervision requires either parallel systems of oversight and accountability or mechanisms by which information from the peer supervision is available to the line manager.

Supervision systems must be appropriate to other structures in the organisation: the staffing structure, the size of the establishment, the team structure, the nature of the task and other professionals. However, systems must also take account of the capacity of the nominated person to supervise. Supervision requires skills. In developing that statement, it is difficult to hold the balance between creating a mystique and denying that the job has skills. There are some organisations that appear to believe that by producing handbooks on supervision setting out the objectives and the mechanics (in the sense of matters such as frequency of supervision and systems of recording), people will be able to do the job. This is as naive as presuming that a teacher will be able to help students to learn by following set procedures. Yet the skills are those that are inherent in good social work, good practice teaching and good social work management: clarity about responsibilities and boundaries; managing the authority inherent in the role; making judgements; being open; listening to the concerns of others; setting out matters that the supervisor wishes to review; reflecting on the process of the supervision meetings; considering ways which might help the supervisee to develop new skills. Perhaps the central point is that the good supervisor is *active*: he or she does more than turn up to the meeting and respond; there is preparation and planning, and a willingness to propose activities. The supervisor will need somewhere to reflect on the supervision, whether to line manager or consultant.

THE MECHANICS OF SUPERVISION

More than most activities, supervision can be carried out according to guidelines, yet largely be ineffective. As has already been set out, the process of the supervision meeting may not allow the central purposes of supervision to take place. Thus the supervisee may recount a version of some activity and the supervisor may note down what is said. Yet the objectives of review of work, learning and accountability may not be achieved. The skills of supervision are not merely administrative, such as ensuring that the times planned for supervision are kept. The skills, as will be discussed in the next section, are related to the manner in which the supervisor listens, the work is reviewed and the individual held to account. The strength of Tash's (1967) work, already cited, lies in the description and analysis of the process of supervision.

> F, (supervisee) who described in a confused way the differing expectations of adults and young people in her situation, was, to the supervisor, obviously confused by them but the supervisor did not know why. The techniques at that point were questions which helped F to clarify the expectations, the attitudes and the parts played by individuals and groups, one by one. The problem had to be sorted out as presented ...

But the supervisor was also asking herself questions – why is F confused? Is it because the situation is impossible to work in? Is it because
she has not known how to clarify it? Is it because she prefers to opt out
– to apportion blame and not think about herself? (p. 88)

Mechanics are a part of the process of supervision. It is no good for the
supervisor to *say* that supervision is important but for the supervision period
frequently to be cancelled, curtailed or interrupted. The reality, as with all
social work activity, is that it is in the detail that the supervisor demonstrates
whether supervision will live up to what is claimed and, indeed, whether the
supervisee matters. I shall not produce precise formula for the mechanics of
supervision, the factors which help to ensure that the objectives are realised,
because these must fit the style of the place and the people involved. Rather,
I shall highlight the areas where the details must be worked out: supervision
must be an integral part of an individual's learning and accountability; there
must be some form of agreement between supervisor and supervisee about
process and content; both parties should be preparing for the supervision
meeting; the whole activity must be reviewed.

Staff in residential and day establishments should have a period of planned
induction, opportunity to examine their work on a regular basis, periodic and
formal examination of their performance and access to someone to discuss
their feelings in relation to their job. These are often termed induction,
supervision, appraisal and consultancy. What matters is that there is clarity
as to how these functions will be carried out and what the relationship is
between them. For example, the supervisor needs to know about the learning
needs of the staff member. Thus, if the supervisor is not carrying out the
appraisal, there must be a formal mechanism to pass across information to
the supervisor.

In day and residential life boundaries often are blurred. People are known
to others through any number of casual encounters such as passing in corri-
dors or serving at a meal time as well as at more set or intimate times such as
bathing. This is one of the great joys and opportunities of such life and work:
you are not meeting people only at set interview times as is largely the pattern
with field work. Yet it has the danger that will be all too familiar: people's
wants and needs may be dealt with on the hoof. 'I'll catch you later, Mrs.
Brown' says the staff member, but Mrs. Brown knows how unlikely it is that
that will happen. This style of work may be too reactive with not enough
planning. Supervision in such establishments is prone to the same tendencies:
'We'll talk about your work when I get a break later in the day' or 'I can't
manage the supervision time again but you know that you can catch me any
time'. These tendencies are compounded by the problems of shortage of office
space or the difficulties for senior staff on shifts to set time aside for the
supervisee from the demands of others.

The setting of boundaries is a key to successful supervision. Supervision
must be regular, rarely cancelled, as guarded as possible from interruptions.
After all, it makes sense that if staff have their protected time, they will be
better equipped to provide that for others.

'Boundaries' refer also to another aspect of this type of work: there is
widespread knowledge of others, their sadness and their happiness. People

will talk about others in the establishment, at best with friendship at worst with malice. Secrets are difficult to keep and staff may not always get the distinction right of when it is appropriate to talk to users about others, and when it is not. The same danger exists in supervision. In these settings, in particular, staff must be informed as to the nature of the confidentiality of the information which is discussed. By and large, the rule should be that everything will be confidential unless there is agreement of supervisor and supervisee *or* the supervisor judges it essential to inform senior managers. There should be a statement in the agreement about this which is reiterated as necessary. A familiar situation is that where a supervisee says that he or she has something important to say but wants it kept confidential. The supervisor ought not to agree to this because she or he has to decide *having heard what is said* whether the information should be passed to managers. For example, the supervisee, having extracted a promise of confidentiality, may say that he or she has concerns about another member of staff or about his/her own capacity to carry out the work.

Insofar as is possible, the agreement covers the major issues: how is the agenda for the meeting constructed, what is to be done before the meeting, the arrangements for protecting the supervision time and space, and the nature of confidentiality (including specifying who may see supervision records).

MATERIAL FOR SUPERVISION

The focus for supervision in field social work tends to be the work that is carried out with a series of individuals, families or groups. Thus, when meeting for supervision, it is possible to review the total workload and decide which of these activities is to be discussed in supervision. Day and residential work involves both direct work with individuals but also a series of tasks which are related to the nature of the work, that is, those activities which are related to daily life: getting up, meals, washing, in between times. It is essential that in supervision both the individual and the general work are considered. Because much of the work is about maintenance of the systems for good daily living, there has to be a considerable degree of structure to supervision. Thus it may be appropriate to focus on 'getting up procedures'. The task would differ with people's responsibilities and abilities. One person might be asked to describe and analyse what happens; another might suggest changes which could be made to the procedures; someone else could ask users for their views; another approach would be to set out the values and objectives of the organisation, and the extent to which these are met by the practice; or the supervisee could be asked to record and analyse their own experiences when they are working at 'getting up' times – this could be a combination of feelings, actions and reflection. In a day centre other activities such as 'mealtimes' could be substituted.

What is essential is that those activities which lie at the heart of successful residential and day care are examined as part of supervision. Workers need to know that these are regarded as vital to the life of the place. However, this is also a key part of empowerment for staff. It is in these repeated, daily living tasks that much of the energy and feeling of staff is contained and the supervisee will benefit from putting the energy into change and improving their own work or that of the place.

Supervision should contribute to the staff member acting with sureness and confidence. Further, supervision must help staff gain control of their work; 'empowerment', in the current terminology. Such empowerment must relate to everyday activities, so staff must assert their views and analyses of what is happening and what would improve performance for them and the users.

The topics for consideration at supervision have to be thought about carefully. So, too, does the material to be examined. Again, there must be variety determined by both supervisor and supervisee. The potential sources are rich: a diary kept by the supervisee, perhaps with description of an event and the trigger questions or ideas that arise; tape or video recordings; supervisor and supervisee doing shared work; role play of a problematic event; observation by the supervisor; various forms of file notes on individuals or events; planning notes for an event which is to take place, something akin to a teacher preparing material, methods and structures in advance of a lesson; focused recording of interaction with an individual throughout a day, rather than just recording problematic events (similar to Dockar Drysdale's 'context profiles' (Dockar Drysdale 1968).

Supervision must be planned. The methods and the material must take account of the issues that supervisor and supervisee determine to be important. Thus the supervisee might be saying that a particular user is withdrawn, never talks at meals, looks unhappy and is teased by others. In part, the feelings that overwhelm the user swamp the worker. The supervisor must take account of her/his knowledge of the staff member: skills, knowledge base current 'solidity' and personal circumstances. The supervision work could follow different lines: reading about depression or talking to someone with theoretical understandings; charting in fine detail observation and interaction with the withdrawn person – the supervisee could be encouraged to look and listen, considering posture, facial expressions, where the person sits and their movements, actual words used in conversations; another possibility is to ask the supervisee to write or record on tape his or her own feelings that are aroused; a further approach would be to ask the supervisee to consider what are the options for action *directly* with the individual *or* indirectly with the systems of the establishment. The worker has to be helped to get a measure of control.

MAKING SUPERVISION WORK

At the start of this chapter I mentioned *outcomes*. What is the outcome of supervision? We can measure the input: the time supervisor and supervisee spend in meetings and preparation; other costs. We can determine the opportunity cost – the activities that are not done because of the resources that go into supervision. We can examine the outputs: the numbers of hours of supervision. But the key questions remains: as a consequence of the energy put into supervision, is there any difference in outcome? Does the worker work better? Is accountability better defined and enacted?

I remain firmly of the view that good supervision does not follow good procedures. Procedures matter, but the heart of supervision is the quality of the interaction. I return to a central theme of this chapter; the skills that are required in supervision are those inherent in good social work: listening to the supervisee involves more than keeping one's ears open, for it has to be active – people want to know that others are listening to them; how does the supervisor demonstrate this? The supervisor is watching as well as listening for emphasis, emotion and the manner in which things are said.

Having listened, something has to happen. There are numerous ways to achieve this, again drawing on all the skills of social work. For example, a response might be to recap along the line: 'If I have understood you right, the issues you are concerned about are ....' Whether to follow this with suggestions of options for action or asking the supervisee for suggestions will depend on the supervisor's analysis of the individual and the situation. The core point is that there has to be that type of searching reflection during the supervision. The consequence might be that, having discussed with the supervisee, the supervisor might be unsure how to proceed. It would be appropriate to say: 'The issue is an important one and I am not sure of the range of options. What I would like to do is to note the matters and set an early follow up meeting when we could both come back with further ideas'. In the interim the supervisor might consult with others as a way of reflecting on what has taken place and what should happen next.

There are dangers in supervision. Perhaps the overriding one is that there can be a belief that the fact of meeting will in some strange way produce results. Other dangers are that supervisor and supervisee may collude to avoid the task, that the supervisor may try to impose a personal, preferred learning style on to the supervisee, that both parties may allow the sessions to move into a comfortable chat rather than a task-focused activity, or that important differences between the two parties may be avoided under the escape of 'a clash of personalities'.

Having just been through a rigorous assessment of the quality of our teaching at Lancaster University, I am only too aware of the tensions that arise from having others oversee and examine our work. Yet I know, too, the importance of the interest in teaching and learning that is generated and the value to me of the way in which assessors reflected on my teaching sessions. The outcome of good supervision is reflection on the task, a searching for understanding of one's own performance as well as of the task, and development. Perhaps above all supervision with its combined thrust of accountability and development has the potential for the supervisee to be valued and enthused by the concerned interest of the supervisor. This is the base for better practice.

REFERENCES

Beedell, C. (1970) *Residential Life*. London: Routledge and Kegan Paul.
Clough, R. (1981) *Old Age Homes*. London: Allen and Unwin.

Clough, R. (1988) *Scandals in Residential Centres,* an unpublished report for the Wagner Committee.

Dockar Drysdale, B. (1968) *Therapy in Child Care.* London: Longman.

Douglas, R. and Payne, C. (1988) *Organising for Learning.* London: National Institute for Social Work.

Menzies, I. (1960) A case study in the functioning of social systems as a defence against anxiety, *Human Relations,* 13.

Payne, C. and Scott, T. (1982) *Developing Supervision of Teams in Field and Residential Social Work.* London: National Institute for Social Work.

Stevenson, O. and Parsloe, P. (1993) *Community Care and Empowerment.* York: Joseph Rowntree.

Tash, M. (1967) *Supervision in Youth Work.* London: National Council for Social Service.

Tilley, M. (1971) Unpublished paper.

CHAPTER 9

SUPERVISION IN A RESIDENTIAL/DAY CARE SETTING

RON WIENER

INTRODUCTION

This chapter is written with a particular slant towards all residential and day care staff.

While supervision has always had a place in fieldwork, it is still possible to read newly published texts on residential work with different client groups and find no mention of supervision in the subject index.

The driving force recently has come from reports such as those by Wagner (1988) and Howe (1992) into residential care, and from *The Children Act* (1989) *Guidance and Regulations* where Volume 4 on Residential Care spells out a framework for supervision: it should be for all staff; it should happen on a one-to-one basis in private and 'staff should ideally receive supervision for one to one-and-a-half hours, not less frequently than once every two to three weeks' (p.10, paras 1.43/1.44). What exists for staff working with children should exist for all staff.

This chapter will be concerned with planned, formal, hierarchical supervision sessions and will look at the importance of supervision both from a manager's and a worker's perspective; the content and format of sessions and the need for their monitoring.

WHAT IS SUPERVISION?

Supervision is a way in which one person helps another to improve their work performance. From a management perspective it answers a number of basic questions:

(1) How do you know that workers are doing what they should be doing? This touches on issues of standards, accountability and governmental and departmental guidelines.

(2) How do you know workers are doing the job as well as they can? This covers: development; training; learning and quality.

(3) How do you know workers are coping? This is largely about stress management.

(4) How do you know that no client/service user is being hurt?

(5) How do you know that no worker is going to land you in it? This is a form of self protection.

From a worker's perspective, supervision provides an opportunity to:

(1) review his/her work to ensure that it meets expectations.

(2) offload feelings and experiences created by the demands of the job and to get support.

(3) look at one's personal and professional needs and career progression.

(4) review one's work to ensure that it meets expectations.

TYPES OF SUPERVISION

There are many different types of supervision:

hierarchical: manager supervises deputies who supervise the staff. The most common form and one which ensures management accountability.

peer: where two people at the same level agree to supervise each other's work. This often happens at the level of first line manager where their supervision from middle managers becomes a limited exercise in crisis management and task completion. The weakness of this type of supervision is that there is no legitimised power to confront each other and this has to be acknowledged and dealt with if collusion is not to occur.

paired: every time two staff members do a piece of work (run a group; work a shift) together, it becomes possible to review and reflect on the quality of that work. This needs to be more than support. It is the sitting down and going through a preset series of questions about how the work was planned, co-ordinated and delivered.

The questions after a shift might include: did we meet the shift objectives? were the care plans for different individuals followed? how did we divide up the tasks? how else could we have handled the incidents? what did we do well? how did we work together? did we spend the appropriate amount of time with each resident? what can we do next time that will improve the quality of care? how aware were we of issues to do with anti-discriminatory practice? ...and so on.

group: the team collectively review each other's work. The risk is that this will become a case discussion, as it is easier to talk about a non-existent client than about how a staff member sitting beside one is delivering their work.

outside: this often happens when the team does not have the expertise to review their work with a particular client and an external consultant is brought in. This needs to be tightly contracted if it is to work well.

ongoing: learning situations happen all the time. Managers, by working alongside staff, can provide positive support and constructive criticism as opportunities arise. This has an important role in residential and daycare where managers often work with care staff. This differs from field work where much of what the worker does is carried out in private and is often not open to public scrutiny. However, feedback on immediate performance is only part of the supervision process.

informal: this is often explained as demand or problem led:

> I have an open door. If anyone is having a difficulty then they only need to come and see me.

This, however, means that someone has to admit to a problem before they can have supervision; or

> 'I give supervision to those staff who need it.'

This assumes that supervision is only about dealing with staff with problems. It also labels these staff as such in the eyes of the rest of the team and is therefore likely to be counter-productive. Also, it fails to take account of the biases that any manager is likely to feel towards their different staff and it is unlikely that in such an informal system all staff will receive an equal amount of supervisory time.

A FRAMEWORK FOR SUPERVISION

Supervision should be part of a *contract* (see Appendix 9A for an example of a local authority social services contract) between worker and manager. This could either be an 'in-house' or a divisional or departmental document. It should cover matters such as: agenda's frequency; length; privacy; confidentiality; and equal opportunities recording.

Agenda setting

There should be a joint activity, with agenda items swapped a couple of days before the session, so that both parties have an opportunity to prepare for it.

If the whole of the agenda comes from the supervisor then the worker is not taking responsibility for their part of the session and the supervisor will end up doing most of the work. Development usually comes from a worker being motivated to tackle issues.

Also, agendas should not simply be a list of problems. The archetypal session:

SUPERVISOR	'Have you got any problems to discuss?'
WORKER	'No,'
SUPERVISOR	'Good, see you next month then.'

is not good supervision – one can learn just as much from things that are being done well as from problem areas. A better reply for the supervisor would have been:

SUPERVISOR	'Then let's start with an area of your work that you're happy with, see what you are doing to achieve that, and how that learning can be taken into other areas.'

Frequency

It is important to set a realistic timetable. With staffing cutbacks and high rates of turnover and resultant stress, supervision is too often one of the first building blocks of a regime to be scrapped. It becomes seen as 'a good' rather than a necessary part of managing people. It is much better to have a session every six weeks if this is adhered to than a fortnightly target which is rarely met. Broken sessions should be replanned as soon as possible.

This is all made much easier if the sessions are planned six months ahead and built into the rota. There is little point in planning a session between a deputy and a care staff if they are the only two on duty.

Confidentiality

This is a difficult issue. Sessions should be confidential in so far as other staff members have no right to know what happened in a session. However, confidentiality is not absolute. First, anything which would, for example, be a suspendable offence, such as hitting a client, could not be covered up if it came to light in a supervision session.

Second, the supervisor needs to be supervised on their supervision. Just as in a supervision session a deputy might want to look at a key worker's case file to review the quality of work, so a supervisor needs to bring their supervision notes along to their own supervision with the officer in charge if they are the deputy. Responsibility must, therefore, be taken for how things are written up during the session.

Recording

A record should be made of each session on a standardised form with a copy for both participants. It needs to cover the issues discussed, actions to be taken and tasks set. Domestic upsets might be recorded simply as that, thus protecting confidentiality, but the important part would be to record what people were going to do to minimise the impact of the upset on the workplace.

Anti-discriminatory practice

This is an important issue to look at in terms of all the sets of relationships that impact on the supervision session. These cover: supervisor and supervisee; supervisee and clients; establishment and clients; establishment and the wider organisation; the wider organisation and the external society.

The supervisor has to be conscious not only of individual aspects of, say, racism, but also its institutional and societal impact on the supervision session. The supervisor, therefore, continually needs to be aware of how issues to do with race, gender, sexual orientation, age, disability and class can be affecting interactions. These might include: power or the lack of it; non-verbal behaviour; religious beliefs and practices; accessibility; emotional consequences of being/feeling victimised; a sense of isolation; ethnocentrism; written and spoken language; physical care; the appropriateness of touch and so on.

WHAT SUPERVISION ISN'T

Supervision isn't:

Counselling

Counselling is about helping another person to sort out a problem largely at that person's pace. While the supervisor might use counselling skills, such as active listening, a supervision session is concerned with a worker's performance and therefore the pace of the session and the need for confrontation are determined by the needs of the establishment rather than by the needs of the worker.

Similarly, a session which is solely concerned with a worker's private life is not a supervision session. It might, on occasions, be necessary to focus on a non-work-related personal issue but this should be seen as a counselling session and another supervision session arranged. It is the job, though, of the supervisor to address how the personal issue affects the work performance and to help the person find appropriate help or support.

A formal management session

If your management style consists of asking people to come into your office and giving them either a formal ticking off or a set of instructions, then trying to run a supervision session in this atmosphere will not work.

There has to be some trust between supervisor and worker because without this there will not be honesty and without this the worker will not be able to talk openly about his/her work. When these conditions are not fulfilled, supervision tends to become a management by objectives sessions and the developmental aspects and the opportunity to learn from mistakes disappear. There is a fine line to be drawn here because, although the supervisor needs to hear the positive and negative aspects of a worker's job, s/he is also the person with line management responsibility for the worker and their performance and the person who writes a reference. Therefore the issues of confidentiality and recording need to be addressed as part of establishing an open working environment.

THE WORK

If supervision is about improving work performance then two things follow:

(1) The workers need to know what is expected of them. They need: a job description; an induction period; guidelines and procedures; training and feedback.

(2) The supervisor needs to know what the worker does. This can be done by: observation; checking records; feedback from other staff; joint working; client reports; what the worker says directly and indirectly. In a session the worker will indicate his/her feelings about particular clients or situations by body language, tone and pitch of voice. The supervisor therefore needs to be alert to what is implied as well as to what is said.

THE CONTEXT OF SUPERVISION SESSIONS

Factual

There is an element of supervision which is about checking up that things are done. Therefore one might expect that in a session a supervisor might be looking to see that:

- departmental guidelines and policies were being followed
- fire and violence drills were being completed
- care plan recommendations were being carried out
- shift tasks were being completed – laundry, cleaning, etc
- administration – logs/file notes were being kept up-to-date
- key worker tasks were being done
- there was attendance at team meetings, reviews etc.

Management

One of the few resources that managers have much control over is the productivity of the hours worked. There are questions of efficiency – is the best use being made of the time – and of effectiveness – what have been the outcomes of the worker's efforts?

The supervisor might therefore want to:

- review how time is used on a particular shift
- look at how shifts/day plans are set up as part of handovers
- look at which service user had what time spent with them to what effect
- look at time spent on administration versus hands on.

Overall, the supervisor is looking for a worker's ability to prioritise, assess, plan and time manage.

In addition to time, there are other resources. These include: physical plant, in other words, all the rooms in the building; equipment on the premises; community resources, for example buildings and people; other team members; other carers for service users; other professionals and advocates.

Again, there is an expectation that the supervisor will explore how the worker makes use of such resources which should ideally have been part of service users' care plans.

Service Users

A large part of the session will need to look at how workers relate to the service users for whom they are responsible. This is likely to include:

- reviewing key client files.
- asking whether care plans still make sense, and what the evidence is for this.
- ensuring entries are up-to-date and meet agreed standards of recording.
- asking which service users are the easier and which the more difficult to work with, and exploring the reasons for this.

- reflect on one good example of practice and one difficult one and draw out the learning from these i.e., what made it a good/difficult instance:
- what did you do?
- what else could you have done?
- what is the theory/practice/research which guided your intervention?
- what would you do differently next time?
- what implication does this have for other clients/staff?

The supervisor would be looking in general for: evidence of planned interventions; use of a range of skills; evidence of learning from experience; that work was client-centred; awareness of ethnic and cultural considerations and examples of collaborative work.

Team Work

Both residential and day care establishments require staff to work together as a team. This is to ensure that: standards are maintained; care plans are implemented irrespective of who is on shift; individual strengths are maximised and shared; staff disharmony does not affect service delivery and people support each other to cope with the stresses and demands that the job brings.

Therefore the supervisor needs to find out how the worker is getting on with her/his colleagues and whether difficulties are best sorted out on a one-to-one basis or brought to team meetings.

It is important that staff feel able to raise questions about their fellow workers' performance. This is where creating a safe climate is important as is being clear about confidentiality. In those cases where there have been scandals over how some workers have treated their clients, other staff usually had some knowledge of what was going on, but didn't want to 'shop their colleagues'.

Knowledge

In order to do their work staff need to have up-to-date knowledge on:

- what is going on for their clients
- treatment methods
- the role of other professionals
- changes in legislation, local departmental re-organisations.

The supervisor needs to check that workers have this knowledge and, if they do not, to help them collect it. This might, for example, involve making sure reading materials are available or arranging for the worker to visit appropriate work sites, or inviting speakers to the unit, for example to talk about diabetes.

Learning/Development

One of the key aspects of a supervisor is to help the supervisee to develop their skills as a worker. Their development needs might come about as a result of looking at the supervisee's work with clients; or as a result of an annual training audit or performance review.

A decision has to be made as to which learning needs can be met in supervision, which by some other form of establishment-based training, which by departmental courses and which by external courses.

In all cases the supervisor and worker need to plan how the training will be implemented in the workplace. There is little point in agreeing to a worker attending a counselling skills course unless the worker has an opportunity to practise these skills in the establishment in some supervised context.

Among issues that supervisors might need to address are: workers' reluctance to undertake training; the working conditions of people going on training courses (for example, residential staff are often expected to attend training courses straight after a night shift); staff who want to attend every course on offer and staff who feel they know it all.

Support/Stress Management

Another function of supervision is to provide support for staff. Part of this will involve looking at an individual's support system; recognising signs of stress; being aware of causes of stress at work, which might range from financial cutbacks to a particularly aggressive individual to working within an oppressive atmosphere, and reviewing the supervisee's workload. As part of this process the supervisor will want to be able to give positive feedback. Feedback, to be useful, should be descriptive rather than evaluative and specific rather than general. It is sad, but not, alas, surprising that, in social service workshops, up to half of participants cannot often remember when they last received praise for a specific piece of work. Yet these are often the same staff who are being asked to implement behavioural based care plans where an emphasis is placed on positive reinforcement to produce the appropriate behaviour. As feedback is often best received as close to the incident as possible, this is where ongoing supervision becomes particularly important.

Recognition needs to be made of the stresses that come with particular types of work such as adolescent residential child care; working with abusers and survivors; and people with severe challenging behaviour. The supervisor needs to be aware that such work is likely to bring up any unresolved personal issues such as the worker's own childhood experiences, and that these need to be recognised in supervision and either addressed there or referred to an appropriate setting.

Tackling the worker whose performance is below par

As we have seen, supervision is not primarily about this, but it is a function of supervision with particular individuals. The first task is to get agreement that the worker's performance is not up to standard. The more objective the measure, the easier this is to do. Otherwise there is a risk of ending up with a pantomime sketch:

SUPERVISOR:	'Your work isn't good enough.'
WORKER:	'Oh yes it is.'
SUPERVISOR:	'Oh no it isn't.'

The second task is to establish the reasons for this. These might be to do with: personal factors such as poor health; organisational factors such as the fact that the job has changed, poor management or the working environment, or because of racist or sexist behaviour.

The third task is then to plan a strategy which will bring the performance up to an agreed level. This might involve goal setting; training; tackling legitimate dissatisfactions; reorganising the work; counselling and improved management.

If the performance still fails to improve then the situation moves from one of supervision to a need for formal management involving the disciplinary procedure.

Task Setting

Finally, as supervision is about improving work performance, setting tasks is one useful way to achieve this, for example, doing a home visit, setting up a quality circle.

Tasks might range from reviewing a care plan to tackling a problem with another staff member. The supervisor might well also end up with tasks such as contacting the training department to find out what courses are available.

The tasks need to be reviewed at the beginning of the next session. If tasks have not been completed then the reasons for this need to be explored.

SKILLS SUPERVISORS NEED

- to listen actively
- to seek information
- to engage staff in formulating alternative explanations of behaviour
- to make a distinction between what is optional and what is essential e.g. in terms of procedures
- to negotiate different ways of dealing with clients, and other workers
- to check that the worker carries out advice
- to challenge and confront. In hierarchical supervision, the supervisor has legitimate power and should be prepared to use it to ensure that policies are implemented, client needs are met and that standards are maintained.
- to discuss issues
- to support.

ACTION ORIENTATED TECHNIQUES

The supervisor might like to consider using a number of techniques, for example:

The empty chair. Useful to represent, for example, a client and to get the worker to sit on the chair and respond to questions from the supervisor and see what the world looks like from the client's perspective. Equally appropriate for gaining insight into inter-staff conflicts.

Sculpting. Using coins or objects to depict a client and his/her caring/professional/family system or the staff team. This is a useful way of looking at relationships. The supervisor can then ask questions such as what would need to happen with whom if the service user were to move into a house of their own.

TRAINING SUPERVISORS

The contents of this chapter provide a framework for a two-day supervision skills course. The part that needs to be added on is the opportunity to practise the skills. This is often done best in a threesome where people take it in turns to be the supervisor, the supervisee and the observer, who gives feedback to the person being the supervisor, at the end of each turn.

The training, however, will only be useful if there is a supervision structure back in the workplace with the newly trained person receiving his/her own supervision so that he/she has the chance to reflect on the implementation of the training.

MONITORING SUPERVISION

As with any system, supervision needs to be monitored otherwise there is no means of knowing whether it continues to meet standards in terms of frequency, coverage, recording and client's interests. Therefore, any supervision sessions carried out by one level of management should become part of the supervision session of the next level. Thus just as a worker might bring care notes to his or her supervision session, the supervisor will bring the record of the supervision of staff members to her or his supervision session.

SUPERVISING FIRST LINE MANAGERS

The content of the supervision session here becomes more complicated (see Wiener 1990, for a fuller account) as in each of the content areas discussed above the manager needs to be supervised as

(1) A worker in his/her own right.

(2) As a manager or leader of the staff team. Therefore the session needs to look at how the manager handles the staff individually and collectively.

(3) As the manager of the establishment of the whole – this ranges from everything relating to the maintenance of the building, control of the budget, relations with the rest of the department through to dealings with other professionals.

(4) The person responsible for the welfare of the service users who attend or live at the institution.

CONCLUSION

The aim of this chapter was to provide a framework for carrying out supervision in a residential or day care setting.

The chapter has argued that a formal supervision system is necessary for both managers and workers to ensure that their different interests, as well as those of service users, are met. For too long, supervision has been seen as a luxury item reserved for field workers. However, given the face-to-face contact time that workers in this sector have with their service users, there is a greater need for a supervision system to be in place. However, such a system will only be effective if it is owned and prioritised by senior management within the organisation. A front line manager cannot be expected to be committed to implementing and maintaining supervision contracts if that is not reflected in his or her dealings with middle management.

REFERENCES

Atherton J.S. (1986) *Professional Supervision in Group Care*. London: Tavistock.

Department of Health (1991) *The Children Act 1989 Guidance and Regulations* Vol.4. London: HMSO.

Hawkins P. and Shohet R. (1989) *Supervision in the Helping Professions*. Buckingham: Open University Press.

The Howe Report (1992) Quality of Care, Local Government Management Board.

Lee K. (1987) 'The Supervision Gap,' *Social Services Insight*, 16 October, pp 16–17.

Moore J. (1986) 'Supervising a balancing act", *Community Care*, 6 November pp.25–26.

The Wagner Report (1988) *A Positive Choice*. London: National Institute of Social Work.

Wiener R (1990) 'Support for all,' *Insight*, 20 June, p.32.

Appendix 9A

SUPERVISION CONTRACT

Between ....

and ....

Frequency ....

Location ....

Duration of Session ....

All information between supervisor and supervisee will be treated with respect and in a professional manner.

Record Keeping

A supervision record will be kept for each session. Both supervisor and supervisee to retain a copy of these records which will be signed and dated by both.

Agenda

Both supervisor and supervisee will agree an agenda at least _____ days in advance of each session.

Preparation for Supervision

Both parties have the right to expect that each will come to the session prepared for the topics on the agenda.

Commitment

Commitment to contracted arrangements should be a responsibility shared between supervisor and supervisee and should form an agenda item in supervision from time to time.

Content

Supervision sessions will cover:

Disagreements

Areas of disagreement between supervisor and supervisee will be recorded on the supervision records. Areas of disagreement that cannot be resolved will be referred to the Line Manager.

This contract will be reviewed ....

Signed ....

Signed ....

Date ....

CHAPTER 10

SUPERVISION OF APPROVED SOCIAL WORK PRACTICE

KATHERINE WILTSHIRE

This chapter is written for approved social worker practitioners (referred to as ASWs) and their supervisors, and highlights the distinctive issues in the supervision of statutory mental health practice. It will explore the organisational context of the supervision of ASW practice, the supervisory requirements of ASW practitioners in the exercise of their statutory duties, the different functions of supervision and their relevance to ASW practice, and the variety of methods of supervision available to practising ASWs in a range of work settings. ASW practitioners and supervisors have been consulted via a structured, written questionnaire (presented as an appendix), and some of their comments have been incorporated into the text to ensure authenticity as far as possible.

PROFESSIONAL CONTEXT TO THE SUPERVISION OF STATUTORY MENTAL HEALTH WORK

Under the 'Requirements and Guidance for the Training of Social Workers to be considered for Approval in England and Wales under the Mental Health Act 1983: CCETSW Paper 19.19 revised edition', CCETSW (1993) state:

> Local authorities will wish to ensure that ASWs receive appropriate supervision of their mental health statutory work by persons with relevant experience and understanding of what approved social work entails. For some authorities, this may mean providing different supervision of this area of their work from that provided by their usual supervisor, particularly when newly approved. Authorities will also wish to have regard to the need to provide appropriate training for ASW's line managers and supervisors.

CCETSW make a clear recommendation about the professional framework for the supervision of ASW practitioners, emphasising the desirability of the supervisor possessing relevant experience and understanding of the ASW role in order to provide appropriate supervision. What, however, should be the benchmark for defining 'appropriate supervision', in the absence of any explicit definition or criteria from CCETSW?

Appropriate supervision is a process which ensures that the individual ASW exercises his or her statutory duties and responsibilities in line with the requirements of the 1983 Mental Health Act, and in line with the professional guidance offered by the Code of Practice (DOH 1993). Each authority will also expect the supervisors of ASWs to ensure that their own departmental policies and procedures on statutory mental health work are adhered to. On the above basis, supervisors of ASW staff need to have a working knowledge of the legislative framework governing work with service users affected by mental health problems, awareness of the principles of good practice laid down in the Code of Practice, and familiarity with their own department's policy and procedures.

Having placed the supervision of ASW staff in its professional context, it is necessary to consider the agency context within which ASWs and their supervisors are operating – frequently against a background of competing operational pressures and priorities.

ASW SUPERVISION – IMPACT OF THE WORK SETTING

ASWs practise in a wide variety of settings. Typically these include area offices, hospital based social work teams, community based mental health teams (which may or may not be multidisciplinary) and out of hours teams. Some authorities operate a generic structure with ASWs deployed in generic teams in relatively large numbers, whereas other authorities are increasingly restructuring into specialist teams, separating adult service provision from children and families services. Some authorities have mental health service delivery subsumed under services for adults (covering elders; physical disability; learning disability; sensory impairment; HIV and AIDS), while others have specialist mental health teams with a concentration of ASWs covering the majority of the Department's statutory mental health work. Some authorities have ASWs located in general and mental health hospital settings: in other areas all ASWs are located in community based settings to ensure greater independence from a medical perspective.

What are some of the key implications for ASWs and their supervision in such a range of organisational contexts?

In a Department organised *generically*, there are likely to be a fairly high number of ASWs dispersed in a large number of settings. Individual ASWs are less likely to have regular and frequent opportunity to practise, and more likely to have a supervisor/line manager with little or no relevant statutory mental health experience. It may also be more difficult to identify experienced practising ASWs to supervise ASW trainees, which may reduce the supply of newly qualified ASWs coming on stream. For supervisors of ASWs in generic teams, ASW practice is likely to compete with other major statutory priorities, resulting in a nominally generic team in reality often prioritising statutory child care work at the expense of general mental health work. The emphasis on child care service delivery makes it difficult for the supervisor to build up and consolidate knowledge and experience of ASW practice, especially if they have no ASW background themselves.

Where Departments opt for *adults teams,* ASW practice is likely to be given a higher profile in a team dedicated to working with vulnerable adults with a range of difficulties and disabilities. However, the resources in adults teams (and adults management structures) may be skewed towards the elderly user group because of their numerical dominance, again at the expense of mental health users.

Where there are *specialist mental health teams* with a high proportion of ASW staff, it is more likely that the team manager/supervisor will themselves have an ASW qualification, and in many cases combine being a practising ASW with their line management function. In addition, the high proportion of ASW team members is likely to ensure access to 'on tap' support and advice from peers working in the same team. Even in these teams, however, statutory mental health work is not always integrated with broader and preventative mental health practice (and its supervision), while the team manager/supervisor may be unavailable to supervise ASWs when they are themselves acting as the ASW in a mental health assessment.

ASWs based on *hospital sites* can be isolated from the mainstream of the department by their outposting in a health environment. ASWs in medical social work departments may not practise frequently enough to maintain their knowledge and skill base, their colleagues may not be ASWs, and their team manager may frequently be absent due to other managerial responsibilities within the hospital setting, leaving the ASW relatively isolated and unsupported. In addition, referrals may be short term, requiring brief intervention whilst the user is in hospital, but restricting opportunities for the ASW to engage in longer term mental health practice as part of their overall workload. Within psychiatric hospital teams, proximity to psychiatrists and medical approaches may compromise the independence of the ASW, and may also make it harder for the supervisor/team manager to retain a strong community based, civil rights perspective whilst operating from within a psychiatric hospital base with its dominant culture of treatment and restriction.

Within *multidisciplinary community mental health teams,* the ASW may be the only ASW within a team of other professionals. Although colleagues from other disciplines may share considerable common ground with the ASW, the more specialist aspects of the ASW's role may need to be addressed outside the team with the ASW's own line manager. The manager of the multidisciplinary mental health team may be a non social work professional, making access to professional supervision from a manager with ASW experience essential if the ASW is to be appropriately supported.

Finally, *out of hours ASWs* usually function autonomously by virtue of exercising their statutory duties outside normal hours. They may have access to a back up system where another colleague is available to shadow, plus access to a mobile phone. They necessarily develop self reliance, having the advantage of frequent, challenging ASW practice where their skills and knowledge are being continuously called upon. Nonetheless, many out of hours ASWs will be practising in this way with little immediate or follow up supervision or support.

Given the wide range of practice situations, and the strengths and weaknesses of different work contexts, many Departments now operate an ASW Rota to ensure the systematic provision of ASW cover for the locality. This ensures that all ASWs have opportunity to engage in ASW practice at regular intervals, and reduces the marginalisation experienced by ASWs in outposted settings where they have only restricted access to other ASW colleagues elsewhere in the department. In addition, ASW Support Forums provide a platform for all ASWs to address policy and practice issues of common concern, and can also help to reduce the isolation of some ASWs.

FUNCTIONS OF SUPERVISION AND THEIR RELEVANCE TO ASW SUPERVISION

Supervision has three main functions, which can be broadly described as *managerial, supportive* and *educative*. Whilst each function has a distinct purpose, there is often considerable overlap depending on the experience of the ASW, the nature of the issues under discussion, and the priority accorded to each function by the supervisor at any one time.

In relation to ASW practice, the *managerial* function is most likely to be carried by the ASW's line manager. Line managers of ASWs perceive their responsibility as:

- ensuring the provision of sufficient ASWs to maintain an appropriate level of service.
- ensuring that the ASW task is being accorded appropriate priority, with other workload pressures being adjusted accordingly.
- ensuring that departmental policies and procedures are complied with.
- providing consultation on the legal and professional aspects of a mental health assessment.
- enabling the ASW to maintain confidence in their ability to discharge their statutory responsibilities.
- taking up issues with other agencies on a formal basis if poor/illegal practice is identified.
- having an overview of standards of ASW practice, with accountability for ensuring that practice meets minimum standards of competence.
- responsibility for evaluating risks to ASW staff, where possible authorising action to minimise those risks – e.g. releasing another colleague to accompany the ASW on an assessment, and re-prioritising workflow to facilitate release.

Line managers of ASWs need to be clear about their managerial function in relation to statutory mental health work, while respecting the personal and individual decision making reached by the ASW in the exercise of their statutory function.

The *supportive* function can be offered from a variety of sources, including, of course, the ASW's Line Manager. The supportive function of ASW supervision recognises that the ASW is working in highly charged crisis situations where there may be a real or perceived threat of physical or psychological abuse to the worker and/or others. For ASWs in front line contact with people experiencing high levels of emotional and mental distress, frequently psychotic in nature, emotional support is essential if the feelings stirred up in the ASW are to be adequately dealt with. The stressful and risky nature of mental health assessments can be safely defused within the context of support from peer ASWs or other colleagues who have an understanding of the complexity of the ASW role, and their unique individual personal accountability for decisions.

The *educative* function acknowledges that ASWs have ongoing training and support needs which must be identified as part of the ASW's continuing professional development. Extending the ASW's knowledge and skill base can be assisted by the ASW's line manager in scheduled supervision, but can also be helped by ASW peers, group supervision, and through an ASW Forum, as well as through refresher training programmes.

WHAT ARE THE MAJOR SUPERVISION NEEDS OF ASWS?

The specific supervision needs of ASWs as defined by practitioners themselves were explored through the questionnaire devised for this chapter (see Appendix 10A). Respondents made it clear that their preference was to seek support and advice from another experienced ASW colleague who may be their line manager, but will not necessarily be. ASW knowledge and experience were valued most highly by practitioners, not the person's line management status, although the supervisor who is a practising ASW may act as the strongest resource in terms of credibility and relevant experience, and therefore authority.

Respondents also noted their need for immediate support and supervision during a mental health assessment, but also for subsequent formal scheduled supervision which allow supervisor and ASW time for reflection and evaluation. Most ASW practice in statutory departments involves requests for mental health assessments, in which ASWs exercise their statutory responsibilities with little or no previous knowledge of the client or their family. ASW respondents identified their supervision and support needs in relation to formal assessments in some of the following ways:

Preparation Stage before an Assessment

- using an experienced ASW colleague (peer/duty senior/line manager) as a 'sounding board' to discuss anxieties, risk level for self and others, strategies for containing the crisis, alternative options for working with the identified client and their family and social network.
- discussing the client/family with other colleagues particularly if already known to the department.
- talking through safety issues on both an emotional and practical level, ensuring colleagues are aware of the ASW's whereabouts, and likely timescale of the assessment.

- deciding on the appropriateness or otherwise of another colleague accompanying the ASW, and being clear about roles and responsibilities.
- thinking through the information gathering stage, the coordination of all parties to the assessment, the paperwork, the need for a police presence and the timescales. Acknowledging that anxiety may hinder the ASW from asking 'all the right questions' at the co-ordinating stage, so a colleague serves a useful 'checklist' function.

Support and Supervision During an Assessment

Most respondents emphasised the importance of access to an experienced colleague – either as a back up to the assessment, or via telephone discussions with a duty senior or supervisor back in the office. A back up colleague provides an opportunity for immediate discussion without the need to resort to telephone contact at one remove. Some of the support needs expressed were:

- consulting with an ASW colleague/senior about what aspects of the situation to focus on during the assessment.
- checking out one's judgement to ensure that the pressures in the situation have not distorted the ASW's perceptions.
- advice about liaising with medical professionals, particularly in the event of disagreement.
- discussion of alternative approaches, including use of other resources.
- access to legal and professional advice about interpreting the legislation and about good practice.
- access to colleagues to check procedures and information.

Support and Supervision in the Immediate Aftermath of an Assessment

ASWs valued support from back-up colleagues, and also from duty seniors or supervisors if it is immediately available. Their support needs at this stage cover:

- opportunities to de-brief
- help to 'wind down' and attend to any distress / feelings in the immediate aftermath. One ASW reported feeling 'high' after completing an assessment, and needed to ventilate feelings once the adrenalin had lessened.
- feedback on one's professional practice, including what was done well / could have been done better or differently
- reviewing the decision making process, especially if particularly stressful or controversial
- sorting out what follow up, if any, would be beneficial, and discussing how to organise it within a short timescale.

After Time for Reflection – Scheduled Supervision

ASW practitioners reported a variety of experiences. Some received most of their support and supervision whilst on duty at the time of the assessment, and reported little or no coverage of ASW practice issues in formal scheduled supervision. Scheduled supervision was sometimes several weeks after a mental health assessment, and so reflection on assessments completed on a duty basis occurred only sporadically. Where ASW practice in relation to assessments was covered in supervision with a line manager, there was a shared responsibility for placing it on the agenda, usually in relation to assessments which had been challenging or problematic. Retrospective supervision provided the opportunity to:

- reflect upon the evidence reached to justify a specific decision
- explore with hindsight alternative interventions or courses of action
- explore the integration of therapeutic approaches with statutory responsibilities and the formal assessment task
- obtain feedback on professional practice, with ideas about how ASW performance might be improved and learning promoted.

Discussion of ASW practice and its general mental health work context was limited for ASWs in children and families and generic settings. This was much less of a problem for ASWs in specialist mental health or adult team settings, where ASW practice is part of a broader spectrum of mental health work reviewed in formal supervision.

SOURCES OF SUPERVISION AVAILABLE TO ASWS

In relation to mental health assessments, ASWs need immediate 'on tap' consultation with an experienced and preferably practising ASW to support them in thinking through risks, statutory tasks, and alternatives to hospital admission. This could be offered by the duty senior, line manager, or other ASW colleagues, depending on their availability for consultation at different stages throughout the assessment. It is valued as an informal, open, advice sharing process outside the structure of formal supervision, with the emphasis on pooling ideas and managing the assessment task.

The ASW's own line manager was the preferred source of supervision for providing an overview of the ASW's professional practice over a period of time, and placing their statutory mental health duties within the context of their other roles and responsibilities. Line management supervision, because of its confidentiality, was also seen as the appropriate forum for addressing the ASW's training and development needs, either specifically or as part of a wider appraisal process. Of the respondents to the questionnaire, several acknowledged that there was no regular review of their ASW development needs in individual supervision, although the line manager might be perceived as supportive of their statutory responsibilities.

One ASW commented:

> My line manager at the local office is supportive of my ASW role as part of my overall development and maintenance of skills, but there has

been no specific discussion in supervision about my development as an ASW.

Another said:

> I have never had my ASW development needs reviewed in one to one supervision, but I am satisfied with the status quo. The informal supervision I receive from an experienced duty senior is satisfactory and meets my current needs.

Despite the major statutory responsibilities shouldered by ASWs, there was a clear tendency for ASW practice to be 'supervised' on a consultative, informal basis outside the structure of formal supervision, particularly where ASWs are almost exclusively involved in mental health assessments on a one off basis. A respondent commented:

> My ASW practice is not part of formal, structured supervision. I could raise issues in supervision with my line manager, but this does not regularly occur because of insufficient time to discuss allocated cases. Reviewing my ASW practice would only get on the supervision agenda if I raised it.

Several respondents agreed that they would benefit from an opportunity to go back and examine basic skills and practice arising from mental health assessments, but often fail to undertake this performance monitoring. Some ASWs identified their development and training needs in Support Forums as part of a collective exercise, feeding their requests up to management teams, either to supplement or replace individual supervision.

In summary, ASWs draw on a variety of sources of advice, consultation, and supervision depending on their needs, their level of experience, their work setting, and the availability of experienced colleagues. The immediacy of informal consultation with experienced colleagues is prioritised during mental health assessments, whereas formal supervision is reserved for retrospective discussion of problematic assessments, discussion of planned intervention following an assessment and, in some instances, performance monitoring and appraisal leading to the identification of future training and development needs.

GROUP SUPPORT AND SUPERVISION

Support can also come from attendance at ASW Forums, and from team colleagues during case discussion meetings. Department-wide Support Forums are increasingly common, but can be compromised by poor attendance, confusion about the remit of the forum, or about responsibility for chairing and co-ordinating the group and lack of senior management recognition that the forum has an important role to play in progressing ASW practice across the Department. Where the forums are successful, one ASW commented that 'it is useful to meet with other ASW colleagues in different districts to see how practice varies, and to communicate any new developments'. A different ASW commented about his department's forum that there is:

varied attendance each month, and the group has lost its direction, probably due to organisational change and pressure of work. It tends to focus on policy rather than on ASW practice issues and the offering of support.

Many ASWs felt 'safer' discussing policy and practical issues, rather than sharing their own practice, in a group with shifting monthly membership. In contrast, however, case discussions in teams with a high level of ownership of ASW practice is likely to promote greater sharing of practice dilemmas and anxieties. Team discussions of ASW practice can also benefit the professional development of non-ASW staff who may nevertheless have a mental health interest, or be considering ASW training.

Whilst departmental Support Forums within Social Services are becoming increasingly common, there are noticeably fewer multi-disciplinary professional forums bringing together all the professionals involved in operating under the 1983 Mental Health Act. The Code of Practice Para 2.39 states:

> Good practice requires that health authorities, NHS Trusts, and local social services authorities should co-operate in ensuring that regular meetings take place between professionals involved in mental health assessments in order to promote understanding, and to provide a forum for clarification of their respective roles and responsibilities.

This 'good practice requirement' in the Code of Practice pinpoints the vital importance of multi-agency collaboration if the standard of statutory mental health service offered to the user is to be promoted by all involved professionals, not the ASW alone. The patchy implementation of this recommendation in the Code of Practice may reflect some of the tension and misunderstanding about roles and duties at the interface between ASWs and medical practitioners. A multi-disciplinary forum can provide an opportunity for clarification and reflection away from the pressures of front line assessments.

ISSUES AND DILEMMAS ADDRESSED BY ASW SUPERVISORS

Experienced ASWs are likely to be approached by their ASW colleagues for consultation, especially if the latter are recently qualified, or only practice infrequently. Whilst they may be willing to offer this support on the basis of their experience, their seniority, or their interest in the work, concern might be expressed about the lack of formal recognition in their job description for this consultation/supervisory role. It appears important for the ASW's line manager to acknowledge the level and frequency of consultation being provided 'informally' to other colleagues, and to take this into account when managing the ASW's overall workload.

Line managers of ASWs may have to address several tensions and dilemmas in their role. Their ability to deal confidently with ASW practice and policy issues will depend on their knowledge and understanding of the complex roles of the ASW. Unless they are practising, or have been recently practising, it may be difficult to keep their knowledge and skill base up to date, leading to a 'credibility gap' with their experienced ASW staff. Departments are increasingly expecting team leaders to manage and supervise, rather than practice, so ASWs may lose the opportunity to practice regularly and maintain their approval once they have been promoted to their first management post. On the other hand, line managers with an ASW background (even if no longer approved) will be equipped to provide an objective, knowledgeable discussion about the statutory responsibilities carried by their staff member.

Where team leaders are not expected to practice as ASWs, the developing 'knowledge and skill gap' which comes from being separated from practice can be addressed by refresher training geared at their needs as supervisors. Such training is likely to include updating on the legislation governing mental disorder, the revised code of practice, and experiential small group work on real practice problems faced by line managers in supervision. Training in generic supervision skills is also an essential basis for the more specialist aspects of ASW supervision, highlighting common areas such as risk assessment, an awareness of the impact of anxiety and how it can distort work and supervisory performance, the dangers of the worker colluding with the 'victim' inside the mentally distressed client, and the importance of clarity about rights and responsibilities between the worker and the supervisor.

Line management supervision of statutory mental health work by a duty senior or line manager shares common elements with others areas of statutory work, especially in relation to management of risk and anxiety. However, there are two vital differences. First, the ASW has the power under the Mental Health Act to remove a person's liberty in the absence of prior judicial scrutiny of the decision. Second, (unlike in statutory child care work) ASWs carry 'individual and accountable professional responsibility for the independent decisions which they must take' (CCETSW 1993). This uniquely accountable role means that the ASW has responsibility for reaching their own independent professional conclusion about what course of action to take, and this cannot be over-ruled by a line manager. The line manager can advise and support the ASW in reasoning through their decision, but they cannot instruct the ASW to take a particular course of action as this would clearly breach the ASW's individual and accountable responsibility.

How does this role affect the power dynamics within the supervisory relationship between a line manager and an ASW? Supervision between a practitioner and line manager usually requires two parties with unequal organisational power to make an effective working relationship. These power dynamics may be further complicated by inequalities based on assumptions about gender, age, ethnicity, disability, or sexuality – for example a supervisor who holds organisational power, but who is a member of a minority group.

Where the supervision of ASW practice is concerned, the supervisor may hold organisational power in relation to other areas of social work practice, but the individual accountability of the ASW over-rides the authority invested in the line manager by their agency. In all their other roles, the social worker can ultimately be instructed by their supervisor, but not in relation to the exercise of their professional duties under the Mental Health Act. Thus, while a line manager may be organisationally senior, in terms of accountability and possibly experience, the ASW holds the power in this transaction. At best this may give a sense of discussion between 'equals', especially if the line manager has an ASW background.

The uniquely independent role of the ASW may not be fully understood by other medical professionals, especially within psychiatry where the hierarchical structure may lead to the mistaken assumption that medical power is dominant and outweighs that of professionals perceived as being of lesser status within the mental health field. The power of the ASW professional subverts these traditional power dynamics, and may leave some doctors frustrated and uncomfortable, resulting in disputes between health and social services. Line managers frequently have a key role to play at the interface between their ASW service and other agencies, taking up issues of poor or illegal practice or formally intervening in inter-agency disputes. Examples include the situation where a consultant psychiatrist puts pressures on a line manager to allocate a second ASW to undertake an assessment because they are dissatisfied with the outcome of the original assessment. It would be inappropriate for a line manager to collude with such a request unless there is clear evidence that circumstances have altered sufficiently to justify a fresh assessment – to do otherwise would be undermining the independence of the ASW enshrined in the legislation.

Other examples warranting line management intervention might include persistent short notice of section expiry dates, Section 136 being wrongfully applied to a person who was not in a public place, inappropriate use of an emergency section because of difficulties in identifying a second medical practitioner, a nearest relative being pressurised to be the applicant when the consultant is dissatisfied with the ASW's independent decision or wanting to avoid an ASW assessment, or a medical practitioner who fails to conduct a proper medical examination as defined by the Code of Practice. In all of the above examples, the line manager with responsibility for the ASW service is advocating standards of good practice to protect both the client and the agency.

The supervisor of an ASW has a fine line to tread between respecting the professional autonomy of their staff member on the one hand, whilst recognising the onerous responsibility the ASW carries for risk assessment and decision making. It is within the supervisory relationship that the ASW can be helped to integrate the feelings, attitudes, thoughts and actions aroused by statutory mental health work – typically including real ambivalence about the extent of their formal autonomy. Thus, supervision which is highly 'task orientated' may underestimate the emotional and attitudinal response of the worker, but conversely, too much absorption in the emotional process might undermine the need for clarity of risk assessment and decision making based on justifiable evidence.

Some departments are recognising the value of self appraisal methods, whereby ASWs are encouraged to appraise their own practice following a statutory assessment. This acknowledges the autonomy of the approved social worker, and the importance of taking active responsibility for their own learning and development. A self appraisal process could be developed from the checklist headings on the standard ASW report following the completion of an assessment, serving as a useful tool to evaluate professional practice.

This could be done as a private activity, or it could be discussed by another ASW colleague on a reciprocal basis, or used as the basis for discussion in one-to-one supervision. However it is used, the process of self appraisal of ASW practice is likely to promote adult learning and professional growth.

AGENCY RESPONSIBILITY FOR THE INDIVIDUAL ASW

Although the ASW holds individual accountability for practice decisions, the employing agency nevertheless has a responsibility for the ASW's welfare in the event of an assessment 'going wrong' or leading to a tragic outcome. ASWs are given authority to practice by their employing authorities, and authorities should insure against legal costs in the event of the ASW being challenged through the judicial system. As well as practical and financial assistance, the ASW may also require emotional support to deal with the distressing aftermath of an assessment which has unforeseen consequences leading to death or injury of the client or other people. Similarly, the ASW's line manager may also need support and supervision of their own to help them deal with their own feelings of guilt, anxiety, and inadequacy in the face of a piece of ASW practice leading to a traumatic outcome, despite the fact that it is the ASW who is professionally accountable.

CONCLUSION

Typically, mental health assessments are given operational priority by duty seniors and line managers, and the ASW is offered considerable support and advice at this stage by both managers and peers according to their levels of ASW experience and 'on tap' availability. However, ASW practice is less likely to be placed on the agenda in structured supervision, thus restricting the opportunity for ASWs to explore their professional practice within the more reflective, analytical climate of formal supervision.

Whilst this may mainly reflect the non-accountability of line managers, it also reflects the competition with other areas of accountable allocated casework, mainly childcare. It also reflects the tendency for mental health assessments to be undertaken by a duty ASW whose involvement frequently stops on completion of the assessment. Other areas of statutory mental health practice, including aftercare planning, attendance at tribunals, preventative input to reduce the risk of admission, joint work with other mental health professionals on allocated cases, are accorded lower priority levels, and are less likely to claim space in scheduled supervision time.

The typical situation can thus result in the ASW having a fragmented overview of their practice, especially if they are on an ASW rota relatively infrequently, with little opportunity for using scheduled supervision to review how interventions and decisions were reached, and how this relates to their knowledge and skill base over a period of time. Whilst discussing each instance of ASW practice in supervision is unrealistic, a periodic review of the worker's practice by another experienced ASW colleague would ensure that ASW work becomes an integrated part of the worker's professional development, not something which happens for the main part outside supervision and separate from their other roles. Focused supervision of this kind need not be from the ASWs line manager and may be provided by an experienced colleague so long as they have a formal remit. The most satisfactory arrangement is likely to involve a line manager with ASW (and ASW supervision) experience being given a remit by the department to give this aspect of supervision to ASWs, including those outside their own team.

References

CCETSW (1993) 'Requirements and guidance for the training of social workers to be considered for approval in England and Wales under the Mental Health Act 1983' (Paper 19.19 (revised edition) 1993).

Department of Health (1993) *Code of Practice – Mental Health Act 1983*. London: HMSO.

APPENDIX 10A

Questionnaire

Thank you for completing this questionnaire. Please could you support your answers with examples where appropriate. **COMPLETE CONFIDENTIALITY WILL BE ASSURED.**

Name (not essential) ....   Current Job Title ....

Length of time practising as an ASW:.....   ....

Are you currently receiving supervision (informal or formal) of your ASW practice?

(i) If YES, from what source and whether a formal part of structured supervision or informal (outside timetabled supervision)

(ii) If NO, any reasons which you'd like to share? (eg not available/needed/ pressure of work)

Do you act as a SOURCE OF CONSULTATION /SUPERVISION to other ASW colleagues? ....

Any comments? (eg what do you offer to other colleagues; is your consultation role given recognition, and if so, how?)......................................

As a practitioner involved at the sharp end of statutory mental health work, how would you DESCRIBE AND PRIORITISE YOUR SUPERVISION NEEDS:

(i) During the information-gathering and preparation stage PRIOR to undertaking a mental health assessment? ....

(ii) During the mental health assessment? ....

(iii) In the immediate aftermath?...

(iv) After some time for reflection?...

(v) In relation to the excercise of your wider ASW duties eg attendance at MHRT's/aftercare responsibilities, ongoing mental health practice on caseload?...

WHO would be your PREFERRED source of supervision/consultation in relation to each of the above headings, and can you expand on WHY?

(e.g. line manager; another ASW colleague in your team/office; an ASW colleague in a different setting; a colleague accompanying you on the assessment as back up; duty senior;any other)

Given your unique individual accountability for decision making in statutory mental health assessments, what do you regard as the DISTINCTIVE ROLE FOR YOUR LINE MANAGER in respect of this area of your practice? (Any comments about what difference it makes to the role depending on whether your line manager has been/is an ASW practitioner themselves).

Do you have access to supervision in which your longer term development as an ASW practitioner is addressed and your training/development needs identified. Any comments about how this gets on the supervision agenda; how frequently/infrequently are your development needs reviewed?

Do you have access to any other of the following to support you in your ASW function:

(i) ASW Department-wide forum.

Any comments?

(ii) Multidisciplinary practitioner's forum (platform for health and social services to debate good practice in relation to statutory mental health duties)

Any comments?

(iii) Self-appraisal procedures (tool to encourage ASWs to reflect upon their own practice and basis for decisions reached)

Any comments?

(iv) Any other forum /aid to developing practice not mentioned?

Any comments?

Does the supervision of your ASW practice challenge and help you to address anti-discriminatory practice issues?

Any comments?

Any examples of where supervision has been the forum for tackling and resolving ASW practice difficulties which have challenged either you or the agency you work in?

Anything else you want to add which the headings haven't covered?

CHAPTER 11

SUPERVISION AND APPRAISAL IN THE PROBATION SERVICE

HAZEL KEMSHALL

INTRODUCTION

The present context for supervision and appraisal in the Probation Service is important. Much has changed since Michael Davies (1988) wrote his review of Probation staff supervision, in which field staff and managers lacked either clarity or agreement over the purpose, function and process of supervision. By the time of this important survey, seniors were already viewed as resource managers rather than case work consultants, and field staff were beginning to lament the loss of individual discussions about client need. Professional development was desired by staff, but seen as increasingly obliterated by managers' concerns with accountability. Seniors were identified as policy monitors, with supervision operating as the main vehicle for both gathering the necessary information, and for directing staff performance towards pre-determined policy goals. Senior and Assistant Chief Officer supervision had already begun to focus upon policy implementation and resource management, with a greater emphasis upon accountability for the achievement of specified targets. The idea of divisional teams and corporate management had been sown.

The intervening years have seen the development of increased accountability for public spending combined with a new managerial style. Criminal Justice has not been exempt from the use of market type solutions to social policy and welfare issues (Raine and Willson 1993). The desire to contain public expenditure has followed three basic stages in the public sector (Flynn 1993); cash limiting, reduction of professional autonomy, and the introduction (real or threatened) of competition.

The Probation Service has also been subject to these reforms, beginning in the mid 1980s with the Statement of National Objectives and Priorities (Home Office 1983), and gaining momentum by the end of the decade with the Audit Commission Reports (1989a, 1989b) on 'Promoting Value for Money in the Probation Service' and 'The Value for Money Audit Guide'. By 1992 the Probation Service was a cash limited organisation, requiring all managers to account for spending, and to control resource allocation and use in line with specific targets. Resourcing would no longer be demand-led. From now on, the Probation Service would have to demonstrate its 'value for money', and have regard to the '3 E's' of economy, efficiency, and effectiveness in its use of resources.

It is within this context that the concern to supervise and appraise staff properly and consistently has arisen. The Financial Management Initiatives throughout the public sector have increasingly made managers accountable for the unit costs of their organisations. Following the Fulton model (Fulton Report 1968), all public sector agencies now have a structure of well defined, inter-related, and accountable management units, accountable for both cost and 'production'. Within this model, staff can be understood as a unit cost, a resource and a source of productivity. Staff activities which are not geared to the Service's targeted activities are potentially wasteful. Increased managerial control is exercised over such activities and consequently professional autonomy is often reduced. This assertion of managerialism over professionalism has been the pattern of much public sector change, particularly in education (Ranson and Tomlinson 1986), and in health (Flynn 1993). Financial accountability in the Probation Service, combined with the legislative changes of the Criminal Justice Act 1991, and the imposition of National Standards (Home Office 1992) has resulted in a need to exercise greater control and accountability over staff performance.

Against this backdrop, the Home Office Inspectorate carried out a thematic inspection on the appraisal of management grade staff in December 1991 (Her Majesty's Inspectorate 1992). The report found that there was a significant gap between 'aspiration and reality' (p.11). Critically, appraisal reports were unpunctual, imprecise, lacking in detail and explanation, and often unrelated to any supervisory process. This inspection began a concerted Home Office effort both to standardise and proscribe supervision and appraisal practice for all grades of staff. This resulted in the 1993 publication of the Home Office's own model scheme for performance appraisal, and Probation Training Unit use of private consultants to formalise core competences for all grades of staff.

This is the context within which supervisors must give and receive both supervision and appraisal. The emphasis is increasingly upon accountability and using staff resources efficiently and effectively. However, this chapter will attempt to provide a policy and practice understanding of supervision and appraisal which focuses upon the enhancement of staff and their performance in addition to accountability concerns. The processes of supervision and appraisal should contribute to effective performance rather than merely managed performance.

Defining Supervision and Appraisal

The Oxford dictionary (1989) defines supervision as: 'To oversee, superintend execution or performance of person, actions or work of person'. The Latin root is even more revealing, with super derived from the Latin word for 'on top of or above', and vision stemming from 'videre' meaning 'to see'. Literally, seeing from above, demonstrating the origins of a predominantly accountable understanding of the supervision function. Appraisal has a literal meaning to 'value, or fix the price of something', and in a sense annual appraisals do have the primary function of valuing staff performance. In some instances, where appraisals are linked to Performance Related Pay, a price is also fixed. However, the encouragement and maintenance of effective staff performance requires more than accountable management. It is important to recognise the other literal meaning of supervision, 'to see beyond'. This definition enables a more balanced understanding of the supervisory function, involving accountability combined with a real focus on developing and enhancing staff, both personally and professionally.

CREATING A CLIMATE FOR SUPERVISION AND APPRAISAL

Supervision and appraisal are inter-related activities which occur within a specific organisational context. They cannot be imposed regardless of such a context, or without an understanding of staff experiences and attitudes to them. The manner in which a supervision and appraisal system is introduced is vital to its subsequent success. Staff should not be the recipients of an imposed system from which they have been excluded, or receive information on their performance through a process which is predominantly geared to the organisation's needs at the expense of their own. The successful design and implementation of a supervision and appraisal scheme should resolve the tension between person centred and Service-led demands. This should in turn: 'counter criticisms that such schemes are purely cost cutting efficiency drives motivated by political rather than professional concerns' (Sawdon and Sawdon 1991, p.7).

Imposition is likely to lead to both resistance and sabotage, thus ensuring that the Service-led agenda is not met. Where such staff, and on occasion supervisor behaviour, is allowed to continue unchecked, the scheme will fall into disrepute and infrequent use.

At the organisational level, creating a climate for successful supervision and appraisal requires active consultation and communication on policy. This policy must include at least the following:

- The purpose and function of supervision
- How supervision of staff will contribute to the agency's overall aims and objectives
- Minimum standards for the content and *conduct* of supervision
- Minimum requirements for supervision contracts, to include frequency, agenda setting, and the use of supervision by both parties
- A statement on anti-discriminatory practice
- How supervision will be recorded, by whom, where stored, content of such records and what status they have, i.e., can they be used as evidence in appraisals?
- An explicit statement on the relationship between supervision and appraisal
- The rights and responsibilities of supervisors and supervisees

- Action and strategies for resolving breakdowns in the supervisory process, or for resolving disagreements
- The level of confidentiality which can be expected and guaranteed.[*]

The policy for appraisal will need to contain all of the above with the following additions:

- A clear statement on how 'poor' performance will be responded to and resolved
- A clear statement on how 'good' performance will be acknowledged and rewarded
- A clear statement on how discriminatory practice will be monitored, censured and removed.

Without these additions, the appraisal process will lack both impact and credibility. Staff will perceive the process as a mere exercise without any relevance to their working lives or future careers, and co-operation may become mere tokenism. The two factors most likely to undermine management credibility and effectiveness are a failure to respond to performance, and a failure to respond to discrimination. If staff perceive that neither really matter then commitment and morale will fall.

At the team or unit level, supervisors should prepare themselves for best practice by asking the following questions:

- What would you like to find when discussing supervision with your staff?
- What do you think good supervision within your team/unit should look like?
- Do you have any areas of good practice which you would like to promote, and how might you use supervision to do this?
- How will supervision in your team/unit take account of issues of inequality, power, and difference?
- How can supervision in your team/unit contribute to improving and maintaining service delivery standards? [**]

The answers to these questions provide a vision of future best practice, and highlight any gap between aspiration and reality in supervision practice. The exercise actively engages supervisors in standard setting, particularly in respect of anti-discriminatory and anti-oppressive practice. Each supervisor must articulate for themselves how they will respond to inequality, differential power relationships and discrimination. The questions are useful, both for supervisors who may be in a position to perpetuate organisational discrimination, and for those who receive it.

This exercise should be complemented by considering the answers staff give to the following:

---

[*]   Adapted and expanded from Tony Morrison: 'A Question of Survival.' *Insight* July 1992, reproduced with the permission of *Community Care*.
[**]   Adapted and expanded from: Metcalf and Curtis: 'Feeding on Support.' *Insight* July 1992, reproduced with the permission of *Community Care*.

- What do you value in the supervisory process?
- Think of the most difficult situation you have had to deal with. How could supervision have helped you to respond more effectively?
- What contract with supervisors is acceptable in terms of length and frequency of supervision? What importance should supervision have in the work place?
- Should the supervisory process be focused in any way, for example on executive, supportive, or developmental issues? What should be the balance between these different areas?
- Who should set the agenda for supervision? Should issues which concern you be the primary focus?
- Should sessions be planned in advance and recorded? If so, who should be responsible for these tasks and what status should supervision notes have?
- What feedback would you like to receive on your performance, both good and below standard performance. How should feedback be given in order that you can act constructively upon it?
- How could supervision enhance your performance, and what role could other forms of supervision play?
- How would you like to see supervisors take account of the issues of inequality, power and difference in their practice?
- What values would you like to see in a supervisor?[*]

The supervisory process should begin with a comparison of these answers. This will emphasise that successful supervision is a mutual activity between supervisor and supervisee, requiring the responsibility and commitment of both parties in order to practise it well. Initial understandings and perceptions can be clarified, 'baggage' cleared and motivation to the process harnessed. Consistency of practice towards all team members should be enhanced by this process, avoiding discrimination through either neglect or favour. If the questions on difference and differential power are explored then practice, whilst more consistent, should also become more relevant. Practice which neglects these issues, and which is heavily proscribed from above can become routinised, distancing already marginalised and vulnerable staff from the process. Standards for supervisory and appraisal practice need to make these issues clear and they must be actively supported by agency policy.

This process of exchange between supervisors and supervisees is crucial. It not only provides information on the current state of supervision in the agency, but is also an indication of how the organisation is performing in the following areas:

- The manner in which authority is either used or abused
- How difference is managed and the level of commitment to anti-discriminatory practice

[*] Adapted and expanded from: Metcalf and Curtis: 'Feeding on Support.' *Insight* July 1992, reproduced with the permission of *Community Care*.

- How differential power relationships are handled in the organisation
- How change is managed, and whether staff are valued as both adult learners and an important human resource. Who initiates change and at what level in the organisation?
- What the organisation sees as effective supervision, and what it values in its supervisors
- What is the current culture and climate of the organisation? Are the perceptions, views, and feelings of staff taken seriously?
- Are staff invested in?
- Does the organisation have a learning culture or an enforcement culture?[*]

The treatment of staff by the agency is often a clear indication of how that agency regards its clients. It will also demonstrate the level of commitment to anti-discriminatory and anti-oppressive practice. Where staff perceive or experience lack of value and oppression, there is often little incentive for them to tackle these issues with clients. The marginalisation of staff can become the marginalisation of clients, as client supervision mirrors staff supervision (Francis 1992). Agencies which value staff, seek to develop them, and engage in a mutual and reciprocal process of supervision that empowers staff to improve their own performance are more likely to see this process repeated with clients. Agencies which are predominantly concerned to discipline, control, and retain high accountability for staff will see staff relationships with clients duplicate this process. Both recipient groups will have their own mechanisms for resistance, sabotage and dis-engagement.

In Practice: Contracts, Recording, Bridging Interviews

The many elements and models of supervision have been well documented (Davies 1988, Payne and Scott 1982, Morrison 1993). This chapter will not re-explore them, but will focus upon the mainstream vehicle of one-to-one supervision and general practice and policy principles which will have applicability to other models.

Engagement, commitment, and reciprocity are the key elements of an effective supervision and appraisal process. Some recommendations have already been made for creating a positive climate at both team/unit and organisational level. These need to be supported by the individual practice of supervisors, who, in their day-to-day practice reflect the agency's care and commitment to staff.

The supervisory process needs to build upon the initial questions outlined above by doing at least the following:

- At the start of a new supervisory relationship each participant should share their past experiences of supervision and their current

---

[*]   Adapted and expanded from Tony Morrison: 'A Question of Survival' *Insight* July 1992, reproduced with the permission of *Community Care*.

expectations. The purpose and boundaries of supervision should be clarified, and a common ground negotiated.

- A written contract reflecting both personal and agency expectations should be agreed. This should cover the rights and obligations of each party.
- The contract should specify the long term objectives for supervision, with review periods clearly stated. These objectives could include performance indicators for appraisal, areas for professional development, training needs, and what will be used as assessment material for that staff member's appraisal.
- Sessions should not be over crowded, or solely dominated by agency concerns and accountability for task performance. The supervisee should have a period of time in which to raise immediate concerns.
- Where possible, supervision agendas should be agreed in advance. There should be a feeling of development and momentum, with the sessions progressing towards the long term objectives.
- Supervision *must* be provided, treated as a priority and professionally delivered.
- Supervision should be recorded, with a copy given to the supervisee prior to the next session. Consider alternating recording or joint recording. Records should note action points with dates for review, and note when something will later be used for appraisal evidence.
- Supervision should be regarded and conducted as a joint experience and as joint learning.
- Agree a confidentiality rule.
- Agree a process for discussing and resolving disagreements, including use of others, the role of facilitators, and higher management.
- Agree how to take account of difference and discrimination, to include defining the legitimate use of power and authority, language use, and mutual commitment to openess.
- Agree how below-standard performance will be discussed, recorded and what might be an acceptable process for improvement.
- Agree how feedback will be given.

Contracts and recording have a particular role in demonstrating to staff the equity, open-ness and mutuality of any supervisory process. However, the real test of any supervisory relationship is how falling standards and ineffective staff performance are discussed and subsequently acted upon by supervisees.

If the supervisory process has been established in accordance with the above recommendations, then supervisors should have both the confidence and the boundaries within which to initiate such a discussion. Staff will not be 'ambushed'. The obligation of the supervisor to provide feedback and enhance performance is already established, and staff know both the rules and procedures for such conversations. In an atmosphere in which supervision has been devalued, and supervisors are viewed as unprofessional or solely in pursuit of the agency's agenda, then conflict and hostility are more likely to arise. Even within the best of circumstances supervisors are often wary about discussing 'poor' performance. This is particularly so where supervisors have come to fear 'difference'. However, difference is a constant reality in people management. The staffing base of the Service has increased in diversity. Not every member of staff will share either the supervisor's or the organisation's values and culture. Race and gender differences are most often to the fore, but there are a range of other possible sites of difference including social class, previous work and economic experiences, routes into the Service, religious and cultural significances, age and sexuality. The organisation needs to value and celebrate such diversity, rather than fear it. Supervision has a powerful role in recognising and enhancing the uniqueness of each individual's contribution. If used oppressively in an effort to seek conformity to organisational norms it can lead to anxiety, anger and marginalisation.

The Bridging Interview has long been advocated as the most effective means of responding to poor performance (Quick 1980). In both technique and philosophy it owes much to motivational interviewing (Aust 1994, Miller 1983, Miller and Rollnick 1991). It concentrates predominantly upon establishing that there is a performance gap, agreeing upon it, exploring why this has occurred, and agreeing an action plan with the supervisee for either skill improvement in order to complete the task, or an increase in motivation and effort. This action plan is sustained and subsequently reviewed. The interview needs to be specific, and focused upon the problem area not upon the person. Using both focused discussion, active listening, and an empathic rather than confrontative technique the supervisor should work towards developing the discrepancy between desired and actual performance. The supervisee's view of the situation is actively sought, and can be an important source of information about barriers to performance, organisational and individual.

It is important at this point to distinguish between those barriers which are solely organisational in source and are beyond the control of the employee, and those which are not. The former may not necessarily be removed by either changes in specific behaviours or through increased effort. Supervisors must recognise where this is likely to be so, and not expose supervisees to unnecessary failure and frustration. On occasion, supervisors, either individually, or with the supervisee, should direct their energies towards the removal of these external barriers rather than focus exclusively on staff performance. The most common barriers are likely to be communication blocks in the agency, the provision of poor information which hinders proper task completion, the inaction or ineffectiveness of key others either within or without the agency, other team members, other teams, other managers and discrimination.

Where the source of poor performance is within the individual's control, then the Bridging Interview should establish what needs to change and how. Wherever possible avoid argumentation. Resistance from the employee at this stage will not be removed by confrontation. Exploration of the disinclination to change will probably be more rewarding, providing information on the nature and source of the resistance. Open questions and reflecting back can be used to establish whether the supervisee can move on from this resistance and formulate their own change plan. The supervisor should endeavour to adopt a self-efficacy model for this stage of the interview, enabling the supervisee both to articulate the desired change and to take decisions about achieving it. Negotiation over time schedule, review date and support structures should follow. The interview is best concluded by checking out the agreement reached and recording it.

To be successful, Bridging Interviews must avoid the following: becoming an interrogative question and answer session during which each party becomes more entrenched; a confrontational session which results in supervisee denial of any fault; a session in which the supervisor plays the expert; a session in which the supervisee leaves feeling labelled and blamed with nothing resolved; or a session in which the supervisor 'jumps the gun' and focuses upon change without exploring the discrepancy and the resistance. These can all lead to either false agreements which fail to last, or to interviews which get 'bogged down' in denial.

Bridging Interviews must be followed through by carrying out review dates and future action. Supervision and training sessions can also be used to support employees through the change process. Most of all, effective change and enhanced performance must be rewarded. Where it is not, supervision will fall into disrepute and morale will be undermined.

APPRAISAL

Supervision and appraisal are both integral parts of the same management function: the maintenance and enhancement of effective staff performance. Neither should exist without the other. Whilst appraisal has the specific function of evaluating staff performance at set intervals, its broader range of functions overlap with, and rely upon the supervisory process. As with supervision, appraisal should be regarded as a mutual process. If staff perceive it as only for management purposes it will be resisted. In broad terms appraisal has the following functions:

- To evaluate performance against set and known criteria.
- To aid accountability. To enable the appraiser to establish that the job is being done and that set standards are being met. To provide feedback to the appraisee about their performance.
- To enable both the appraiser and the appraisee to evaluate whether the performance is appropriate and effective. This may involve re-negotiation of future standards, new tasks, and different performance.
- To negotiate and agree upon what can be developed and improved.
- To give reward – money, status, praise. To value the employee.
- To socialise staff into the life of the organisation. To say 'you belong'.
- To highlight, and where possible, rectify incompetence.
- To demonstrate how the organisation will reward good performance and respond to incompetence – will it do either, and will it do it equitably?

In order to carry out these functions, the appraisal process must be carried out in an equitable fashion and in a climate conducive to its success. This requires:

- An agreement about the overall process with all staff
- Open and known criteria against which performance will be evaluated
- A clear and agreed time scale for the process
- Support structures, i.e., supervision and training
- A clear policy statement about what happens at the end of appraisal, and how disagreements will be resolved
- A clear policy statement on how the organisation will respond to poor performance
- A clear, known and equitable reward system, applying to both monetary and non-monetary rewards
- Assessment procedures which are anti-discriminatory, open and respected
- Genuine space for appraisee participation
- The process is consistently applied
- There is a quality control system which is regularly used and the results are shared with staff.

In carrying out an individual appraisal, the appraiser should prepare for the event in advance and seek to place it within the context of the employee's working life. The criteria for appraisal must be rooted in the job specification and any work or developmental contract agreed through supervision. What will count as evidence that tasks have been completed and standards met should be agreed in advance, and the process for evidence collection clearly articulated to the employee. This should ensure that evidence is collected in an on-going way, contributing to the appraiser's knowledge of the employee's performance, rather than collected retrospectively in order to confirm 'assessments' already made. The latter does not enable on-going feedback or encourage discussion of performance as a routine part of supervision. Nor can it provide many safeguards against discrimination, as the tendency is to use evidence to confirm opinions already held rather than to collect evidence in order to establish that a standard has been met. Assessment is not a value-free exercise; power, prejudice, stereotypes, values and misunderstanding all affect our perceptions of performance and of evidence (Kemshall 1993).

Whilst competences and performance indicators have been defined as objective phenomena which can be discovered and measured, assessment is not such a simplistic exercise. It is affected by the views of the assessor and the context within which it takes place. Competences and performance indicators may reflect little more than the agency's priorities and values, and in this way the construction of appraisal forms can often: 'signal(s) the organisation's value structure and personnel philosophy rather than real behavioural standards' (Randell *et al.* 1990).

Competence is agency specific, dependent upon the context of operation and the overall philosophy of the agency towards employee performance. It is also the product of a complex relationship between appraiser and appraisee, and of their supervisory relationship. To some extent, competent performance is the point at which the worker's performance 'fits' with the subjective views of the appraiser and the aims and objectives of the agency. Where they do not, failure is often an issue.

The implications of over-confidence in competency-based models of assessment have been more thoroughly discussed elsewhere (Kemshall 1993). The key points for appraisers must be to avoid dependency upon 'competent language' which reflects the white, male domination of much Probation Service culture, or to over-value personal characteristics which fit well with agency norms and expectations. Black and women workers join a Probation Service that embodies and reflects the dominant white, male culture of British society. Whilst frontline recruitment is changing, changes in senior management remain slow, and the value base of managers and the occupational structure of the Service remains white and male. The 'business culture' of the private sector has reinforced this, through attitudes, language use, and who and what is rewarded by the agency. This is the context within which appraisal takes place.

Perceptions and collection of evidence are also affected. Berger and Luckmann (1967) have argued that we do not experience the world as a set of random objects and experiences. Rather, our initial experiences become set as a pattern, assisting us in de-coding future events. In this way, a random world becomes ordered through a set of 'typifications' or 'commonsense knowledge'. Assessment procedures draw upon these typifications, both in determining what can count as evidence and also in literally determining what can be seen. Direct observation is itself dependent upon, and mediated by, the appraiser's typifications, ideas of what constitutes a 'good worker', a 'professional person' and so on. Evidence will be chosen according to whether it confirms or negates these typifications. The reality of direct evidence is neither very direct or very real. It may, however, be that of a white, often male appraiser, and the reality of the organisation and the culture from which it is derived and which it reinforces. Simplistic attempts to ground appraisal in direct evidence and the language of performance indicators may only serve to hide discrimination rather than eradicate it.

No assessment or appraisal procedure can hope to guarantee equity. Critical awareness must be exercised by appraisers about the nature of the competences and performance indicators they are using. Negotiation between appraiser and appraisee is essential to the setting of performance indicators and for the collection of evidence. A variety of assessment methods should be used to ensure a holistic view of performance. This should enable a 'checking out' approach to performance issues which tests one piece of evidence against another in an attempt to gain *verification* of one's view rather than mere confirmation. The collection of evidence should be approached as a joint task between appraiser and appraisee, offering the facility of an on-going checking mechanism and higher participation by staff. This is less likely to feel like the oppressive imposition of another's view, and supports the self-efficacy model of staff as active learners capable of their own self-assessment and development. Within this negotiation staff should be recognised as unique individuals with the potential to contribute actively to enhanced service delivery. Any appraisal procedure which fails to recognise this, and substitutes uniformity for creativity, will ultimately de-value the most important Service resource.

CONCLUSION

Public sector managers are at the interface between their organisations and the political process in a way in which private sector managers are not (Flynn 1993). This crucial difference is often overlooked when the importation of private sector management techniques into the public sector is advocated. Unlike private sector managers, public service managers do not have an easily identifiable group of shareholders to whom they are accountable. Their accountability structures are far more complex, involving politicians, significant stakeholders, user groups and ultimately the tax payer.

In this scenario, the management values which predominate will tend to reflect the values of the most powerful group (Flynn 1993). At present, these are the managerialist values of 'the right to manage', increased accountability, and management by objectives. They in turn, reflect a political desire to limit the public sector, impose market solutions onto state provision, and decrease resources to a residual state sector. Whilst the usefulness of these management techniques has had some success in the private sector by keeping companies competitive and outward looking, responsiveness and flexibility are increasingly advocated as successful business characteristics (Peters and Waterman 1982, Peters 1989). These characteristics are not always guaranteed by managerialism.

Within the public sector the usefulness and applicability of managerialism must also be treated with caution. Whilst the intention is to ensure greater management control, increased accountability of staff, higher and more consistent work output, and quality standards within low growth resources, there is a real danger that the commitment and motivation of the work force will be eroded by this approach. Within a situation of little resource growth, managers will become increasingly occupied with rationing and controlling resources. This includes the activities of staff, and managers may well become more inward looking, focusing on budgets and internal control systems, than outward looking to users and major stakeholders. Increased specification of task and heightened control are not necessarily the best ways to enhance quality standards. Job satisfaction and responsiveness to users is often lost, and increased 'automation' can lead to a decrease in professional commitment and subsequent low standards and morale.

This management approach is not the way to produce a quality and effective service, but this is the task for the Probation Service if it wishes to remain 'in business' beyond the late 1990s. A quality service is more often produced by active listening to users, stakeholders and staff and balancing these views against the pressures of a political process which will always impinge upon the public sector in some way. This, rather than excessive control of staff is the true management task.

Supervision and appraisal processes should reflect the pursuit of quality rather than the pursuit of control. In a world of diminishing resources, the retention and enhancement of staff will be the most significant contribution to the future of the service that managers can make.

REFERENCES.

Audit Commission (1989a) *Promoting Value For Money in the Probation Service.* London: HMSO.

Audit Commission (1989b) *The Value For Money Audit Guide.* London: HMSO.

Aust, A. (1994). Unpublished lecture, Department of Social Work, University of Birmingham.

Berger, P.L. and Luckmannn, T. (1967) *The Social Construction of Reality.* London: Allen Lane.

Davies, M. (1988) *Staff Supervision in the Probation Service.* Aldershot: Avebury.

Flynn, N. (1993) *Public Sector Management. 2nd edition.* Hemel Hempstead: Harvester Wheatsheaf.

Fulton, Lord John. (1968) *The Civil Service, Report of Committee. Cmnd 3638,* London: HMSO.

Francis, J. (1992) Results Without Racism. *Community Care,* July.

Her Majesty's Inspectorate (1992). *Appraisal of Management Grade Staff in the Probation Service.* London: Home Office.

Home Office (1983). *Statement of National Aims and Objectives.* London: Home Office.

Home Office (1992) *National Standards for Supervision in the Community.* London: Home Office.

Home Office, Probation Training Unit, (1993). *A Model Scheme Devised by the Home Office Staff Appraisal Working Party.* London: Home Office.

Kemshall, H. (1993). Assessing Competence: Scientific Process or Subjective Inference? Do We Really See It? *Social Work Education, 12, 1, pp.36–45.*

Metcalf and Curtis (1992). Feeding on Support. *Community Care,* July.

Miller, W.R. (1983). Motivational Interviewing with Problem Drinkers. *Behavioural Psychotherapy, 11, pp.145–152.*

Miller, W.R. and Rollnick,S. (1991). *Motivational Interviewing: Preparing People to Change Addictive Behaviour.* New York: Guilford Press.

Morrison, T. (1992). A Question of Survival. *Community Care,* July.

Morrison, T. (1993). *Staff Supervision in Social Care.* London: Longman.

Oxford English Dictionary. (1989). Vol. i and vol xvii. Clarendon Press, Oxford.

Payne, C. and Scott, A. (1982). *Developing Supervision of Teams in Field and Residential Social Work, Part 1.* National Institute of Social Work, paper no. 12.

Peters, T. and Waterman, R. (1982). *In Search of Excellence.* New York: Harper and Row.

Peters, T. (1989) *Thriving on Chaos, A Handbook for a Management Revolution.* London: Pan Books in association with MacMillan.

Quick, T. (1980). *The Quick Motivational Method.* Business Books.

Raine, J. and Willson, M. (1993). *Managing Criminal Justice.* Hemel Hempstead: Harvester Wheatsheaf.

Randell, G., Packard, P. and Slater, J. (1984). *Staff Appraisal: A First Step to Effective Leadership*. London: Institute of Personnel Management.

Ranson, S. and Tomlinson, J. (1986). *The Changing Government of Education*. London: Allen and Unwin.

Sawdon, D.T. and Sawdon, C. (1991) *Developing Staff Supervision and Appraisal in the Probation Service*. Humberside Probation Service.

CHAPTER 12

SUPERVISING STAFF IN FAMILY COURT WELFARE TEAMS

SUE LANE AND STEVE MACKEY

INTRODUCTION

Developing successful supervision in Court Welfare Teams is essential given the high emotional charge which accompanies the work, the potential for abuse of power, and the long term impact of any outcome on the lives of children. This chapter will look at some of the characteristics of Court Welfare teams and some strategies for supervisors. This chapter is not the place for debating the merits of co-working arrangements in Court Welfare Teams or specific theoretical frameworks for understanding family conflicts. Co-working arrangements are in place in many teams and the issues discussed and the practical suggestions have come from such team and agency practice; however, we make specific suggestions for adapting our ideas where practice is more individualised. We are not advocating any particular model for understanding families, but we do advocate that teams and their supervisors should be clear about the models they find helpful and have the flexibility to respond to different ideas.

We have not attempted to indicate how our ideas might be adapted for clerical staff attached to Court Welfare teams; however, supervisors with direct responsibility for such staff will need to take account of the impact of family distress and include those issues in their supervision.

GETTING TO KNOW THE TEAM

For supervision of any group of staff to be successful, supervisors need to know the team both as individuals and as a group and to have ways of working with the group both individually and collectively. Court welfare teams present particular challenges in this respect as their make-up can be rather different from many field teams, so techniques and strategies need to match the skills and experience of the team.

However, experience of working with families, and particularly with children, can be minimal amongst new recruits and, depending on recent experience, other essential elements can be missing such as recent court work or even report writing.

Despite the experience that staff apparently bring to the job, supervisors cannot afford to make assumptions about the competence individual staff will have in their new tasks. It is crucial, however, if staff are to make a successful transition, that the skills and experience that they do bring are recognised and have a place and value in the total team experience. Part of these skills and experience are the personal and family experience which shapes our responses to families in difficulty.

This would be demanding enough for most supervisors but many Senior Probation Officers may find themselves managing Court Welfare Teams with very limited knowledge themselves of family court work while some members of the team have been engaged in the task for many years. Supervisors need to establish their own credibility with teams while learning about the task, if new to it, or returning after a long break. Only those who are lucky enough to be promoted from recent assignment to a Court Welfare Team are likely to avoid the need to learn about family disputes and they have a great deal to learn about supervision and team management.

The initial task for new supervisors is, therefore, to establish themselves and to get to know enough about each member of staff to form the basis for the supervisory relationship. Those who are already established in role will find that they need to review their practice from time to time and a useful starting point is to check out what the supervisor and team members 'know' about each other. Co-working lends itself to 'live supervision' and where such arrangements are in place supervisors need to take advantage of them and incorporate them into their supervisory arrangements.

The following exercises (12.1, 12.2 and 12.3) aim to encourage sharing of personal and professional experience which is significant to the individual and relevant to the job.

Exercise 12.1: Getting to Know the Team

Each person brings in an object which has significance for them; different ways for using this is a starting point; each person has time to share information (can be pairs); each team member has opportunity to get to know others better; supervisor can structure and vary event to develop specific issues of current relevance to members of team.

For example, define type of object, its range of significance, location in time, and symbolism in terms of self, exchange objects by choosing a different one and explain its significance or appeal.

Exercise 12.2: Life Chart

Each person is given a wide sheet of paper which is marked out as in the example. They then mark in events of significance in their lives, giving them a score, which might have relevance in working with separating and divorcing families. Each person shares the reasons for identifying particular events and the score they gave them with another. These charts can be reviewed from time to time on a team or individual basis.

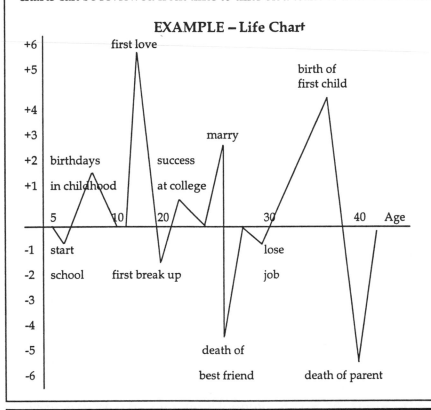

EXAMPLE – Life Chart

Exercise 12.3: Skills and Task Analysis

This framework provides an analytical tool for describing the range of skills required of Court Welfare Officers and can assist supervisors to identify gaps in individual repertoires. It should assist supervisors to demystify the Court Welfare task and help staff to transfer skills to other roles and tasks in the probation service and social work generally. As competencies become more widely established as a framework for training and appraisal other frameworks are likely to be widely available.

EXAMPLE - Skills and Task Analysis

TASKS	SKILLS	KNOWLEDGE
Write reports	written expression	structure of reports for family proceedings;
Interview child	list techniques for talking to children about families;	understanding of child development; impact of family breakdown on child;
	ability to manage own feelings of distress; ability to convey child's views to parents.	
Attend Court	present opinion clearly	family court procedures

DIVORCE AND SEPARATION

Divorcing and separating couples bring their conflicts to the encounter with the Court Welfare Officer and supervision needs to recognise that this will have an impact on the personal lives of staff. This is not an issue for debate and supervisors must negotiate ways of dealing with this emotional burden both individually and collectively. Some team members will resist such supervision and issues need to be discussed with sufficient openness to provide support while maintaining the privacy of individuals in respect of their personal lives.

Resistance may be perfectly proper if team boundaries have become hazy and support has degenerated into uncritical acceptance or the intrusive expectation that there are no areas of personal privacy. In this respect the principle challenge for the supervisor is to recognise the significance of co-working arrangements and to ensure that they are neither collusive nor destructive. All teams contain pressures towards conformity but this is especially so in Court Welfare Teams where members depend greatly on one another to complete the day-to-day task. The conflict demonstrated by families is directly opposed by the agreement of team members between themselves. Conflict risks becoming a property of the outside world which has to be kept at a distance, like the divorcing couple. Supervisors need to strive to create an environment which allows differences to be explored safely, which enables individuals to separate themselves from other people's problems, and which promotes trust between team members as colleagues committed to the work. It goes with this that Senior Probation Officers (SPOs) need space for themselves in a supervisory relationship that recognises the inherent risks of the task and provides opportunities to reflect on experiences.

WORKING WITH CHILDREN

Children present particular problems for staff working in Court Welfare. First, their problems are usually only capable of solution by the adults who are their parents or the wider family network. Second, parents do find it enormously difficult to face the consequences of divorce, an adult solution to an adult problem, in terms of the pain, distress, and disruption to children's lives. Court Welfare Officers (CWOs) have to face the unreal expectations of parents while also working with them to produce the solution. This creates a real conflict of loyalties which raises the vulnerability of all staff at different times. The solution most frequently advocated and adopted is to maintain a position of neutrality while facilitating communication between parents about the choices realistically available. The capacity required of the Court Welfare Officer in these circumstances is to ensure that parents take responsibility for understanding their child's perspective and incorporating it into the arrangements. The danger of this strategy is that the pain of the children may often be avoided by all participants, including the CWO, in pursuit of a negotiated settlement which meets everyone's needs except the child's.

All Court Welfare Officers will sometimes find themselves responding to the parents' difficulties either by representing the child's view or those of one or other of the parents. In some circumstances it is entirely proper that such a judgement is made but at other times it may represent a real difficulty for the individual member of staff. Co-working arrangements are intended to avoid this difficulty but co-working partnerships are not universally equal and supervisors need to be sensitive to individual workers' strengths and weaknesses and ensure the work with children does not become distorted by the different qualities of individual staff members. It is most unlikely that any of us can develop both the skills in interpretation and the self-discipline required without reliable supervision and, while much can be achieved within the co-working arrangement, supervisors need ways of checking this out.

Most commonly this is done by participating in the co-working practices, ensuring attention to all staff, and being willing to share skills and to be challenged by team members. Supervisors need to know the style and preferences of individual officers, to ensure that co-working arrangements promote a balance of approaches to children. They need to be confident that CWOs in confronting the distress of children, neither ignore their needs in pursuit of parental ownership of decisions nor undermine parents by imposing or promoting options which reflect the officer's own views.

These issues have been brought into focus for the Court Welfare Service by the implementation of the Children Act 1989 and considerable work has been undertaken by services to improve the quality of work with and on behalf of children. The supervisory challenge in this to provide a climate in which staff review each other's practices constructively and critically. The exercises discussed in relation to getting to know the team have great value in providing a framework of knowledge for the supervisor to be sensitive to the different capacities, qualities and skills of different staff members in their work with children.

Exercise 12.4: Ensuring children are heard

All members of staff should have an opportunity to watch their own interviewing of children on video and have space to discuss the issues raised in supervision.

Role play exercises which require members of staff to be children dealing with specific problems, e.g. telling your best friend about your mum and dad; or telling your absent parent you want time to see friends at weekends.

These exercises can help to develop a more concrete awareness of the distress and difficulty children feel about ordinary dilemmas faced when parents split-up, as well as the unusual.

COURT CONTEXTS

Staff need to develop their confidence in their role in court, emphasising the importance of maintaining their identity as social workers in the court setting and avoiding the dangers of over-identification with legalistic approaches to families. Supervisors can assist greatly in this both by developing confident relationships with the Court themselves and by including team members whenever appropriate in contacts with the Court. Court-based conciliation and duty services are useful points of contact as are opportunities to participate in Directions. Staff are unlikely to feel confident if their only encounters with courts are in the small minority of cases that are heavily contested where they are subject to rigorous cross examination.

Probation Officers do not universally come to Court Welfare Teams with a positive experience of courts and in reality this is a particularly daunting aspect of the job for many new recruits. This needs to be a significant part of local induction programmes and well supported by simulation and training exercises. Opportunities to observe colleagues in action are also useful and careful preparation in supervision of evidence-giving is essential. Supervisors will not themselves always feel confident of these issues and it is particularly important to use the experience of team members and to value their contribution to colleagues' development. Court clerks and district judges can be particularly helpful in developing local induction and training events and their interest and goodwill can be very valuable to supervisors. There is no real substitute for the confidence that comes with experience in this aspect of the task but good advice and careful preparation and rehearsal are a shared responsibility for supervisor and staff member.

AGENCY AND TEAM PRACTICES

Agency and team structures are significant in shaping supervisory practice. Many Court Welfare Teams have developed in an environment of benign neglect. Senior Probation Officers have often found themselves essentially alone with their team and the Courts to get on with the task, only to receive attention if backlogs become an embarrassment to the service. Any survival strategies which they and their teams have developed can be treated with suspicion in such a context and the cohesion of the team is experienced as a threat by the wider Service.

Good quality practice which achieves consistent levels of satisfaction for families and Courts is a practice which is open to scrutiny and is understandable. Legal worries about the status of a conciliatory approach to families has encouraged Court Welfare Teams to be guarded about practices and to protect working protocols from external review, particularly where these practices have sought to encourage families to reach agreement. This history both of neglect and collusion with the Courts about what really happens has often provided supervisors with considerable power and responsibility with little effective support.

There has been considerable change in this environment, as the expectation of greater accountability in the Probation Service generally has eventually reached Court Welfare Teams through the Home Office thematic inspection, the implementation of the Children Act, the revision of the Assistant Chief Probation Officers' Handbook, the participation of senior managers in Family Court business committees and the drafting of National Standards. Most supervisors will have varying aspects of this legacy in their teams, affecting individual relationships both in terms of supervision and perceptions of the task. This can on occasions become a highly charged environment which can make even simple supervisory tasks seem insurmountable. Exercises can help team members to take stock with the supervisor; in preparing for this the supervisor needs to think about strengths and opportunities, while giving team members space to reflect on the weaknesses and threats in a structured way that contains them.

In addition to this whole team exercise supervisors can encourage an environment of openness between staff, checking that all staff are using team structures for co-working, that these are not becoming closed arrangements between particular pairs and that a programme for reviewing practices is in hand which encourages constructive criticism.

DEVELOPING TEAM PHILOSOPHIES

While the history of the team can be an important factor to acknowledge, supervisors may find a more constructive strategy is to encourage the positive articulation of team theory and practice. This can be developed either as a local policy document within the frameworks generally used in the service,

Exercise 12.5: SWOT analysis

An opportunity for team members to evaluate the team environment and their contribution to its work.

STRENGTHS	OPPORTUNITIES
lots of experience	court confidence
Y can train others	X is attending course on work with children
WEAKNESSES	THREATS
No black members	need to be more efficient
New CWO's lack of experience in work with children	GALs (Guardian Ad Litem)

Exercise 12.6: Team Sabbaticals

Each member of staff takes it in turn to have a sabbatical month, free of new work allocation. In return for this space they agree with the supervisor an area of reading or practical research which they undertake on behalf of the team. An opportunity to feedback to the whole team is structured into a team meeting at which the whole team can explore the implications for practice in the team. At an individual level this activity can be developed for personal skills development as well as contributing to appraisal and career development discussions.

or more specifically as a team document. It is important that any such document is developed as something which can be shared more widely than the team itself. It is of course expected that any team statements are not in direct conflict with National Standards but there is space for teams to develop a clear framework of practice which can provide both staff member and supervisor with a framework for supervision. This can be a particularly helpful framework for identifying theoretical assumptions and ideas used by a team within which the conduct of interviews and co-working arrangements can be articulated. Such documents are not static and need regular review, which also ensures that assumptions are made explicit and the reasons for particular strategies and practices are clear to everyone.

This approach also enables the supervisor and the team to debate issues of style, the extent of team democracy and the authority of the supervisor.

These can be difficult issues in any team, but surface more regularly where members are very experienced, and can become positive forces in the team if acknowledged within the team practices. Teams and their supervisors need to find ways of working together effectively and having ways of coping with change.

Exercise 12.7: Team Handbook

Supervisors work with the team to develop a statement of team practice which is agreed by all members. Each team member takes responsibility for drafting a section and all participate in regular reviews. Such documents clarify co-working responsibilities and etiquette and provide a framework for induction.

This exercise is useful where supervisors find they are less experienced in working with families than team members and can be particularly helpful for staff who are identified as the team expert. It can be very easy to ignore the supervisory needs of such staff. Open recognition of team and individual skills will assist inexperienced supervisors to establish their position in the team and can remind experienced supervisors of the different supervisory needs of each member of staff. Exercise 12.8 can complement a handbook or stand alone as a review exercise. It can provide much information for the supervisor at a team and individual level.

This is a helpful exercise when there are new members in the team but has validity at any time as it helps to articulate the informal assumptions which develop in any working environment. It can also provide much useful information for individual supervision.

Exercise 12.8: Team Rules

Each team member writes down what they believe are the unwritten codes of behaviour within the team. For example, each person takes their fair share of Friday duty; I must always work with a co-worker when seeing family members together; we do home visits when ...

As 'rules' are shared and explored exceptions and variations can be validated and considerable diversity of practice encouraged.

ANTI-DISCRIMINATORY PRACTICE AND GATEKEEPING ISSUES

In our work on these issues we have taken the view that equality issues should be an integral feature of general quality management involving shared responsibility between supervisor and the supervised.

Court Welfare Teams have been slow to benefit from the work of the Probation Service in respect of equality issues. History and staff profile are important aspects of this. Ensuring that reports and the interviewing which informs them is properly grounded in an anti-discriminatory approach which respects family cultures is a primary responsibility of the supervisor. Participation in monitoring and effective gatekeeping systems are essential and need to reflect the procedures established elsewhere in the service. However, the content is necessarily different and Court Welfare Teams need to find language which presents information about families positively, analysing accurately those issues of family life which are relevant to the dispute and avoiding unlawful stereotypes. This can be very difficult and raises difficult issues for supervision.

Each team member needs space within supervision to explore their own beliefs about families and to identify those lifestyles that challenge their own practices and hence their neutrality in family enquiries.

All team members need space to discuss techniques which enable families to identify what is subjectively significant rather than working from assumptions about families.

All team members need to be sufficiently confident of these issues not be passive or intimidated when dealing with family arrangements in cultures other than their own.

All team members need to recognise the statutory limits of self-regulation by families and be able to identify the conditions which warrant public intervention in family arrangements and supervision to support them in initiating such intervention.

It is the role of the Senior Probation Officer to model good practice and create a safe environment for team members to challenge each other and discuss different practices and their impact on different families. This will also require attention in individual supervision as some matters will remain unresolved if left to team and peer group pressure. This requires the supervisor to be sensitive to recurring issues between staff and to ensure that individual supervision gives space to explore feelings and their link to working practices.

Court Welfare practice is especially vulnerable to power differentials between partners and this can of itself lead to practice which, when examined closely, is discriminatory. In particular, it is important to ensure that staff are alert to the conflicts of interest between mothers with care and their children and to ensure that in meeting the child's need for continuing contact with father, that the mother's need for privacy and independence is not compromised. Indeed, the pursuit of Court Orders is, of itself, a method of continuing to exercise power over women's lives and may only incidentally have benefits for the children. These issues are inevitably further complicated when staff are working across cultural, racial, and language differences. Supervisors need to have access to consultancy on these issues both for themselves and their teams, and to have interpreting and translating services which meet the demand. Supervision needs to ensure that staff are using such services appropriately and are open to suggestion and development. The way power is mediated within the team can reflect the conflicts which families present and supervisors need to consider carefully how their role within the team provides realistic and appropriate models. This can be a particularly sensitive issue for male managers with predominantly female teams.

APPRAISAL SYSTEMS

The Probation Service is now working towards national systems for staff appraisal. In Court Welfare Teams the collective working practices suggest that it would be sensible to ensure that appraisals reflect colleagues' experiences of each other. Team meetings can usefully incorporate opportunities for giving colleagues feedback, and the Senior Probation Officer can also have open systems for identifying volume and through-put of work which give staff confidence that their performance is openly measured. Appraisal also offers a regular opportunity to explore career development issues and to provide a framework for identifying training needs. Assistant Chief Probation Officers (ACPOs) can also usefully consider using team feedback in respect of Senior Probation Officers' performance. Appraisal practices which are integrated into the routine supervisory relationships are likely to work better for both supervisor and the supervised. Appraisal procedures can provide a framework for supervision contracts so that the two processes support one another properly.

STAFF MOVEMENT

The strategies discussed for developing an open and accountable style of supervision become particularly useful to supervisors faced with significant movement within a team. Most Probation Services have policies and procedures for managing the movement of staff between specialisms and Senior Probation Officers can expect regular changes to Court Welfare Teams. Each change presents an opportunity for review and development of team practice and this can of itself help to value new members' experiences. The most frequently described sense in respect of changing work focus is the sense of being de-skilled. Newcomers to Court Welfare Teams particularly report this effect and it remains a difficult issue for supervision. Those leaving often report a sense of loss and uncertainty. These are the disadvantages which come with valuing the skill and expertise of experienced Court Welfare Officers. Supervisors can, however, assist staff with these transitions by reviewing individual skills, planning the process and relating the timing to training opportunities.

Exercise 12.9: Reviewing and Planning

Prior training/learning review of personal and professional development; identify specifics which are open to development and those which need to be left behind; consider strategies for development, e.g. formal and informal training, co-working, individual planning and review.

SUPERVISION FOR SUPERVISORS

It is unlikely that any individual supervisor can achieve all this, particularly as many Senior Probation Officers in Court Welfare Teams are working in relative isolation from colleagues and carrying much of the day-to-day responsibility for the relationships with family courts. Each of us finds it easier to support staff if we are well supported ourselves and we should expect a high standard of supervision for ourselves. ACPOs in many areas have little recent direct experience of the task and this can become a block to a good managerial relationship and lead to a situation where the emphasis is on the issues and the supervisor feels safest with – finance and resource management – leaving the Senior Probation Officer to cope with their own emotional issues within the team. We hope some of the ideas we have shared in this discussion will be useful for ACPO–SPO supervision also, as teams cannot be expected to support their managers routinely, although all do from time to time.

CONCLUSION

In this discussion we have approached the task of supervision from its team context, believing that supervision is most effective when it uses the information which team life generates. We think this is particularly important in Family Court Welfare teams because of the need to share work issues with colleagues and because of the benefits of co-working in work with families. We have shared ideas we have found useful but there are likely to be many more which others are using successfully. Family Court Welfare teams have provided the environment for the development of many of these ideas but we do not see them as exclusive to this context. Indeed, we think they can be applied in many other social work contexts, not least fieldwork teams in the Probation Service.

CHAPTER 13

SUPERVISION IN PROBATION AND BAIL HOSTELS

MARTIN ROSCOE

INTRODUCTION

The purpose of this chapter is to examine the practice of supervision in probation and bail hostels. The nature of the hostel environment in probation and bail hostels is dwelt on at some length because this is seen as a key determinant of both the content of supervision and the way in which supervision is delivered. Similarly, the nature of team working in probation and bail hostels merits attention, again as a key determinant of supervision practice. In particular, the structure of teams in this environment means that models of supervision derived from field probation and social work settings are largely inappropriate.

Although the basic themes of supervision dealt with in this chapter have much in common with supervision delivered in other settings, they again reflect in their specific content the dilemmas and problems arising from the hostel environment and the methods of team working needed in that setting.

Finally, in looking at the basic thematic strands in supervision, the chapter addresses some issues of balance in supervision; that is to say, the relative weight which should be given to the different concerns and purposes of supervision. Imprecise though it is, the notion of getting a "feel" for the relative weight to be given to different issues is seen as an important part of successful supervision in probation and bail hostels.

THE PROBATION AND BAIL HOSTEL ENVIRONMENT

There are at the time of writing 113 probation and bail hostels approved by the Home Office in England and Wales. They provide places for some 2500 residents annually at a cost of around £30.5 million. Of the population resident in approved hostels during 1991/2:

- 69 per cent were on bail awaiting sentence
- 25 per cent were on probation
- 6 per cent were under supervision on release from custody (HM Inspectorate of Probation 1993, p.10)

In most approved hostels, the resident group will contain individuals at very different stages of the criminal justice process whose attitude to the hostel will be affected by this. Residents on bail may live in a hostel for a few days; others, mostly awaiting a Crown Court appearance, may be there for several months. Offenders living in a hostel as a condition of a probation order will have tried out hostel life as part of an assessment period, but more will be expected of them in terms of involvement in programmes and activities run by the Probation Service to tackle offending, address underlying problems and develop skills and confidence.

Released prisoners under probation supervision will have completed a prison sentence; for them, the hostel will provide a temporary address acceptable to the prison authorities in which a conditional part of their sentence can be served in the community while they adjust to independent life following the very restricted setting of a prison.

Just over a quarter of the hostels cater solely for residents on bail, split evenly between those which cater solely for male residents and those catering for a mixed population. The remaining three-quarters cater for offenders under probation supervision. The number of hostels in each category is shown in Figure 13.1 below.

Figure 13.1		
	Bail Only	Probation and Bail
Mixed	14	28
Men only	16	48
Women only	1	2
(HM Inspectorate of Probation 1993, p.11)		

In addition to the variety of legal status, the resident group will contain a wide variety of ages. Just over half will be young men aged between 18 and 25 years with a significant incidence of drug and alcohol problems and a significant minority with psychiatric problems. In "mixed" hostels, there will also be a minority of female residents - typically one or two women, often young women, in an otherwise male group, vulnerable to pressure and sexual exploitation. Black residents will, again, in most hostels be in a minority and will have a range of religious, dietary and cultural needs in addition to their frequent difficulties in sharing the same living space with sometimes hostile white fellow residents.

Hostels, particularly probation and bail hostels, are generally unstable environments bringing together anxious, disorganised and volatile individuals under a variety of restrictions. Tension is endemic, arising as much from the heterogeneous mix of residents as from the personality and behaviour of any one individual. Tolerance of frustration is low, inflammatory incidents are never far away, arising often from apparently minor irritations. Staff need to be constantly alert to mood and atmosphere and be able to intervene rapidly to defuse tension and confrontation. Adding further pressure is the need constantly to maintain high occupancy levels (generally over 80 per cent of hostel capacity). Hostels which fail to maintain high occupancy levels are now, with cutbacks in the Home Office hostel budget, vulnerable to closure.

Despite the variety of hostels, settings and types of residents, there are common issues and problems. At the most basic level, all provide 24-hour care, seven days a week, of individuals from a variety of backgrounds who have not chosen to live together. Approved hostels provide continuous care for groups of residents by groups of staff working mostly on a rota basis. At this most fundamental level, issues which are central to the supervisory process begin to emerge. Field workers tend to work on their own or with one or two colleagues. Their encounters with clients are usually not witnessed directly by their seniors and managers. Clients in field work settings tend not to share workers. In the residential setting, however, hostel workers work alongside their immediate managers and have the opportunity to refer to them at some point in most of their working hours. In addition, they take over the care of a group of residents from a colleague and hand over to another. Their work and their decisions are subject to relatively immediate and public scrutiny both by colleagues and residents themselves. Consistency with the working styles of peers and with the policies of management becomes a key and immediate issue for these groups of staff. Consistent management of routines, interpretation of hostel rules quickly becomes the over-riding day-to-day issue for hostel staff faced with the scrutiny in the first instance of hostel residents ("Sarah lets us do this" or "Jim wouldn't respond like that"). Inconsistency with colleagues or management policy is the subject of immediate and often heated comment.

SUPERVISION AND TEAM STRUCTURE

The need for consistent and continuous care is based, however, on a setting which implies a great deal of heterogeneity. The staffing structure of an approved hostel contains a wide variety of staff and roles. Although there is some variation, the usual composition of staff teams in approved probation and bail hostels is:

- Warden
- Deputy Warden
- A team of Assistant Wardens
- Admin/secretarial officers
- Cook (sometimes part time)
- Cleaners (part time)
- Maintenance worker (part time, if at all).

In addition, in many hostels, the introduction of waking night staff is being implemented and many will also employ sessional relief staff to cover absences through sickness and holidays.

The variety of roles in a typical staff team in an approved hostel setting also implies a variety of professional backgrounds and levels of experience. Wardens and deputy wardens may generally be experienced senior probation officers and probation officers. For many assistant wardens, though by no means all, the hostel setting will be their first experience of professional social work. Other staff will have roles which are not directly focused on resident care (although all will have varying degrees of contact with residents). Their common interactions with residents may be mediated through a professional background and value system which has little in common with social work.

The issue for supervision in the hostel setting is to weld together a disparate group of individuals with a variety of roles and backgrounds into a staff team capable of delivering consistent care to a group of residents, who themselves have a variety of needs.

It is almost a paradox. One group of individuals, disparate in roles, experience and professional background, working together sometimes simultaneously and sometimes sequentially as part of a rota, are responsible for delivering continuous and consistent care to another group of individuals, disparate in legal status, age, sex, ethnicity and personality in a fundamentally unstable setting, characterised by frequent tension and frequent changes in the resident group. Staff have to be able to work as a team, taking a consistent approach to the work. The task of ensuring a common approach falls mainly on the senior staff who must ensure consistency of care both while they are there and in their absence. The vehicle for delivering consistency among the staff group is the supervisory process.

The whole staff team needs to be aware of the ground which supervision ought to cover and of the activities which contribute to it. In particular, it needs an understanding of how supervision is delivered. Staff from a variety of backgrounds will have different expectations not only of the content of supervision, but also of the structures through which it is delivered. Staff groups deriving their expectations of supervision from fieldwork models may be overly focused on the one-to-one relationship with their manager as the exclusive setting for supervision. In this model, team members appear to be the spokes on a wheel with the manager at the hub. All communication in this model flows through the manager.

In reality, though, hostels are not like that. There are many settings in which supervision can occur, if defined broadly as the 'process of talking, to someone else involved in the same system, about what one is doing, in order to be able to do it better' (Atherton 1986, p.3).

A prime focus of supervision can be, if adequate time and space is given over to it, the 'handover meeting' as staff from one shift discuss issues and problems with incoming staff. How handovers are used needs to be the subject of team agreement and a consistent format needs to be maintained. It is not commonly, though, a process which directly involves senior staff, but is one in which fundamental issues of supervision will arise. Some rota systems will create natural and consistent linkages between members of staff who will generally hand over one to the other. Where, by accident or design, a rota system creates such consistent linkages, there should be a conscious utilisation of the supervisory possibilities they present. The manager's role may be to review formally their effectiveness from time to time with the staff concerned.

Similarly, the accidents of the rota system may mean that where more than one member of staff is present at a particular time, consistent pairings or other linkages occur. Again, these need to be the subject of conscious planning and evaluation.

Depending on their role, some members of staff may occupy relatively 'fixed' positions and will need to work with a variety of other staff members who come and go as part of the rota system.

Typically, support staff such as hostel administrators, cleaners, cooks, maintenance staff will need to work with other more 'transient' staff such as assistant wardens on the rota. Clarifying role boundaries, the support each needs from the other, and working to make these relationships consistent across the staff group will be an important part of the supervisory process which may be tackled in a variety of different ways - one-to-one meetings, group discussion and feedback with or without the presence of senior staff.

Another kind of supervisory arrangement may occur when new staff in an introductory period 'shadow' more experienced members of staff. Here, again, participants need to see this relationship as one that is involved in the process and purposes of supervision. It is, again, a relationship which needs to be evaluated.

Finally, most approved hostels will involve an allocation of management responsibilities between a warden and a deputy warden. The two participants should spend considerable time in ensuring that they understand each other's role and boundaries and in ensuring that other staff understand their arrangements for the division of responsibilities. Deputy wardens may be responsible, broadly, for day-to-day 'live' supervision of some or all staff with the warden taking responsibility for more formal processes of appraisal, design and review of job descriptions, leading team meetings and so forth. Clearly, this kind of pairing needs to achieve management consistency and will need a lot of open discussion about different leadership styles, personal strengths and weaknesses, different types of experience and different values and attitudes.

Effective supervision in the setting of an approved hostel is, then, a whole team issue. It is not simply the responsibility of one person to deliver supervision. Supervision covering the range of issues from hostel objectives, the design of staff roles, individual professional development, methods of communication and decision making, and coping with stress will occur through a variety of relationships. The effectiveness of these relationships in delivering good supervision across the range of issues needs to be the subject of open discussion, planning and evaluation.

THEMES OF SUPERVISION

Following the work of Payne and Scott (Payne and Scott 1982), it is possible to identify a number of core themes in the supervisory process. Payne and Scott identify two principal aspects of teamwork which supervision needs to encompass. First is the instrumental function of achieving the task of the group through the allocation of work and the maximisation of individual contributions to the group task. It involves the group in managing its own decision-making in relation to agreed goals. The second function they identify is the expressive one by which team members provide personal support and stimulation for each other.

Within the instrumental function of teamwork there are a number of important themes for supervision. First, there is the need to develop team goals and plans and to relate these to the wider purposes both of the Probation Service and the criminal justice system as a whole. The report of the Probation Inspectorate notes the isolation of approved hostels from the wider Probation Service:

> They felt they had little credibility with field colleagues and that their work was not seen as being professional or useful. This had an enormously damaging impact on morale...' (HM Inspectorate of Probation 1993 p.67)

The report makes clear that this is not a problem simply to be resolved by re-organising things to ensure greater contact between field and residential staff. In the first place comes the need for each hostel team to be able to articulate a clear set of measurable hostel objectives which contribute in identifiable ways to the goals of the Probation Service. National standards published by the Home Office (Home Office 1992) require hostels to publish a statement of aims and objectives, an admissions policy, and information to their local Chief Probation Officer on at least an annual basis about the outcome of referrals. These standards provide a useful impetus to hostel teams to review their aims and associated outcomes regularly. As a focus for team effort and as a counter to the inbuilt tendency toward isolation and collective lack of self-esteem, these are key concerns. The results of monitoring and evaluation should be a regular concern (and certainly not an annual formal exercise). Particularly in bail hostels, where admissions and departures are frequent, there is scope for monthly discussion and analysis of trends and a goal of supervision ought to be primarily to encourage regular discussion but also to see the connections between day-to-day hostel activities and routines and monthly outcomes.

Hostel rules and routines can often tend to be the product of history, instituted in response to special past circumstances, which have often now lost their meaning. An 'experimental' orientation allows for routines which have become rituals to be challenged and encourages staff to think critically about the minutiae of hostel life. Hostels can be enclosed self-referential worlds and a constant focus on objectives and their contribution to the wider aims of the organisation can be a day-by-day antidote.

An effective tool for linking everyday hostel issues with the more abstract levels of agency goals and purposes is the 'slow motion action replay'. In individual supervision or in team meetings a member of staff can replay the thought processes leading to decisions taken in particular circumstances, such as when, for instance, a resident arrives late for the hostel curfew. The point of the exercise is to see each situation as individual and complex – not simply one of a general class ('curfew breach'). The consistency reached through regular discussions of this sort is far more valuable than simple 'rule-book' consistency.

A second important aspect of the instrumental focus of supervision is the attention paid to the design and demarcation of staff roles. It is a useful practice first for each member of staff to have access to the job descriptions of all other staff (including the wardens) and for these job descriptions to be reviewed regularly in team meetings. A particularly useful exercise is for staff involved in resident care to review with administrative and support staff the extent to which their roles overlap and to identify where the performance of each role impacts on the other. Where, for instance, residents are involved in domestic cleaning duties the enthusiasm of assistant wardens may directly impact on the ability of hostel cleaning staff to carry out their responsibilities. Three-way meetings between the staff involved, structured by warden or deputy, can help to focus what in many hostels can simply be an area of dissatisfied grumbling and tension.

A third instrumental focus of supervision is the need to manage the group's own decision making. Not only does this involve regular weekly team meetings (protected from the intrusion of the telephone, residents and their visitors) but also the review of the effectiveness of team meetings, preferably by an evaluation at the end of each meeting.

Finally, supervision needs to manage and plan the development of each individual member of staff. For many staff, hostel work is the first experience of professional social work and may be seen as a means of gaining practical experience before seeking further qualifications. A structured approach to staff induction is essential. An outline induction programme for assistant wardens in the Hampshire Probation Service is given in Figure 13.2 below.

At the root of the expressive functions of supervision, Payne and Scott (1982) identify helping staff cope with stress as a major theme. Hostel life is full of stress. Tension and the likelihood of inflammatory and sometimes violent incidents among the resident group are ever present. While effective strategies for preventing and managing violent or aggressive incidents are important (including careful attention to the physical design of the environment, use of safety alarms, etc.) there is nevertheless a continuing impact on staff individually and collectively of living with relatively constant threat and low-level aggression as well as more serious incidents.

Managing the aftermath of aggressive incidents is a crucial theme. The long-lasting after effects of aggressive incidents can be manifested in cycles of confusion, self-blame and damage to self-esteem. The processes by which support from colleagues and managers is asked for and offered needs to be regularly addressed in supervision with a recognition that the effects of aggression can be long-lasting and can resurface at unexpected intervals. Post incident counselling and support should allow the expression of anger at the perpetrator of the assault (verbal or physical) and should acknowledge the feelings of isolation and loneliness provoked by being the victim of such incidents. Some of the areas to be covered either in a group or individually might be:

- explore how people got involved and their preparation
- explore their own experiences in the incident
- how did they see things happening and what were their reactions

Figure 13.2

INDUCTION PROGRAMME	DATE TO BE DONE BY	DATE DONE	BY WHOM
Workplace introduction - this begins the bonding process of the more informal relationship, in motivational terms 'the belonging' aspects, and gives attention to workplace 'social' norms/expectations Familiarisation with hostel plan Appropriate staff introductions Explanation of staff structure Fire prevention systems and alarms			
The geographical layout – familiarity of orientation to the physical surroundings. Comfort and social facilities.			
Job instruction – focuses on the fit between what 'I/she/he does' as an individual member of staff with the overall purpose of the organisation as a whole. Hostel programme and routines Chores, projects and policies Published statement concerning equal opportunities Anti-racism training Complaints and grievances procedure Record keeping; log diary Message book Accident report book Violent incident report form Residents' daily record log			
Organisational structure – the infrastructure and the interaction of other sections/functions of the organisation			
Trade Union/sports/social facilities – how to access the formal/informal staffing networks.			
Data protection – the organisation and individuals can be prosecuted for incorrect holding, using or disclosure of computerised personal data in contravention of the Data Protection Act.			
Hostel philosophy – philosophy and purpose. Hampshire Statement of Purpose and Strategy Confidentiality Code of Ethics Equal opportunity/anti-discriminatory policy			
Conditions of employment (where appropriate) – this covers the statutory and contractual relationship between the employer and employee ie what each expects of each other under the common law concept of the contract of employment. **Hours of work/shifts** Leave entitlement			

INDUCTION PROGRAMME	DATE TO BE DONE BY	DATE DONE	BY WHOM
Health and Safety policy – of vital importance and often forgotten. We have a statutory duty to inform members of staff about mechanisms for their safe employment and their obligations in that respect. Familiarisation with policy folder/sign as read Use of personal alarms explained Security – importance of keys etc			
Hostel manuals – familiarise/sign as read.			
Office procedures: Record keeping – log book, message book, NWC book, accident report book, violent incidents, damage report Familiarisation with all relevant forms Referrals Chores Hostel programmes and routines Complaints and grievance procedure Personnel manual folder Administration manual folder			
Management Effectiveness Programme – explain programme and county fit/wall charts etc.			
Security procedures: Knowledge and use of keys Hostel lock up procedure Knowledge of hostel rules Knowledge and use of staff phone numbers			
Training needs: Breakaway Performance appraisals Health and hygiene Management of violence Anti-discrimination			
Assistant Wardens: Shadow shift supervisor for two days shifts and one night shift Learn daily programme and routines Read hostel manual Read hostel policy folder Court and bail procedures Breach procedures Probation awareness Referral procedures Team meetings Rota Resident induction 24 interview Key worker system Criminal Justice system/explain Offending Behaviour Group Rent collection procedures DSS and Housing Benefit procedures Relevant agency visits Fire prevention systems and alarms			

- what were the most difficult things for them to do and what were the worst aspects of the incident
- what were the things that were done well (very important in the process of rebuilding self-esteem)
- what were the close and distancing things they felt about other colleagues
- present feelings toward those involved
- the difficulties of getting back to the 'normal' work situation.

THE BALANCE OF SUPERVISION

While responding effectively in each of the areas identified is a major criterion of effective supervision, it is equally important to achieve the right balance between each of these areas. First, there is a need to ensure an appropriate balance between the instrumental and expressive elements of supervision. An overemphasis on the rational, cognitive elements of objective setting, policy formulation, reviewing job descriptions and so forth can dangerously marginalise the emotional components of developing interpersonal communication and support among the staff group. An anonymous assistant warden writing in *Probation Journal* (1993) describes how destructive an over-rational supervisory process can be, particularly in the aftermath of stress produced through the aggression of residents:

> The content of the abuse I suffered was particularly sexist. I was terrified. I felt unable to talk about that terror to my male colleagues. I kept my feelings neatly tucked out of sight, even in the debriefing I participated in with my manager. No space for my feelings to be aired and understood was offered to me by the men I work with. I felt safe only in talking about issues and ideas... My emotional responses are not welcomed or acknowledged. Focus is planted firmly on cognition and behaviour. (pp.145–50)

A lack of emotional solidarity among the staff group can disable the important cognitive purposes of supervision. Conversely, though, an overemphasis on staff solidarity can lead to an overemphasis on the needs of the staff group and not enough on the needs of residents and the need to achieve the objectives and purposes of the hostel.

Where the balance needs to be between these, rational and emotional components of supervision will vary over time according to the nature of the current resident group and the stage of development of the staff group. At a given period the emphasis given to the five themes of supervision may need to change and getting the balance right needs the conscious reflection of senior staff and the staff group as a whole.

The questionnaire shown in Figure 13.3 or variants of it may be a helpful device in 'taking the temperature' of the team and getting the 'feel' of where the balance of supervision ought to be. It can be used as a basis for team discussion or with individuals either verbally or as a written questionnaire.

Figure 13.3: Team supervision questionnaire

For each of the 25 statements given below please indicate the extent to which you agree or disagree.

Strongly agree   1

Agree   2

Disagree   3

Strongly disagree   4

OBJECTIVES:

1	I am clear about the main purpose of the hostel	1	2	3	4
2	I can see how our work is important in the Probation Service	1	2	3	4
3	I get clear feedback on hostel performance	1	2	3	4
4	I can explain to others the primary purpose of the hostel	1	2	3	4
5	I can justify the work of the hostel	1	2	3	4

ROLES:

6	I feel too much is asked of me	1	2	3	4
7	I feel underused in my job	1	2	3	4
8	I feel my decisions will be backed up	1	2	3	4
9	I know when to seek advice	1	2	3	4
10	I am confident that asking for help is not a mark against me	1	2	3	4

TEAM COHESION:

11	I trust all my colleagues in the hostel	1	2	3	4
12	I feel I have a voice in important decisions in the hostel	1	2	3	4
13	I can disagree with my colleagues	1	2	3	4
14	I feel we do good work here	1	2	3	4
15	I feel we can take collective decisions	1	2	3	4

STRESS:

16	I can discuss personal problems if I need to	1	2	3	4
17	My colleagues notice when I am unhappy	1	2	3	4
18	If I am angry I can say so	1	2	3	4
19	I can express negative feelings about residents	1	2	3	4
20	If I have a bad shift, I can talk about it	1	2	3	4

PROFESSIONAL DEVELOPMENT:

21	I am confident I have the basic knowledge to carry out my job	1	2	3	4
22	I feel my skills are improving	1	2	3	4
23	I get the opportunity to think about hostel objectives	1	2	3	4
24	I understand developments in the Probation Service	1	2	3	4
25	I feel that I learn from my colleagues	1	2	3	4

Indications of dissatisfaction may give the clue as to where the balance of supervision ought to be.

Getting the balance right needs not only the conscious attention of senior staff. The whole staff team needs to be aware of the ground which supervision ought to cover and of the activities which contribute to it.

REFERENCES

Atherton J.S. (1986) *Professional Supervision in Group Care: A Contract Based Approach*. London: Tavistock.

HM Inspectorate of Probation (1993) *Approved Probation and Bail Hostels: Report of a Thematic Inspection*. London: Home Office.

Home Office (1992) *National Standards for the Supervision of Offenders in the Community*. London: Home Office.

Payne C. and Scott T. (1982) *Developing Supervision of Teams in Field and Residential Social Work: Part 1*. London: National Institute for Social Work.

Personal Account (1993) 'My life as a Woman in a Bail Hostel.' *Probation Journal* Vol 40 No 3 pp.149-150.

CHAPTER 14

Supervision in the Voluntary Sector

Christine Stanners

A Practitioner's view

Over a number of years I have been providing supervision in the voluntary sector:

- as a study supervisor for students from voluntary organisations taking the Certificate in Social Service (CSS) where I was paid as an independent consultant (i.e., not part of the management structure)
- as a manager supervising staff and volunteers within a voluntary organisation where I was the paid Director
- as a 'professional' supervising lay volunteer counsellors providing a bereavement service, where I was unpaid.

For all three activities I drew on my professional training and experience as a medical social worker, and the experience of being supervised as a student and as a practitioner.

In this chapter I shall make observations on the differences between supervising students, staff and volunteers within the voluntary and statutory sectors and identify common ground. I shall emphasise the importance of supervision in a voluntary organisation in today's climate of quality assurance and control and note some of the contextual differences between the statutory and voluntary sectors which affect supervision. I shall make distinctions between managerial and non-managerial supervision and, drawing on experiential work with students and trainees, evaluate the difference between one-to-one and group supervision. I shall also address issues around the power structure of the supervisory relationship and its potential to become destructive rather than supportive.

Finally I shall present three practical guidelines for implementing supervision:

- a generic model which can be used for staff, students and volunteers
- an outline of a session of supervision drawn up for one-to-one supervision
- a 'contract' agreement which I drew up for the group supervision of volunteer counsellors.

Much of what I describe as the supervisory task will be generic to all settings but throughout the chapter I shall highlight features of supervision which are of particular relevance to the voluntary sector.

SUPERVISION AND THE VOLUNTARY ETHIC

Definitions

'Supervision' and 'voluntary' – there is a tension between the two concepts since 'voluntary' implies freedom to do what you want to do when you want to do it, and 'supervision' implies restraint and control. I have discovered several definitions of supervision which accord with the voluntary ethos:

> Supervision is the process of reflecting on what you are doing with the help of another, in order to help you do it better. (Atherton 1987)

> Ordinarily the word means overseeing, or a responsible person inspecting the work of someone with less responsibility, but in the caring professions it has come to mean the process through which support, guidance and increasing insight are gained by all workers. (Cruse 1987)

As definitions of the *process* these apply equally to supervising staff, students and volunteers in the voluntary sector. However, a definition for the *function* of supervision must go further and I would suggest that it is to provide a safe environment for:

- assessing and monitoring the practice and workload of the individual worker
- clarification of the agency policies and procedures, levels of decision-making and prioritisation
- information exchange
- learning and development
- modelling good practice
- problem solving
- support.

To be effective, the supervisory relationship must be founded on mutual trust and respect for individual knowledge and experience, and must seek to preserve non-judgmental attitudes on personal and cultural differences.

As Sandy Adirondack inimitably comments:

> The purpose of the sessions is not to give supervisors the opportunity to insult or criticise workers. (Adirondack 1990)

DIFFERENCES BETWEEN VOLUNTARY AND STATUTORY SECTORS AFFECTING SUPERVISORY ACTIVITIES

The paid employee in a voluntary organisation

For paid employees in the voluntary sector there is rarely a career structure within the organisation. There is often no training policy or budget. There is frequently a lack of clear objectives, priorities and clarity about decision-making levels of responsibility. Lines of accountability may be unclear. Job descriptions may lack precision, and boundaries between jobs are characteristically 'elastic'. In statutory organisations these structures are usually clearly defined.

Voluntary Management Committees may see supervision as a bureaucratic activity which is not appropriate in a voluntary setting and may not give a 'right' to the time spent. Staff themselves may be resistant to 'formalising' supervision. The distance between the supervisor and the supervisee in the management structure may not be great and the supervisor may even find they are supervising people with more experience than themselves. Further, since there may be only one person carrying out a particular operation within the agency the supervisor may have a different skills set from the staff member they are supervising. He or she may not be the worker's Line Manager but is able to offer 'professional' supervision from their own area of expertise.

There is an ethos that people choosing to work in the voluntary sector are altruistically motivated so they are not expected to make demands over working conditions, nor to object to taking on areas of work which are not reflected in their contracts. Union representation may not be common.

All these factors make it difficult to provide effective supervision in the voluntary sector. However, the present competitive market in the provision of care is making demands on voluntary organisations for greater accountability, requiring explicit management skills in target setting, monitoring performance and evaluating outcomes. I would suggest that these are the tasks of supervision which makes it an essential component of quality assurance.

SUPERVISION IS AN ESSENTIAL COMPONENT OF QUALITY ASSURANCE

THE STUDENT IN A VOLUNTARY ORGANISATION

When I was employed as a study supervisor I found that students from the voluntary sector were at a disadvantage when starting the CSS Courses since they were unfamiliar with Social Services and Health Service structures and practices. They were isolated by the use of initials and jargon. In the statutory sector pre-course preparation was provided in a planned programme, and group supervision in addition to study supervision was provided for students. Some large voluntary organisations with a number of establishments were able to offer support through a training department, but often students were sponsored singly by their agency and had no peer support. Jealousy and resentment from their work colleagues were not uncommon, particularly if supernumerary cover was inadequate, or non-existent, which could be the case, although contrary to the Course requirements.

Re-entry to the workplace was often painful and qualification not rewarded by salary increments. In the voluntary sector where there may be a small and static staff, the opportunity for promotion to senior posts within the organisation is limited. Supervision after the end of the Course is not included in some of the voluntary sector contracts, but it is essential to the successful management of a student's return from a training course to the workplace.

SUPERVISION IS ESSENTIAL TO THE SUCCESSFUL MANAGEMENT OF A STUDENT'S RETURN FROM A TRAINING COURSE TO THE WORK PLACE

THE VOLUNTEER IN A VOLUNTARY ORGANISATION

The agency using volunteers to provide a service is often challenged on the impossibility of requirement performance standards from the voluntary workforce. It is perceived as a powerless situation for 'employers': that is, no pay – no sanctions. Volunteers are seen to be holding the power. They can walk away and they cannot be required to undertake tasks they do not like.

Supervision, as it is being defined here, can be a means of managing the power, recognising the volunteer worker as having the same needs of supervision and the same right to it as the paid worker.

In order to understand how to provide effective supervision for volunteers some insight is required into the motivation behind volunteering. Research by the Volunteer Centre suggests that 'status' is an important motivator and association with professionals is one way in which this can be achieved (Hatch 1982).

Supervision, therefore, can be seen as enabling volunteers to work in a professional manner, and as a means of according them the status of accredited workers within the organisation.

It can also meet the needs of 'professionals' working as volunteers; those with specialist skills often join voluntary organisations in order to develop their own skills and technology, according to Kramer (1981). Supervision can be offered as an appropriate means of meeting these volunteers' needs for validation and enhancing their skills.

SUPERVISION CAN MEET THE NEEDS OF VOLUNTEERS FOR VALIDATION AND ENABLE THEM TO WORK IN A PROFESSIONAL MANNER

However, Penelope Hall (1981) notes that 'human service professionals seem to be effective in moulding organisations to suit their interests'. In research I carried out into the factors bringing about a change of goal in a voluntary organisation, it was evident that the drive of the 'professionals' working as volunteers to extend their own skills had a significant influence on change (Stanners 1987).

Supervision can help to ensure that the activities of volunteers fall within the objectives and goals of the organisation, and that creative ideas are brought into the planning processes of the organisation and do not subvert its direction.

Volunteers may not want their volunteering to be formalised or bureaucratised. 'Supervision' may sound too controlling, just as 'training' may sound too demanding, but every serious volunteer will want *induction* and preparation and ongoing support.

Supervision, whatever it may be called, is one way in which standards can be agreed and upheld, information exchanged, and skills development targeted to the agency's objectives, in the voluntary setting.

SUPERVISION IS ONE WAY IN WHICH STANDARDS CAN BE AGREED AND UPHELD, INFORMATION EXCHANGED, AND SKILLS DEVELOPMENT TARGETED TO THE AGENCY'S OBJECTIVES

DIFFERENCES IN MOTIVATION BETWEEN THE PAID AND THE VOLUNTEER WORKER

When a group of CSS students (i.e., paid workers) were asked in a seminar I was running on supervision to consider what motivated them in their work, they said:

- conviction about the value of the job
- recognition of the value of their contribution
- adequate and appropriate pay.

When asked to identify what they needed in order to carry out their work to achieve satisfaction they said:

- clear understanding of what they were required to do
- clear understanding of the level at which they could make decisions
- knowledge of agency policies
- training to enhance their skills
- support in carrying out the work effectively
- feedback on outcomes and practice.

When they were asked what they thought might motivate and give job satisfaction to volunteers they were surprised to recognise that the needs were the same except for the pay.

THE TASKS OF THE SUPERVISOR AS SEEN BY THE STUDENT

Another group of students on a CSS course were asked in a workshop to say what they thought the tasks of a study supervisor were. They described the role as an enabling one, in which the supervisor:

- listens
- reflects
- clarifies and interprets
- confirms and approves
- probes
- directs to sources of information
- re-labels
- adds new data
- identifies options
- proposes criteria
- recommends
- prescribes
- helps plan implementation
- teaches
- follows-up
- enhances self-esteem of the student.

They defined supervision as providing:

> a flexible framework within which the student and study supervisor can build a mature relationship within professional boundaries, in order to promote personal and professional growth and in which the student will feel supported, enabled and valued.

The characteristics they required in the supervisor included:

> flexibility, honesty, patience, enthusiasm, commitment, ability to keep cool, to keep perspective, and to be punctual. They felt the supervisor also needed skills as a moderator and negotiator.

MODELLING GOOD PRACTICE THROUGH THE SUPERVISORY RELATIONSHIP

The emphasis the students laid on punctuality, helping to plan implementation, identifying options, directing to sources of information, re-labelling, and so forth, provides the supervisor with the opportunity to demonstrate good management practices. The listening, clarifying and interpreting which they included in the repertoire of tasks of the supervisor are techniques used in counselling and can be used as a model of good counselling practice. Lynn Franchino (1989) says that techniques of clarification, reflecting back, probing and challenging are appropriate to the supervisory task.

POWER RELATIONSHIPS IN SUPERVISION

When the same group of students were asked to give examples of bad experiences of supervision, they described destructive practices such as breaking confidentiality, domination, not being valued, not being supported, being put down, own agenda disregarded, incorrect assumptions, lack of structure, irrelevance of personal issues, anger, and personal battles. They identified that supervision can be destructive if:

- it undermines confidence and self-esteem
- it makes the student too dependent
- if the supervisor wants to *teach* rather than facilitating the student's learning
- the supervisor needs to control
- the supervisor needs to feel important
- it is experienced as restraint or criticism.

It becomes clear that the supervisor must be aware of his or her own needs in the supervisory relationship. Supervision for the supervisor therefore becomes an essential requirement.

SUPERVISION FOR THE SUPERVISOR IS ESSENTIAL

The destructive elements defined by the students highlight the need to recognise the power each participant holds in the supervisory relationship. The role of the study supervisor was an interesting one in the power relationship. In my own experience as a freelance study supervisor employed by several voluntary organisations I was independent of line management and of the policy-making processes of service management within the agencies.

The strength of this position was the ability to take an objective view so that the student could safely feed back on practice, management and relationships within the agency without fear of compromise.

The weakness of the position was that as a supervisor with no management role I was not always aware of the policy and politics within the agency. The holding or withholding of information could become, therefore, a source of power for the student.

James Atherton (1987), in an analysis of different types of supervision, makes a distinction between managerial and non-managerial supervision which is helpful in considering the power held by the supervisor. He describes managerial supervision as being directly linked to the management of the organisation as a whole, and to the management of the individual's work within the organisation. He says it identifies work to be done, and monitors how well it is done. The supervisor has the authority to make sure it *is* done and that it is done in accordance with the policy of the organisation.

Professional or non-managerial supervision, on the other hand, he sees as concerned with values, skills and knowledge and, he says, may involve a supervisor who has no direct link with the management of the individual's work, and may not even have a direct link with the organisation.

The supervisor in the non-managerial or professional role has no authority to effect change in the student's working environment, which can induce a sense of powerlessness. On the other hand, the supervisor's role in assessment gives power over the student. Since it is outside the line management control of the organisation there is inherent in the relationship a danger of collusion, cosiness and over-involvement in the student's personal issues. These dangers point yet again to the need for supervision of the supervisor.

POWER DIFFERENCES IN GROUP AND ONE-TO-ONE SUPERVISION

In a workshop which I ran for an organisation providing a bereavement service by voluntary counsellors, the participants were asked to share their bad experiences of supervision. They were customarily supervised in groups, although one-to-one supervision was available if required. They identified that group supervision can be destructive if:

- there is over-domination or passivity of members
- there is an over-critical leader or group members
- the leader is too dogmatic, authoritarian or judgmental
- the leader asks too many questions – or not enough.

It is evident from these observations that supervisors providing group supervision require training and skills in groupwork.

SUPERVISORS SUPERVISING GROUPS REQUIRE
GROUPWORK SKILLS

In the same workshop comparisons were made between group and individual supervision. Some counsellors saw one-to-one supervision as offering a safer place to risk exposure of practice and weaknesses but others did not agree. They thought the individual being supervised would be more vulnerable, indeed, open to *sabotage*!

Atherton (1987), evaluating the potential and limitation of group supervision against individual supervision, suggests that group supervision is the riskiest option in terms of effective outcomes. One-to-one is less threatening for the individual with problems, but then he or she cannot 'hide' behind others. He warns against the possibility of collusion in groups. I have already suggested that this can also be a feature of one-to-one supervisory relationships. It may be that one-to-one support, through supervision, is most appropriate where interpersonal skills are the resource the agency is offering, as in a counselling service. However, the organisation may not be able to afford this level of support and group supervision may be a more cost-effective option. A combination of both would give the maximum opportunity for volunteers staff and students to develop their skills and knowledge. Group supervision and training sessions can often be shared by paid workers and volunteers, with each learning from the other's life experience and perceptions.

SUMMARY OF NEEDS IN SUPERVISION

From the above review it becomes possible to summarise the needs of both the person receiving supervision, and the supervisor.

The supervisee needs

(1) safety

(2) being valued

(3) respect

(4) support.

achieved by:

(i) clear agreements on confidentiality

(ii) self-awareness in the supervisor

(iii) the supervisee's own agenda addressed

(iv) a structure for the supervision sessions

(v) accurate feedback from the supervisor

(vi) a recognition by the agency of the 'right' to supervision and time designated to it.

The supervisor needs:

(1) authority

(2) self awareness

(3) skills in counselling, groupwork, giving feedback

(4) support.

achieved by:

(i) developing clear understanding with line managers about the style and boundaries of the supervisory role being undertaken

(ii) gaining knowledge of agency policy and procedures and of the supervisee's role and function

(iii) supervision for themselves

(iv) training in groupwork and counselling skills.

Each requires honesty, punctuality and commitment from the other, and mutual respect.

SUMMARY

In this brief survey of supervision in the voluntary sector I have tried to identify the basic needs of supervisors and those receiving supervision, including paid staff, students and volunteers.

I have emphasised the important role of supervision in today's voluntary organisations. I have drawn on experiential work with students and volunteer workers to identify the needs and the potential dangers which the mis-management of power can generate in the supervisor relationship. I have identified six key points of particular importance in the voluntary sector:

- supervision is an essential component of quality assurance
- supervision is essential to the successful management of student training and return to the work place
- supervision is a means of enabling volunteers to work in a professional manner and to validate their skills
- supervision is a means of upholding standards, exchanging information, and enabling skills development to be targeted to the agency's objectives
- supervision for the supervisor is essential
- group-work skills are necessary for the supervisor providing group supervision.

I have also tried to identify why supervision may be more difficult to implement in a voluntary organisation where lines of accountability may not be clear, staff development opportunities are limited and the concept of supervision likely to be in conflict with the views of both the voluntary management committee and the volunteers.

Finally, for those who may be setting up supervision processes in the voluntary sector or reviewing their practice I offer three practical guidelines:

(1) A practical model of supervision including a 'contract'.

(2) The process of implementing a supervision session, including a sample record sheet.

(3) A model of a 'contract' for group supervision.

Supervision can be a mutually satisfying professional activity for all participants: staff, students, volunteers and the supervisor. The value to the agency in sustaining and drawing out the potential in the workforce, clarifying roles, management structures and operational objectives, makes investment in supervision essential for voluntary organisations as they strive to meet quality standards in the new market economy of care.

REFERENCES

Adirondack, S. (1990) *Just About Managing*. London: LVSC.

Atherton, J. (1987) *Workbook on Professional Supervision in Group Care*. (Unpublished) Bedford H.E. College, Bedford.

CRUSE Bereavement Care (1987) Guidelines on Supervision from the Yellow Handbook.

Franchino, L. (1989) *Bereavement and Counselling, A Handbook for Trainers*. Privately printed, Weybridge.

Hall, P. ((1981) *Professionalisation and Bureaucratisation*. In R. Kramer op. cit.

Hatch, S. (1982) *Volunteers: Patterns, Meanings and Motives*. Berkhamstead: Volunteer Centre.

Kramer, R. (1981) *Voluntary Agencies in the Welfare State*. Berkeley, CA: University of California Press.

Stanners, C. (1987) *The Levers of Change, a study of a change of goal in a voluntary organisation*. Dissertation paper, Brunel University.

Appendix 14A: A Practical Model of Supervision

1. The supervisor should prepare two loose-leaf files to include:

　　1.1　Statement of the purpose of supervision

　　1.2　the ground rules

　　1.3　the contract

　　1.4　record sheets.

1.1 Statement of purpose:

To provide an opportunity for the worker to plan, prioritise, monitor and evaluate their work in a supportive relationship by:

- clarifying tasks, duties, responsibilities, and resources
- setting performance targets
- identifying the standards of performance required
- understanding the policy framework within which they are carrying out their work
- considering the implications and potential outcomes of alternative courses of action
- reflecting on the demand the job is having on their personal and practice resources
- monitoring the workload
- giving and receiving feedback on outcomes and performance
- identifying training and development needs
- modelling good practice
- considering personal issues which are affecting work performance.

1.2 The Ground Rules:

- time will be set aside for supervision on a regular basis and will have the highest priority (1 hour minimum at weekly intervals for students, monthly for staff and probably volunteers)

- supervision shall not be interrupted except by an explicit agreement
- a comfortable venue will be provided, booked in advance by agreement
- confidentiality will be guaranteed and what may be shared outside the supervision session will be explicitly agreed
- the supervisor and the supervisee will each keep a copy of the record sheet showing what has been discussed and agreed in each session
- agendas will be drawn up by each party and exchanged at least one day ahead of the session.

1.3 The Contract:

- who is to be involved ....
- the time of meetings ....
- the place..
- the duration ....
- the frequency ....
- the preparation required...
- the way the sessions will be recorded..

Signed by supervisee ....

Signed by supervisor ....

Date ....

Appendix 14B

Guideline No. II: The Process of Implementing a Supervision Session

(1) agree priorities from the two Agendas (supervisor's and supervisee's)

(2) agree who goes first – ideally the supervisee will take the lead

(3) the supervisor listens, reflects back, clarifies, (modelling good practice)

(4) the supervisor probes, challenges and interprets (modelling counselling techniques)

(5) the supervisor confirms good work practice and acknowledges achievement of tasks (modelling good management practice)

(6) the supervisor encourages self awareness in the supervisee

(7) the supervisee encourages self-awareness in the supervisor

(8) targets set previously will be reviewed

(9) goals and targets will be agreed.

Counselling techniques which can be used in supervision are described by Lyn Franchino in a Handbook on Bereavement and Counselling (1989).

A SUPERVISION RECORD SHEET

Date	Name of Worker		Name of Supervisor			
Item No	Topic	Issues arising	Action	When by	Who by	Done

Figure 14A.1 Supervision record sheet

Figure 14A.2 *Model contract for group supervision*

A MODEL 'CONTRACT' FOR GROUP SUPERVISION IN A VOLUNTARY ORGANISATION PROVIDING ONE-TO-ONE COUNSELLING

Responsibilities of Supervisor	Responsibilities of Counsellor
1. To convene and attend regular meetings	1. To attend regular meetings and notify supervisor if unable to attend
2. To make explicit the boundaries of confidentiality.	2. To understand and maintain agreed boundaries of confidentiality
3. To ensure that the counselling work is of the standard agreed by the Management Committee	3. To understand that the work carried out in counselling must be to the standard agreed by the Management Committee

Fig 14A.2 (continued) Model contract

4. To provide support for counsellors by:	4. To enable the supervisor to offer support by:
(i) Monitoring the caseload to see that counsellors are not overburdened by numbers or intensity or personal issues. Responsible for proposing reduction in work load or temporary (or permanent) withdrawal.	(i) Being open and honest in the supervision group and in individual consultation and keeping supervisor informed of workload.
(ii) To be available at all times for consultation.	(ii) By using supervision to develop self-awareness, to enhance skills and extend knowledge.
(iii) To provide opportunity for each counsellor to present their 'cases' to the group.	(iii) To be prepared to present their 'cases' openly in the group.
5. To provide the opportunity for growth and development, by using the group as a teaching medium	5. To use the opportunity for growth and development
(i) Through shared experience of group members	(i) By offering experience and knowledge appropriately to the group
(ii) By acknowledging and discussing issues	(ii) to take responsibility for raising issues

Fig 14A.2 (continued) Model contract

6. To consult appropriately in uncommon circumstances where client might benefit from more professional insights.

7. To give space for private needs to be explored when affecting the well being of the counsellor

8. To be aware of own needs for support and consultation, and to ensure that opportunities for this are available.

6. To seek consultation promptly with supervisor when anxious or in doubt.

7. To acknowledge private needs when they are interfering with counselling work.

8. To be aware of supervisor's needs.

CHAPTER 15

Supervision or Practice Teaching for Students?

Jacki Pritchard

It has been acknowledged throughout this book that the number of texts on supervision has increased considerably during the past two decades and certainly books on student supervision are not in short supply. In this chapter I do not wish to repeat what the reader can find elsewhere. I wanted to write this chapter because I feel very strongly that many students are not currently getting 'quality supervision', possibly because of the emphasis placed on practice teaching.

I felt this chapter had to be written because during the past five years I have seen many students on placement and have been able to witness what has happened to them from different perspectives. This is because I have worked alongside students as a practice teacher, as a social work colleague on a team, as a team leader and now as a tutor at a local University.

I am appalled by what I have witnessed during some placements. Some students have been left totally unsupported, even though the role and importance of a practice teacher has been developed and given a high profile in recent years. There are still some workers who think having a student 'might be fun' and do not realise what an enormous commitment it is, because of the preparation and the volume of work it requires. Then there are those workers who thought that, because they have had students for years, they do not have to do anything differently. With the introduction of practice curricula they now realise they have to play a very different part.

Professionals sometimes find it hard to be honest about good and bad practices because it involves criticising colleagues. In regard to student placements there are two truths which need to be addressed:

(1) students are sometimes 'dumped' in placements which are inappropriate

(2) some practice teachers are not up to standard.

Lack of resources is, again, the root cause why students may not get the placement they want or need for their personal development. The reality is that there is a shortage of placements and consequently students often do not know where they are going to be placed until the very last minute, so preparation and pre-placement meetings cannot take place.

Because of the shortage of placements, workers may feel 'pressurised' (e.g. by the training section) into having a student. These workers may not be totally committed to the student because of having been forced to take a student. Having a student is time consuming and involves a huge amount of work before, during and after the placement. This situation may be overcome by more agencies adopting the idea of having specialist practice teachers – in other words, workers spend half their time working on a small caseload, and the other half supervising students.

At the same time, some workers have been taking students for years and have become set in their ways, even though the concept of practice teaching has been developed and given a high profile in recent years. Even though standards have been set by CCETSW (1991), few practice teachers are ever told that they are not good enough. There is a great deal of inconsistency in practice, in spite of the guidelines laid down by CCETSW.

The purpose in writing this chapter is to outline what supervision should involve for both the practice teacher and for the student, by giving actual examples of good and bad practice. There is a need to distinguish between practice teaching and supervision, and also to explain the importance of each. Some consideration will also be given to how good supervision can be achieved, but I anticipate that many of the exercises in preceding chapters can be used to achieve this for students whilst on placement. The recommendations in this chapter will apply to students being placed in any work setting.

WHAT DOES SUPERVISION MEAN TO A STUDENT?

Throughout this book reference has been made to definitions of supervision. Authors elsewhere have addressed the issue of what supervision means in different work settings (Payne and Scott 1982). So what might be meaningful to students? No matter where they are placed (in fieldwork, residential setting, voluntary agencies) they need the same support as workers who are there on a permanent basis.

At the outset students need to consider what supervision means to them. It is a fact that many qualified staff do not receive regular supervision and their expectations about what constitutes good supervision may differ considerably. Therefore, the whole topic of supervision should be discussed at the beginning of the placement in order for the student to be able to use supervision in a constructive way.

Supervision is usually discussed at the pre-placement meeting when discussing the practice teaching sessions and the placement agreement is formulated. However, I doubt that many students think beyond frequency and duration of the sessions at this stage, because they are anxious during the first meeting and have lots of thoughts going round in their heads. Other things may be more significant at the time (e.g. what is the practice teacher going to be like? What sort of cases are they going to be given).

On the placement agreement form there will be a section about practice teaching sessions, but this needs to be developed further and a firmer contract agreed once the placement has started. On the placement agreement form it is usually agreed that the practice teacher and student will meet on a weekly basis for between one and one and a half hours and a venue is agreed. These considerations should not be dealt with lightly. The practice teacher should be committed to keeping the weekly appointment and should not make excuses for rearranging it because other things 'have cropped up'. It is crucial that if a practice teacher reneges on the agreement then some action should be taken immediately, so that time is not lost. On one placement, a practice teacher could not see the student as arranged because the first week he had a 'personal problem' which had to be sorted out and as a result of that he took a week's leave the following week. He came back for a week and did not rearrange supervision, then went on sick leave for three weeks. The student said:

> The first four to six weeks were really wasted. It was a large chunk out of the placement. I felt totally deskilled, inadequate; a complete failure. I was lucky that the rest of the team were around. It was OK because I am gobby and asked things. The other student was very quiet and did not push herself forward to find things out.

The situation was resolved by the student contacting her College tutor, who immediately arranged to see the practice teacher's team leader. The team leader then agreed to give supervision to the student himself until the practice teacher returned. However, this should have been offered as a matter of course rather than the tutor having to step in. When the practice teacher did return it was felt he could not commit himself to the student and as a result of this another practice teacher was found.

The lessons to be learnt from this example of bad practice is that there should be contingency plans in place for when a practice teacher becomes unavailable, for whatever reason. A team, no matter in what setting the placement occurs, should take some responsibility for ensuring that the student is not left to drift.

The venue for supervision sessions is important because of the need for privacy, and arrangements need to be made to make sure that interruptions do not occur. Sometimes practice teachers suggest venues away from the workplace in order to achieve these objectives. It has been known for some practice teachers to make use of their own homes because no room is available at work. Some people may question whether this is 'professional'. An example of when this arrangement went horribly wrong was when a student did agree to have supervision at her practice teacher's house but then discovered that this was so that he could look after his four children, who were on holiday from school. There was no privacy and constant interruptions.

DIFFERENTIATING BETWEEN PRACTICE TEACHING AND SUPERVISION

When I undertook my practice teaching course I found it extremely difficult to get into the habit of saying 'practice teaching' rather than 'supervision'. The emphasis was on the *teaching* of students, which is very valid. Now that I am on the other side of the fence in my tutoring role, I seriously question whether we have done students a disservice by not giving equal importance to the role of supervision.

There is a difference between the tasks involved in practice teaching and those involved in supervising a student. Practice teaching is directed towards helping the student to learn the job, that is, developing skills and knowledge. Supervision is about helping the student to do the job better. Teaching will be focused on many different areas, for example methods, policies, legislation, values, attitudes, anti-discriminatory practice. Supervision has three functions, which will be discussed further below, in other words, accountability, education (which is part of the practice teaching element) and support.

Practice teachers and students do alternate between calling their sessions 'practice teaching sessions' and 'supervision sessions'. It is therefore important to agree a firmer contract once the placement begins to sort out *what* is going to be done *when*. An example of a supervision contract drawn up with a student is given in Figure 15.1.

Figure 15.1: Supervision Contract drawn up with Student

STRICTLY CONFIDENTIAL

Name of practice teacher: ....

Name of student: :..

Date contract agreed: ....

Supervision sessions will take place as follows:

Frequency: Weekly

Time: Monday 10.00 – 12.00

Venue: Meeting Room at local Family Centre
                         (to be booked in advance by practice teacher)

AGENDA

1. Time management

2. Discuss cases **(student to give case files, written up to date, by midday Friday each week)**

3. Discussion on issues resulting from team meetings/other meetings attended

4. Social work methods. The student wishes to concentrate on looking at certain theoretical models during her placement (specifically – behaviour modification, task centred approach, attachment theory) and wants to spend part of these sessions discussing a theory and application to practice. The practice teacher has agreed to suggest relevant reading to be undertaken by both practice teacher and student in preparation for supervision.

5. Bereavement counselling. Student to undertake specific piece of work with a group of bereaved parents. Student to feedback on tasks/work done each week, i.e., setting up the group, group sessions, etc. Time will be given to consider groupwork skills, counselling skills, student's own feelings concerning loss and grief.

6. Other issues (**other items can be added to the agenda either by the practice teacher or student in advance of the supervision sessions, by latest midday Friday**).

Practice Teacher ....

Student...

The student and practice teacher should spend a considerable amount of time together during the induction period and will begin to 'know' each other, but the first formal supervision session should address specific issues, namely:

(1) the format of future sessions

(2) how the student can learn best.

It was said above that the student may have little notion about supervision, depending on his/her previous work experience. It is therefore important for the student to gain an overview of the theories on supervision (e.g. by reading Chapter 1; or Morrison 1993), but also to be told how their practice teacher views supervision (what has his/her own experiences been regarding supervision?). It would also be important for the student to talk about their own experiences of supervision if they have any at all. I have written elsewhere that it is useful to design an exercise about what the supervisor and supervisee expect of each other (see Chapter 7 Exercise 7.1 in this book; Owen and Pritchard 1993, pp. 220–22).

The purpose of supervision needs to be explained clearly and differentiated from the purpose of practice teaching. Ford and Jones (1987) believe that the student supervisor has two roles to perform

> ... that of supervision and that of practice teacher. The supervisor is accountable to both the agency and the client; the practice teacher has a responsibility to the educational establishment and the student. The

supervisor has, first, to ensure that a good standard of service is offered to the agency's clients, and, second, to develop skills in teaching so as to maximise the learning of the student. (p. 64)

IMPLEMENTING THE FUNCTIONS OF SUPERVISION FOR THE STUDENT

The three main functions of supervision (i.e., accountability, education and support) apply to student supervision in very much the same way as to a permanent worker.

Accountability

The supervisor is responsible for the student and so if 'anything awful happens' the supervisor would be held responsible. Supervision should not be regarded as a process whereby the supervisor is seen to be 'checking up on' the student and is therefore viewed with suspicion. Supervision is a professional tool by which the quality of service being delivered to clients can be measured.

I have been aware of situations where some students have felt that their practice teachers do not 'trust' them when their use of time is questioned. For example, one practice teacher in a mid placement meeting said that she was concerned that she had *never* seen her student in the office at the end of the day and felt that there must have been some occasions when the student was not visiting at the end of the afternoon and could have returned to the office rather than go straight home. The student became very angry about questioning her use of time. It may have been more helpful if the practice teacher had raised this matter with the student in a supervision session rather than bringing it up for the first time in a meeting with the College tutor. Supervision should be a forum where work practices are discussed.

The practice teacher does need to know what the student is actually doing. Therefore, it is important during supervision sessions to allocate some time to looking at time management issues. It is helpful to discuss how the previous week has been by asking about where the student has been and what activities have they actually been engaging in (observation visits, joint visits, visits to clients, units, meetings, resource panels, case conferences, reviews etc.). The student's diary can form the basis for discussion during this part of the session. It is also important to plan for the week ahead.

Another part of the supervision agenda should be discussion of cases. By going through the student's cases the supervisor will be able to gauge how the student is working, what skills and knowledge s/he possesses already and what areas need to be worked on/developed for the future. This is crucial as the role of supervisor is to provide appropriate learning opportunities. The initial placement agreement will have highlighted areas of learning which the student needs to focus on during the placement. Supervision is a way of checking that the agreement is being met, but also other areas which need to be worked on, or specific difficulties may come to light during the sessions. This leads on to the educative role of supervision.

Education

The educative role in supervision brings in the practice teaching element. At the beginning of the placement some time must be devoted to ascertaining how the student can learn best. Every individual has 'their own way of doing things'. Some people can read and write essays with loud music blearing out; others (like myself!) have to have complete silence. Some like to get up early in the morning to work; others prefer to 'burn the midnight oil'. We all know what we *like* to do, but is important to find out how we learn best. It is not the purpose of this chapter to go into theories regarding adult learning because there are now many texts which can be referred to.

However, I would recommend Honey and Mumford's (1986) 'Learning Styles Questionnaire'. The authors explain that

> this questionnaire is designed to find out your preferred learning style(s). Over the years you have probably developed learning 'habits' that help you benefit more from some experiences than from others. Since you are probably unaware of this, this questionnaire will help you pinpoint your learning preferences so that you are in a better position to select learning experiences that suit your style. (Honey and Mumford 1986)

Once ways of learning have been identified, the supervisor and student must decide which methods they are going to use. They have many choices:

- Reading – books, articles, policy documents, procedures, case files
- Written pieces of work (process recording, reports, observation critiques)
- Exercises
- Role play
- Simulation exercises
- Tape recording (interviews; role play)
- Video recording (actual situations; role plays; using triggers to practice interviewing skills)
- Organised workshops (e.g. for students placed in different agencies within a geographical area)
- Group meetings (e.g. for all students placed within an agency).

Support

A student will have many anxieties during the course of the placement. In the beginning there will be the usual thoughts:

- will my practice teacher be OK?
- will I get on with the rest of the team?
- what if I can't cope with the work?

There may also be additional/personal worries:

- *the distance to travel everyday*

  Some students commute up to 45 miles to a placement each day, which can be extremely tiring especially in bad winter conditions. Others have to rely on public transport, which may be unreliable and consequently causes another type of anxiety.

- *child care*

  What if my child gets ill and I have to take time off?

  I have to pick up my child early every Friday because the childminder goes away for weekends.

- *what is it going to be like being the only black worker in a predominantly white community (e.g. pit village).*

Any such concerns should be voiced and dealt with at the beginning of the placement, or else they will dominate the student's mind.

As the placement progresses and the student gets 'stuck in', s/he may find him/herself dealing with some very stressful situations and the supervisor must enable him/her to vent his/her feelings. The student must feel 'safe' to be able to do this. Students must not think that if they say how they are feeling they 'might fail the placement' because they will be seen as 'not coping'.

The supervisor and student are not in enviable positions. They have limited time together and it is unrealistic to expect any two human beings to build a completely trusting and honest relationship within a few weeks. Some established workers still feel uncomfortable about raising certain issues with their managers after years of working together!

It may be useful to cite some typical examples of difficult situations which students have found themselves facing and as a result needed to talk about their feelings:

- seeing horrific injuries on a child
- taking a child into care, when the child is screaming to stay with its mother
- working with an older person who wants to die/may be considering suicide
- witnessing bad practice within a residential unit
- after writing a court report, a client has been sent to prison
- a client reoffends
- you find out a client has been lying to you and you've been completely taken in
- a client dies.

All these situations can bring out different emotional feelings – anger, horror, disbelief, sadness, despair, uncertainty, failure, stupidness, naivety, loss – which need to be vented openly and dealt with for future development and good practice. Such situations may bring the student to a point where s/he is questioning their own values, attitudes, long-held beliefs.

It is very important that the student learns that it is all right to have all these feelings, but that they must be dealt with properly. Discussion needs to focus on being professional (when you find yourself face-to-face with a client and a difficult situation), getting things out of your system (e.g. by crying once you are safe), cutting off from work (how do you do this?).

PROPER ENDINGS

The last few weeks of the placement are usually dominated by the final report. The practice teacher is anxious 'to get it right' and the student is hoping 'that it will all be OK'. Together with getting the report done, the student has to do final visits, complete write ups, close/transfer cases, say 'goodbyes' to clients and colleagues, which can be quite emotional. It is equally important for the practice teacher and student to finish off properly too – not just breathe a sigh of relief that it is all done and dusted.

A great deal of work will have gone into evaluating the student's work and how this is going to be presented in the final report. It may be useful to think of this evaluation as 'an appraisal'. Appraisals should take place as a form of good practice for permanent workers who have regular supervision. Such an appraisal should take place for a student and the end product will be the final report. This appraisal should be conducted during a formal supervision session before starting to write the final report. A fitting ending may be using or repeating an exercise carried out at the beginning of the placement about what constitutes good supervision or what would the student expect from a supervisor in the future?

REFERENCES

CCETSW (1991). *Rules and requirements for the diploma in social work*. London: CCETSW.

Ford, K. and Jones, A. (1987). *Student supervision*. Basingstoke: Macmillan Press.

Honey, P. and Mumford, A. (1986). *Using your learning styles*. Maidenhead: P. Honey.

Morrison, T. (1993). *Staff Supervision in Social Care*. London: Longman.

Owen, H. and Pritchard, J. (1993). *Good Practice in Child Protection: A Manual for Professionals*. London: Jessica Kingsley.

Payne, C. and Scott, T. (1982). *Developing supervision of teams in field and residential social work*. London: National Institute for Social Work – Papers No. 12.

CONTRIBUTORS

Jacki Pritchard is a Freelance Trainer and Locality Manager with Sheffield Family and Community Services.

Catherine Sawdon is a Freelance Trainer and Training Officer with Wakefield Social Serices.

David Sawdon is a Freelance Trainer.

Elizabeth Ash is an Independent Consultant in Education and Training.

Paul Borland is an Independent Trainer, and Senior Probation Officer and Training Officer with the South Yorkshire Probation Service.

Patricia Riley is the Director of Wheatfields Hospice in Leeds.

Jean Moore is a Freelance Trainer and Child Abuse Consultant.

Cherry Rowlings is a Professor in the Department of Applied Social Science at the University of Stirling.

Roger Clough is a Professor in the Department of Applied Social Science at the University of Lancaster.

Ron Wiener is a Freelance Trainer and Community Psychologist, and Associate Consultant in the Department of Adult Continuing Education at the University of Leeds.

Hazel Kemshall is a Lecturer in Probation Studies in the Department of Social Policy and Social Work at the University of Birmingham.

Sue Lane is an Assistant Chief Probation Officer with the West Midlands Probation Service.

Steve Mackey is a Senior Probation Officer with the West Midlands Probation Service.

Martin Roscoe is a Senior Probation Officer with the Hampshire Probation Service.

Christine Stanners is Development Director (Community Care) with Camden Age Concern.

Katherine Wiltshire is an Independent Trainer and Consultant.

Subject Index

Name Index

Good Practice in Child Protection
A Manual for Professionals
Edited by Hilary Owen and Jacki Pritchard
ISBN 1 85302 205 5 pb
Good Practice 1

'Each chapter is fully referenced, and some include case studies and exercises. I found *Good Practice in Child Protection* not only interesting but educational. It was harrowing to read the case studies and descriptions, and this shows the vital need of good training, supervision and support for workers in this field or for those who come into situations in which a child may be being abused in any way.' – *Nursing Standard*

CONTENTS: Introduction, Hilary Owen and Jacki Pritchard. 1. Managing Your Own Learning in Child Protection, Ann Hollows *Senior Development Officer, National Children's Bureau.* 2. The Children Act and Child Protection, Pat Munroe *Solicitor.* 3. Recognition of Abuse, Dr Alice Swann *Senior Clinical Medical Officer, Belfast.* 4. Awareness and Recognition, Jo Crow *Sister in Accident and Emergency, The Children's Hospital, Birmingham.* 5. Recognition of Abuse by Workers in Other Specialisms, Jacki Pritchard. 6. Preventing Female Genital Mutilation: A Practical Multidisciplinary Approach, Hilary Owen and Lola Brown *Senior Race Relations Trainer (Child Protection), Lambeth Social Services.* 7. Children with Disabilities – A Challenge for Child Protection Procedures? Philippa Russell *Director, Voluntary Council for Handicapped Children.* 8. On Becoming a Tightrope Walker – Communicating Effectively With Children About Abuse, Eve Brock *Trainer & Team Leader of teachers, HM Prison Lindholme.* 9. Promoting Inter-Professional Understanding and Collaboration, Tony McFarlane *Multidisciplinary Training Officer, Co. Antrim.* 10. Developing Skills in Contributing at Child Protection Case Conferences, Hilary Owen and Lindsey Savage *Child Protection Administrator, Sheffield Family & Community Services Department.* 11. Child Protection Conferences: Maximising Their Potential, Marion Charles *Senior Lecturer, School of Social Studies, University of Nottingham.* 12. Formulating Child Protection Plans, Hilary Owen and Jacki Pritchard. 13. Victims of Child Abuse Giving Evidence: Helping to Reduce Trauma, Isobel Todd *Probation Officer, Nottinghamshire.* 14. Child Protection: The Police Perspective, Sergeant Colin Walke *Surrey Constabulary.* 15. Supervision and Support of Workers Involved in Child Protection Cases, Professor Dorota Iwaniec *Department of Social Work, Queen's University of Belfast.* 16. Support and Supervision for Social Workers Working in the Child Protection Field, Jacki Pritchard.

Jessica Kingsley Publishers
116 Pentonville Road, London N1 9JB

Good Practice in Risk Assessment
and Risk Management

Edited by Jacki Pritchard and Hazel Kemshall

ISBN 1 85302 338 8 pb

Good Practice 3

'The difficulty of balancing the management of risks and the rights of the individuals is tackled with sensitivity and skill... The book is well referenced throughout and should be required reading for practitioners, managers and policy makers.' – *Therapy Weekly*

'...this book does not shirk the 'big issues' and, by doing so, begins to unfold the complex nature of its subject. To their credit in general, the authors do not lose sight of their portfolio and therefore the body of the text is peppered with case studies and examples of direct work with clients... a book which every practitioner, manager and student should be able to draw from... This work should be viewed as a benchmark from which the concept of risk can be developed through better training both in terms of understanding how we make judgements and the way in which those decisions are then managed.' – *Probation Journal*

Jacki Pritchard is a qualified social worker who has worked as a practitioner and manager in both fieldwork and hospital settings. She is also an accredited practice teacher and has been employed as a trainer and consultant in England and Northern Ireland. Her previous publications include *Good Practice in Child Protection* and *Good Practice in Supervision*. **Hazel Kemshall** is a lecturer in probation studies at the University of Birmingham. She spent ten years as a probation practitioner and manager in a range of fieldwork and specialist settings. Her current research interests are in service delivery to women offenders and risk assessment in work with offenders. She has published a range of articles on probation practice and management.

CONTENTS: Introduction, *Hazel Kemshall and Jacki Pritchard*. 1 Risking Legal Repercussions, *David Carson*. 2 Risk Assessment in Child Protection Work, *Brian Corby*. 3 Children with Disabilities, *Philippa Russell*. 4 A Framework of Risk Assessment and Management for Older People, *Jane Lawson*. 5 Risk and Older People, *Rosemary Littlechild and John Blakeney*. 6 Risk for Whom? Social Work and People with Physical Disabilities, *Liz Ross and Jan Waterson*. 7 Risk Management and People with Mental Health Problems, *Tony Ryan*. 8 Risk Work and Mental Health, *Ann Davis*. 9 Facts, Fantasies and Confusion; Risks and Substance Use, *Ronno Griffiths and Jan Waterson*. 10 Offender Risk and Probation Practice, *Hazel Kemshall*. 11 Sex Offender Risk Assessment, *Sue McEwan and Joe Sullivan*. 12 Violence and Aggression to Social Work and Social Care Staff, *Brian Littlechild*. 13 Applying Risk in Practice: Case Studies and Training Material, *Avril Aust, Hazel Kemshall, Jane Lawson, Sue McEwan and Joe Sullivan, Jacki Pritchard, Tony Ryan*.

Jessica Kingsley Publishers
116 Pentonville Road, London N1 9JB

Good Practice in Counselling People Who Have Been Abused

Edited by Zetta Bear

ISBN 1 85302 424 4 pb

Good Practice 4

CONTENTS: Introduction. Men as victims/offenders, *David Briggs*. Abuse and Self Harm, *Lois Arnold and Gloria Babiker*. Counselling Children, *Madge Bray*. People with Learning Difficulties, *Steve Morris*. Empowerment, *Sandra Samuels*. Abuse of Elders, *Jacki Pritchard*. Beyond Survival, *Sharon Gilbert*. Abuse and Substance Misuse, *Ronno Griffiths*. Ritual Abuse, *Sara Scott*. Survivor's Perspective, *Runa Wolf*. Complex Post Traumatic Stress Disorder, *Liz Hall*. Race and Abuse, *Jalner Hanmer*.

The Abuse of Older People

A Training Manual for Detection and Prevention 2nd edition

Jacki Pritchard

ISBN 1 85302 305 1 pb

'The book is directly relevant and useful to training courses leading to various professional qualifications, to staff development within agencies, and to post qualifying studies. It would provide an especially valuable focus for inter-agency and interdisciplinary training. I warmly recommend the book to all people engaged in the promotion of effective community care.' – *Professor Eric Sainsbury*

'This book provides a ready-made training package containing an abundance of carefully thought-out scenarios, simulation and role-play exercises which are ideal for multidisciplinary workshops. Of particular interest is the exercise designed to help staff learn how to prioritise their workload...this is a good, practical guide to the subject and will be of use to all staff involved in care of the elderly in institutional and community settings.' – *Nursing Times*

Jessica Kingsley Publishers
116 Pentonville Road, London N1 9JB

Working with Elder Abuse
A Training Manual for Home Care, Residential and Day Care Staff
Jacki Pritchard
ISBN 1 85302 418 X pb

This practical training manual is written for home care, residential and day care staff, who need to be able to recognise elder abuse, but may not be trained to do so. Its large format, range of exercises and photo-copiable worksheets makes it a valuable source of training material not only for training teams, but also for managers who train staff and teams on site.

Each chapter contains exercises, a reading list and a simple discussion of the theory behind each of the key areas covered by the manual. These include:

- defining elder abuse
- recognizing elder abuse
- what to do when working with elder abuse
- case conferences
- long term work with victims and abusers
- abuse in institutions
- issues for managers
- case studies

CONTENTS: 1 Elder abuse - what is it? 2 Recognizing abuse. 3 What to do when working with elder abuse. 4 Handling disclosure. 5 Monitoring and reviewing. 6 Case conferences made simple. 7 Medium and long term work with victims and abusers. 8 Residential/day care 1: the theory. 9 Residential/day care 2: the exercises. 10 Issues for managers. 11 Role plays. 12 Case Studies.

Jessica Kingsley Publishers
116 Pentonville Road, London N1 9JB

Community Care Practice and the Law
Michael Mandelstam with Belinda Schwehr
ISBN 1 85302 273 X pb

'...a comprehensive and up-to-date guide to community care law which discusses in detail, and with knowledge and insight about policy and practice, how the law provides both the framework for the delivery of services and the means by which decisions and services can be challenged... valuable for students and for others trying to make sense of how law and practice should and do interact. Planners and managers will also find the book invaluable... this should serve as a valuable reference book for many years.' – *Issues in Social Work Education*

'this book has to be a must on any occupational therapist's bookshelf for reference by both the independent practitioner and those employed in the statutory services. It is also an important work of reference for occupational therapy education establishments and their students as they prepare new practitioners for the increasingly complex and litigious world in which they will be providing services.'
— *British Journal of Occupational Therapy*

'This book fills a gap in describing the legal framework of the new legislation and relating that to day-to-day questions that arise amongst those administering services or receiving them...will be of great benefit in dealing with the knotty questions around health or social care, the definition of the need and the role of the NHS in long-term care...exceptionally clear and impressively up-to-date. All those who read it will be significantly better informed.' – *Care Weekly*

'Anyone looking for a practical guide to the legal implications of community care practice will find this book by Michael Mandelstam and Belinda Schwehr of immense help. Their practical approach makes *Community Care Practice and the Law* equally suited for service managers and practitioners, voluntary organisations, service users and carers, as well as lawyers, lecturers and students.' – *Disability News*

'This book appears to be the first real attempt to provide a complete and comprehensive guide to application of community care policy and practice... The back cover of this book declares that it is 'an essential work of reference for managers in the social and health services in both the statutory and voluntary sectors, and for the legal profession, it will also be a useful text for students of social work and social policy'. It is difficult to fault this claim save that the work essential ought to be underlined.' – *Therapeutic Communities*

Jessica Kingsley Publishers
116 Pentonville Road, London N1 9JB

'...indispensable...the material is well presented in an accessible way and the authors analyse some of the more contentious aspects of community care' – *Baseline*

'Using non-legal language this book provides practical assistance... It deals objectively with controversial issues and will be of considerable help to workers in this field.' – *Aslib Book Guide*

'Excellent and much needed text for students and practitioners'
– Peter Storey, Senior Lecturer,
Stockport College of Further and Higher Education

Staff Supervision in a Turbulent Environment
Managing Process and Task in Front-line Services
Lynette Hughes and Paul Pengelly
ISBN 1 85302 327 2 pb

This book focuses on the relationship between supervisor and supervisee. The authors explore ways of thinking about how the processes of supervision interact with the accomplishment of supervisory tasks and provide an introduction to supervisory dilemmas in the current turbulent environment of statutory services. A theoretical exposition of some concepts relevant to understanding supervisory processes is accompanied by a fuller exploration of how these concepts are relevant to supervisory dilemmas. The authors conclude that safe and effective practice with service-users continues to depend on agencies providing the 'thinking space' that supervision can represent, and challenge supervisors and supervisees to explore their own thinking and practice.

CONTENTS: 1. The Turbulent Environment. 2. Piggy in the Middle. 3. Supervisory Triangles. 4. Stages and Styles. 5. Drama Triangle of Victims/Rescuer/Persecutor. 6. Reflection Process/Mirroring. 7. Institutional and Professional Defences. 8. Calling a Halt. 9. Challenge and Containment. 10. Care and Control.

Lynette Hughes is Senior Marital Psychotherapist at The Tavistock Marital Studies Institutes. **Paul Pengelly** is a marital psychotherapist and consultant in private practice, an Associate staff member of the Tavistock Marital Studies Institute and a visiting lecturer at the Tavistock Clinic.

Jessica Kingsley Publishers
116 Pentonville Road, London N1 9JB